# Contents

The plates are between pages 80 and 81, 144 and 145.

Unless otherwise stated all the photographs are the author's.

# Introduction to the Second Edition

ALTHOUGH not published until 1971, the bulk of the first edition of *Salmon* was written as far back as 1969. During that time I have enjoyed a great deal more experience in salmon fishing and it would be smug and self-opinionated to suggest that some of my originally-held views have not been subject to slight change. It would be pompous to imply that in 1969 I knew it all and that the ensuing years have taught me nothing. Any angler – no matter his experience or life-span – should continue to learn and profit from additional experience. There are some, however, who might accuse the writer of contradiction when, in effect, and as a result of this additional experience, he has done little more than modify his opinion.

With the exception of a few literal errors and an erroneous transposition, I have decided not to alter one comma of the text of the first edition; but, where I have thought it worthy of mention or new developments have occured, I have added short appendices at the end of certain chapters. Also the work has been enlarged by the inclusion of four extra chapters. Although it is no yardstick or great milestone, I have now caught over one thousand salmon and there is hardly a day spent by the riverside when I do not increase my knowledge of this fascinating sport. I hope that I shall have the wit and the wisdom to continue to learn, for there would appear to be no place for a closed mind in the sphere of salmon fishing.

# Preface

Change comes slowly to the world of the salmon fisherman. The methods we have inherited tend to stick. Books on the subject have come and gone. Some have left their mark; others have fallen by the wayside. Very few have provided the reader with facts; and it is a shattering admission that, so far as the salmon is concerned, we are still desperately short of *facts*. Fancies there are by the million. I am not alone in having my share of these. It is my aim to explore such facts as are known; and to speculate with my fancies, and on those of well known authorities of past and present. Moreover, to be frank, I cannot pretend that I shall bring any great revelation to my reader. The only road to successful salmon fishing is, in my opinion, through the hard school of experience.

Unfortunately it is still true to say that one of the greatest factors in successful salmon fishing is determined by the size of the angler's bank balance. Those who can afford the best beats usually have a head start on lesser mortals; and in some instances, where these anglers have the services of a good gillie or boatman, they may well catch fish which have not been fully earned by their own skill. They come back home with their tales of monster catches and are credited for being expert anglers; when, had they been left to their own devices, many would have made a poor showing. However, I have always reasoned that an angler should catch at least five hundred salmon before he goes into print with any of his theories; and nearer to a thousand before he attempts a book. Mercifully, at the time of writing, the good Lord has permitted me to catch just short of this latter number; but I am still well aware of the fact that even this number of fish is dismally small when compared with the vast numbers caught by some earlier writers on the subject. I approach my task humbly, therefore, in the knowledge that there are many with greater experience than myself; many, indeed, who quietly go about their task and never commit a word to print; and many who shun the limelight. I console myself with the thought that there are also quite a few, less humble than myself, who have breathed dogma and pedantry, ruthlessly and plentifully, from their vast, or in some instances (believe it or not) limited, experience.

I commenced my fishing days as a boy of eight. In those far off days, trout of the rock-girt streams near my home in Northern England were the quarry. Pike and roach came to the net from nearby ponds and rivers. Worms and maggots were the most used baits; and it was not until the end of military duty, in the Second World War, that I took to the fly-rod. For the next ten years the epitome of fishing came, for me, in the form of dry-fly fishing for trout. Salmon were fish I occasionally caught, usually by accident; and I became convinced that there could be no sane approach to salmon fishing. Gradually, however, this outlook changed as more and more opportunities for salmon fishing presented themselves. Success followed upon success as I began to realize that there were more factors involved than pure good luck. There was even a formula of sorts; but it was a vague formula – one that could not be defined or proved. It was basic, with many variable permutations; and the words *never* and *always* had no place.

As experience increased and confidence grew, I inevitably went into print. The aura of truth about the printed word is still a mystery to me; but my writing led me into wider fields and brought introductions to well known names. Opportunities to fish more exotic waters also came my way; and further experience brought more successes because, to a large extent, the two are interdependent. I say to a large extent because mere experience cannot be the final hallmark. There are some who either cannot, or will not, learn from experience. My grandfather may well have driven more miles than Graham Hill. But there can be little doubt which of them was the most experienced; and, for reason of that experience, the better driver. The champions of most sports achieve their acclaim while they are young men. Yet the angling world will not acclaim the youngsters. Accolades are not due until senility approaches; the time when cynicism and dogma are to be noted in reflections. At this destination, therefore, I have not yet arrived. Accolades and acclaim are not my aim; but for the past twenty years I have had a wide and varied salmon fishing experience. I have learned what it pays to do; and what, sometimes, it pays not to do. I have also learned when it pays to fish hard; and when it seems preferable to sit and watch.

There will be no pearls of wisdom in this book, except that I have caught salmon by every legitimate method – and a few the other way! I have listened to the pundits and read their writings; but, a more important factor, I have fished – and fished diligently. I have learned all the mechanics of casting from the tournament experts. I have learned how to tie flies that catch fish, even though they may not catch fishermen! I have found the method of tailing my fish from the water, instead of stabbing them in the vitals with a gaff. My salmon fishing has taken me to exotic places like Scandinavia and the United States of America, and has introduced me to a hundred and one friends – and, I hope, few enemies! It has brought me immense enjoyment; and also some treasured memories.

No success would have been possible, however, without friends. In the immediate post-war years, I had the good fortune to meet the man who was to have the greatest influence on my angling career. I refer, of course, to that very controversial figure, Eric Horsfall Turner. Eric and I have spent many happy days together, and still do. At the time we first met he was solving many of his own angling problems; and was on the threshold of a writing career that was, through the years, to instruct and amuse his many readers. Through him I met many of the well known names in angling; and was coached and encouraged in my own progress. We do not, nowadays, always see eye-to-eye on certain topics; but we agree to differ, and respect facts and considered opinions. Perhaps the man who was to have the greatest influence on pure technical ability was the late Captain T. L. Edwards. Tommy was a tough teacher, demanding nothing save the best. He taught me not only how to cast to a reasonably high standard, but he also gave me an insight on how to teach others. In my opinion, he was the greatest professional angling tutor we have ever had. No man, in a lifetime of angling, can ever learn all there is to know about it. It would take several re-incarnations to enable the angler to reach even the threshold of full knowledge. Moreover, to think like the fish we should have to be as dim-witted as the fish! We can never understand their ways; nor accustom ourselves to their environment. We are merely hunters, after the style of primitive men of old; but with the sophisticated difference that instead of doing it to live, we are purely concerned to face the challenge of outwitting creatures, by the most sporting methods that appeal to our environment. If some of the facts in this book help the reader to a greater understanding of salmon fishing problems, and some of the fancies show the worth of a trial which brings success – then my object will have been achieved.

Thanks are also due to the publishers of *Anglers' Annual* and to the editors of *Angling, Angling Times, Au Bord de l'Eau, The Field, Field and Stream, Shooting Times,* and *Trout and Salmon* for permission to reproduce, either wholly or in part, some of my articles that have appeared in these journals. Thanks are also due to my good friend Reg Righyni for his great kindness in permitting me to fish his water on the Lune until I could pay for my share of the rent; to Mr Richard North, the owner of this water, on which I have had so much sport; to my good friend Odd Haraldsen, for all his past kindness, and his promise to continue to invite me to his

Norwegian rivers until I catch a fifty-pounder; to Ken Morritt, of Intrepid reels fame, for his kindness in inviting me to fish waters as his guest which I could not have afforded at that time – and for the pleasure of his wit and company; to that talented photographer and dry-fly fisherman, Roy Shaw, for some of the illustrations; and to photographers Keith Massey and Ken Pettinger for some of the others; to Jenny Axtell and Wendy Sellers for typing all this; to Richard Walker, the editor of this series, who first encouraged me to write this book, and who, along with Eric Horsfall Turner, steered it through the rough into final publication form, despite Dick's one-time comment that he cared little for salmon-fishing – and less for the people who pursued it (I hope with his tongue in his cheek). Lastly I bow to my wife, herself a keen salmon angler, who has given me every encouragement throughout the tedium of writing by sweeping away the cigarette butts and occasionally filling my glass with Scotch!

# 1
## Facts and Fancies

---

MOST salmon anglers are agreed that when we come to discuss
the broad canvas of all that appertains to the question of
salmon, we are very short of the full facts. We know that the
salmon has its birth in the highly oxygenated waters of our
upland rivers, where it then spends approximately two years
as a parr; growing little, but feeding voraciously on the
quantity of small available food. Then, during the early
spring, it dons a silvery coat as it progresses to the smolt stage;
and drops downstream to meet what fate awaits it. On this
downstream migration the fish are subjected to many trials.
They have to negotiate weirs, and possibly the turbines of
hydro-electric schemes. They have to face the danger to survival from the pollution of industrial or housing communities
near the estuary. They have to seek out a track past the
various predators awaiting them in the sea. At this stage they
become an unknown quantity. We lose our knowledge of the
facts, and the fancies take over. Not all is man's fancy, however. In his never-ending quest to reap a harvest from the sea,
he finds certain sea-feeding grounds (notably those in the
vicinity of Greenland – see Chapter 26) where it has been
established that grilse-sized salmon can be netted in pro-
digious numbers. A similar fishery was established by the
Danes and Faroese on the high seas off Greenland; and also
by the Danes and Swedes on one of the migration routes of
Norwegian salmon; but as most of these latter fish are thought

to be kelts returning to the sea, a greater concern is for the devastating number of fresh salmon taken off Greenland by heavy commercial fishing.

With our increasing knowledge of some of the sea migrations, however, further information concerning the salmon's sea diet continues to come to light. An article in the *Atlantic Salmon Journal*, published during the autumn of 1968 and entitled 'Atlantic Salmon in Northern Latitudes', written by T. B. Fraser, claims that salmon eat herrings, alewives, smelts, capelins, sprats, eels, small mackerel, haddocks, shrimps, and crustaceans; and follow gatherings of such sea life in their migrations. Sea-water temperatures are said to have great bearing on where the shoals move; and it is stated that it has been scientifically proved that salmon can navigate by the sun. This comment is based on the assumption that they sometimes *see* the sun in Northern wintery latitudes! Anglers interested in salmon navigation are recommended to read *Homing of Salmon – Underwater Guideposts*, by Arthur D. Hasler, of the University of Wisconsin.

This, however, does not solve our problem. We lose our 6-ins to 9-ins smolts from our estuaries; and do not hear of them again until they have acquired a weight of some 4-lb to 10-lb off Greenland. Even then, we are still uncertain whether the entire migration goes to Greenland; but if there are other selected destinations it is a merciful blessing that they have not yet been discovered. Atomic submarines are alleged to have recorded packs of salmon feeding under the arctic ice. Their location has never been divulged, however; and if this is the location to which the bulk of them go, it is fortunate that the ice affords them protection from the destructive tactics of the commercial fishing world.

Tagging experiments give us the next fact. After varying periods at sea, the salmon make every endeavour to get back to the river of their birth. Having found an abundant larder somewhere in the sea depths, sufficient to take them from mere fingerlings to fish around 5-lb to 7-lb in their first year of sea feeding, some may well return during the summer following the year of their first migration. These young returning fish are termed 'grilse'. Salmon may, however, prolong their marine feasting, and feel no urge to return until the second or third year at sea; by which time they are mature salmon, and may weigh anywhere between 12-lb and 30-lb. The greater part of their sea life behaviour, therefore, is unknown. Many fancies and just a few facts, have been put forward concerning their sea life; the most notable fancies, perhaps, coming from the pen of Richard Waddington in his book *Salmon Fishing*.

It has been pretty well established that the salmon return to the rivers of their birth for the purpose of meeting the natural instinct which leads to reproduction of the species. Somewhere, way out at sea, the instinct comes upon them. They stop feeding and, like a homing pigeon, begin their long and often arduous pilgrimage back to fresh water. Certain return migration routes have been discovered by man; and drift netting with nylon nets reaped a rich salmon harvest off our coasts until banned by law. Other predators lie in wait. Packs of seals, for instance, indulge in salmon feasts as the main run make for the estuaries, where the commercial fishermen lie in wait to operate their various salmon netting systems. The salmon may well have to negotiate polluted estuaries, with a risk of mortality, in order to find upstream water of greater purity. But slowly, as spring turns into summer, the rivers fill again with fresh-run fish who anxiously seek peace and quiet until, in the autumn of the year, they find their mate and fulfil the requirements of species generation.

We know that as far as feeding for sustenance is concerned, the salmon do not feed in fresh water. People who continue to maintain that they do are like the Flat Earth Society members who still maintain their tenets, despite having seen factual space pictures. The digestive organs of the salmon are said to cease to function upon entry into fresh water. But the full facts are not known. There is a deal of evidence for the theory that salmon then become *incapable* of feeding in fresh water;

but some eminent authorities have expressed the view that
should the salmon have the inclination to feed there is no
reason why the digestive processes should not continue to
function. Which comes first, therefore, the chicken or the
egg? Does the stomach occlude, and become inoperative, due
to fasting, or does the occlusion compel the fish to fast? All
authorities seem agreed that salmon do not feed in fresh water
in the full sense of the word; and that they are maintained by
the built-up fat and protein in the body tissue. The entire
process of staying in fresh water is a slow process of wasting
away. The eggs or milt have to be formed from these natural
reserves. The salmon lose their girth; and scale-readings show
a recession in growth. The flesh loses its natural fat; and by
the time a spring-run fish faces the rigours of spawning, it is a
sorry looking creature. Even after its completion of the sex
act, the Atlantic salmon (unlike its Pacific cousin) is not
necessarily doomed to die. Many females drop back into
quieter water while the males guard breeding grounds,
termed 'redds'. While many do, in fact, succumb and die, a
good proportion make their way back to the sea as 'kelts'; and
even though a high percentage of these kelts may fall to
hungry marine predators, there is evidence that a worth-while
percentage, at least, survive to make the journey again.

Richard Waddington argued that for reason of birth
location the salmon is basically a fresh-water fish. The specific
gravity of a salmon egg would make it float in sea water. This
may induce fresh-water laying; but by reason of feeding habit,
salmon may well be classed as sea-fish. Assuming this to be
fact, why is it that salmon sometimes take our flies or baits
whilst they are in fresh water? What prompts them to do this?
Is it the memory of their younger days in the river, as parr,
when they fed on every available morsel the river could
produce? Is it the memory of their rich sea feeding? Is it their
anger at having the peace and tranquillity of their fresh-water
lie shattered by a wobbling spinner or a fluttering fly? Or is
it purely habitual reflex action, as Waddington postulated?
Might another factor even be the great competition which

goes on between salmon and salmon, for a good lie? When
the individual salmon finally finds a suitable lie, is the taking
of a lure a show of resentment of the intrusion, not only of
some other salmon, but of some other form of natural life?
The fact is – we do not *know*. It may be any, or all, of these
influences. If it were only one of them, why is it that the
angler should not catch every salmon in the river? Why is it
that, at some periods, they are on the take; and at others,
nothing on earth will induce them to move? Why is it that
fresh-run fish are easier to catch than the, obviously, more
hungry stale fish, which have been in the river for a much
longer period? Why is it that sometimes a fish will grab any
fly, bait or spinner as though it represented the last meal of
its life – which well it may do? The fact is we do not *know*;
and to think that we do is mere fancy. The angler, of course,
is perfectly entitled to his fancies. The facts are so desperately
obscure that unless fancies had been there to fall back on,
there would have been no progress at all in the techniques of
salmon fishing. This is based on presumption that there has
been some progress – which, in the full sense, I doubt!

If an angler were asked to catch a fish which he had never
seen or heard of before, one of his prime questions would be
'What does it feed on?' Armed with this knowledge, he would
then be able to devise the necessary lure, whether fly, spinner
or bait and go forth with reasonable confidence. He would,
with some assurance, obviously present the right type of lure
to induce the fish to take it. We already know, however, that
the salmon neither feeds, nor, rather, takes food for nutriment
in fresh water. Yet over the past decades, man has devised lures
galore which will all take salmon under varying conditions.
Have we yet arrived at definite conclusions that any one of the
various designs we adopt for salmon fishing is the best design
to induce a take? Might there not be some lure, undiscovered
as yet, which would hook more consistently? We don't know,
and as the fish does not take food, it is reasonable to suppose
that it would take a spinning wrist-watch just as well as the
most beautifully contrived lure! Indeed, well they might do.

I have never tried a spinning wrist-watch, a wobbling carrot,
or any such lures, for a simple reason; the salmon is never
likely to encounter such things in his normal life. We realize,
of course, that as predators they must feed on something in the
sea; but we have, as yet, little knowledge of their staple diet.
We have quite a deal of information on their infant-feeding
habits while in fresh water. We know that they take flies and
small aquatic insects; we know them to be close relations of
the brown trout, who are some of the most intensive predators. Dare we assume, therefore, that the salmon's general
behaviour is very similar to that of trout? We know, for
instance, that certain types of trout have accustomed themselves to a sea-going migration, and have thus earned the term
'sea-trout'. We know these fish to be predators in both their
river and sea lives; so it seems reasonable to accept that the
salmon find a more bountiful larder of small fish to prey upon
while they are at sea.

    It is not difficult, therefore, to understand the reasoning of
the salmon fishermen of earlier years. If a small fly catches
trout, then a larger fly should catch salmon. It seems reasonable to presume that the first salmon caught was probably
hooked entirely by accident when the angler was wet-fly
fishing for trout. With the fine horse-hair casts of those far-off
days, the hooked fish could easily have been lost. But these
early findings would, at least, bring some clue about what a
salmon is prepared to take; and the flies, spinners and baits
that are in use today doubtless have their evolution from these
primitive findings; rather than from any knowledge of the
salmon's staple diet. It could be argued, therefore, that the
old-fashioned types of lure would be equally effective on our
salmon rivers today; and that it is purely fancy which invests
our modern patterns with belief that they have magic
qualities. Have we, in fact, made any progress at all? We are
certainly no nearer knowledge as to why a salmon takes our
lures; and although it cannot be logical to fish for them with
a wrist-watch (even if this could be made to flutter like an
ailing prey) who is to say that it will not be as effective as

modern designs of the Devon Minnow? The movement of a Devon Minnow through the water is surely most illogical, for nothing in nature moves in such a fashion. Yet I have caught far too many salmon on the Devon to discard it lightly as a take-inducing lure. It has been the standard spinning lure for successful fishermen through past decades; and although most of our lures have undergone minor changes over the years, it is only fancy which invests them with preference beyond that of the originals, today.

We know, therefore, that, quite by accident, man has stumbled upon ways and means of catching salmon. We can only *assume* that we have found the better ways. Indeed, if better lures are there to be discovered, it could well be argued that they are best unfound; since their effective use would cause further depradations on our diminishing stocks. If the present ravages of trappings in the estuaries, polluted waters, and commercial Greenland netting (not to mention the present outbreak of salmon disease) continue unabated, then the prospect is indeed bleak; but so long as the salmon remain, man will seek to catch them. Moreover, as anglers (and, of course, conservationists) show the main concern about the future of our salmon stocks, and not the commercial fishermen, it is the anglers who have, logically, the greatest entitlement to catch the salmon.

We know that salmon will take a worm, fly, spinner, prawn and shrimp since they have been caught with all of these lures. We know that while in fresh water salmon do not take these lures for food to ensure their sustenance. Let us examine some of the old methods, and some of the new. Many opinions will be based on fancy; but on the fancy born of experience, and set against the yardstick of success.

AUTHOR'S NOTE:—*On the question of high seas netting for salmon off Greenland there have been some new developments, but there is still some cause for concern. Chapter 27 deals at greater length with the problem.*

DRIFT NETTING. *In error I commented that all drift netting had been banned by law. This, while true of Scotland, is most certainly not true of the rest of Britain. Further information may be found in Chapter 27.*

## 2
## Seasons and Methods

We have already seen that salmon may be caught in fresh water with a great variety of lures. As yet, there is little more than a basic formula to guide the novice in his choice of season or method; and it is indeed important to have knowledge of several factors before a particular section of a river is likely to be exploited to the full.

If we take the Tweed as, perhaps, the most prolific salmon river in Britain it is an interesting exercise to examine the movements of salmon in that river at varying times of the year; and try to determine the best methods for each season. There is no doubt that most forms of fly-fishing for salmon take pride of place in method; and from the opening of the Tweed season, on 1 February of each year, fly-only is the rule until the commercial netsmen begin their operations on 15 February. Following this, all legitimate angling methods are permitted until the close season for the netsmen commences on 15 September, after which the fly-only rule comes back into force. In a sense this is a nonsensical rule which is obviously imposed on the angler to appease the netsmen; but to overcome the early season ban on spinning, some very heavy flies have been devised. These, when fished expertly, are almost as effective as the spinner. There are those who hold the belief that the fly disturbs the water less than the spinner; and, therefore, proves more effective over a period. I think that a lot depends, in this instance, upon the skill of the angler. Speaking personally, I have little doubt that, during the early season, the spinning bait – either natural or artificial – is the most effective. Big, heavy flies are brutes to cast; and it requires strong muscles and a stout heart to spend a day with the essentially heavy salmon fly-rod.

There are even a few rivers which open on 15 January (and even earlier in Ireland); notably the Tay, the Eden and the Wye. On these rivers spinning or harling with big baits is the general order of battle; and this style of fishing (usually with a double-handed bait-casting rod and a multiplying reel) is in common and frequent practice until early April. There is no doubt that a mild spell in January induces many fresh fish to run into our more noted salmon rivers. If the weather stays mild and water temperatures rise correspondingly, the fish will tend to run up fast. If a cold spell either continues or intervenes, it has a slowing-down effect on running salmon. The old rule about warmer water making the fish run faster, is a good old basic; and the knowledge of these facts often enables the angler to intercept a run of fish on a particular beat of the river; always provided, of course, that he has access. Let us look at the Tweed for examples.

In a normal year, it was almost unknown for fresh fish to be as far upstream as Makerstoun during February. Beats below Kelso, and down to Lennel, were having the cream of the sport. Then, since 1963, we have had a succession of comparatively mild winters. The beats at Lennel have had a lean time; whereas those around Floors, and higher upstream, have been taking fish earlier than ever before. I regularly fish the Upper Hendersyde water, immediately below Kelso. Over the past ten years some great changes in the running habits of the fresh-fish have been observed. I have taken this beat regularly during the first two weeks of February. Examination of the records over the past ten years, during what is considered to be the most productive period, show that sometimes salmon have not come up in any number, if there has been a cold spell in January; and that the bulk have gone through if January has been mild. Finding the beat full of fish on arrival,

is something which has only happened to me twice during the
last eleven years. Needless to say, we have taken advantage of
this situation when it occurred; and twice the record of fish
taken from the beat has been equalled during this period. I
keep hoping for the next season to come along to bring me the
chance of breaking this record. I recall, however, that when I
was on this same beat during the bitter February of 1963,
there was hardly a fish in the river. For the most part, the
river was an ice rink; but I was fortunate enough to have
access to the same beat during the third week of March, by
which time the thaw had arrived and our pools were full of
fresh-run fish. This was one of those two occasions of heavy
catches, which I have mentioned.

It can be seen then that to take the same beat at the same
time, year after year, will give the angler fairly long odds
against hitting it exactly right. It is always a gamble; and the
only way to shorten the odds is to review the records of the
beat over the previous ten years. This will give a sound guide
to the most productive periods. The rest is up to fate, upon
which depends the elements – and the whims of nature!

In an average season, by the time April arrives, the beats
below Kelso will doubtless be showing a shortage of fish.
There will only be spasmodic runs throughout the season. A
few fish may tarry long enough to get themselves hooked; but
these beats will not now produce the big bags until, with the
advent of autumn, the water temperatures drop. Then the
autumn-run fish will slow down their pace of running and
fill these lower beats once again.

The reason I have outlined this specific instance of a salmon
river is to show that knowledge of fish habits on the particular
river the angler is to fish, can be fairly vital to the achievement of regular success. There will rarely be much point in
fishing with anything other than spinning tackle or large sunk
flies when water temperatures are between 32° to the low
40°s; and the flies or spinners should be fished as slowly as
possible, well down in the water.

It is generally accepted that as soon as water temperatures

rise to near the 50° mark, fly-fishing, with a floating line and small flies, comes into its own. By such time the fish should be well spread out in the middle and upper reaches of the river; and some will be losing their lovely silver sheen, and colouring up a little. They may well be more difficult to tempt with either the small spinner or the small fly; and there could be a period when they appear to take nothing at all. Normally, however, I find that there are good early periods for the spinner or sunk-fly, followed by an interesting spell of greased-line fishing in late April or May. At the end of May, however, the difficulties seem to commence; and it is at such time that prawning and worming seem to save an otherwise blank period. In some quarters, these methods are frowned upon; but they offer the frustrated angler a means of taking salmon that are apparently uncatchable by other tactics. This is not to infer that such methods act in any magical fashion. Expert use of the worm or a prawn can, however, turn the risk of a fishless day into a productive one at certain times and seasons. It must be borne in mind that indiscriminate use of the prawn, however, can do general angling more harm than good. A water which has been heavily prawned will rarely provide good sport for the fly-fisherman until fresh stocks of fish get into the river.

There is an unsolved mystery about the times and seasons when salmon are likely to run into our rivers. The more noted rivers like Tay, Spey, Tweed and Dee all seem to have a good early run; whereas other rivers will not see a glimpse of fresh-fish until late spring or summer. Despite all attempts to induce spring runs, little rivers like the Yorkshire Esk rarely see fresh-fish until June, dependent on the weight of water flow. I have seen dry summers there when the Esk fish have not been able to run up to any extent until the season was virtually over. Again, what makes fish run Tweed in February when they are not ready to spawn until November? What makes other fish run the same river in November when they are already on the threshold of spawning? Why are most Tweed springers small fish, and the autumn ones much larger? Why are Eden springers the largest salmon likely to run the river during any year? Why won't the Esk fish go near the river until the first floods of summer? Doubtless, the length of the river system has some bearing on this. The Tweed, Tay, Spey and Dee are all long rivers, whereas the Yorkshire Esk is barely twenty-nine miles from source to mouth. It seems reasonable to suppose that the fish know when they must enter the river to reach their chosen spot by the time they are ready to spawn. The Argyllshire Awe gets a run of fish in April and May; but these fish are rarely caught in the Awe. They go straight through the river, into Loch Awe, and up the Orchy. It is not until June that the Awe fish come in; and fishing of the river commences in earnest about this time.

There are many imponderables about the ways of salmon. The fact that any river has earned the label 'salmon river' is little guide to the sport which may be expected from it. There are several factors with which the angler must make himself aware before he can expect a river to yield its best; and on some spate streams it is almost essential to be on the water at a precise hour of the day, when the gillie or keeper tells you the fishing is likely to be good. Again, the height and colour of the water plays a very important role on all rivers; but it is especially important on most spate streams. Having ascertained a reasonable assurance that there will be salmon in our beat during the time of our visit, we are better able to decide the tactics we shall adopt. It will also help us to know whether the fish are likely to be fresh-run; and the height of the water will have strong influence on the assessment of chances of a catch.

My fishing venues are very varied. First there is the Tweed during February, when I am usually limited to the big sunk fly, or a $2\frac{1}{2}$-ins to 3-ins spinner – or even a Toby spoon later in the month. Then comes late April, which sees me on the banks of the Spey, instructing on the Scottish Council of Physical Recreation angling courses. I get some opportunities to fish there, however; and may find myself using anything from 2-ins Devons to small flies on a greased line. Much will depend on the height and temperature of the water; but with the amount of spinning which is done by anglers, I frequently resort to a medium sized fly on a floating line, with a sinking tip. This gives a compromise between true sunk-line and floating-line tactics; and also gives the salmon an alternative to the numerous spinners which have fluttered over their heads. As April warms into May, I tend to fall back on true greased-line methods, and only spin if the water is too high for fly.

During June, I may be on a middle beat of the Dee; or trying early season conclusions with the Norwegian salmon. June seems a bit late for the best of the Dee fly-fishing; and I have frequently had to resort to spinning, worming or prawning in order to get fish. Over in Norway, however, the snows are just beginning to melt; and although the weather may be semi-tropical, the water is still maintained very cold by the melting snow. I have fished there in an air temperature of 80° when the water had to struggle to make 42°. As the snow melts, the rivers run heavy and strong. The tactics which were used on Tweed, back in February or March of the year, are once again in fashion. The cream of Norwegian fly-fishing will not come until late July or August, when, with luck, I shall be over there once again. In between these times, however, I may well be spending many of my free weekends on a private stretch of the Lune; or on the Association water of the Yorkshire Esk. On these waters, I could be using anything from tiny flies to prawns and worms. As September cools into October, the floating line with the sinking tip gets used for fly-fishing; and flies and spinners gradually go up in size. By the end of November I am once again hurling out the big, leaded, sunk flies on Tweed. This then, gives but a brief picture of seasons and methods. Let us go from here to examine these in greater detail.

AUTHOR'S NOTE:—*The exceptionally mild winters of 1971, '72 and '73 have seen some dramatic early upstream migrations with consequent poor sport in the traditional spring beats.*

# 3
## Fly Fishing Techniques

---

*No. 1.   Sunk Fly*

WE have already discussed the premise reasoned by earlier
anglers that if a small fly caught trout, a larger one should
catch salmon; and that the evolution of the salmon-fly was
based on nothing more than speculation. In 1850, 'Ephemera'
(E. Fitzgibbon) in *Book of the Salmon* was giving detailed
dressings, with lists of salmon flies, 'for every good river in the
empire'! Little did he know that 120 years would do little for
salmon flies, yet it was destined to knock hell out of the
empire. In 1855, William Blacker gave us the *Art of Fly
Making*, with many detailed descriptions of how to dress flies
for salmon; but it was not until 1895 that George Kelson
unloaded his tome *The Salmon Fly* on the angling public at
large.

It seems strange that such a work should have been taken
so seriously. Doubtless Kelson was sincere in his beliefs that
the multitude of fly patterns he illustrated in his book had
their times and seasons. But, today, as I glance through page
after page of coloured plates, I am struck by the overall similarity of many of the illustrated designs. It is crediting the
salmon with a great deal more sophistication than I think they
possess to think that they would have a preference for one fly
and not for another. I think that Richard Waddington produced some logical thought in his postulation that salmon in
cold water require a much larger fly than those in water over
50°. Certainly my experience has been that for early spring

and late autumn fishing, there seems little point in fishing
with a fly of less than 2-ins in length; and that the fly has to be
fished well down, near the bed of the river. Balfour-Kinnear,
in his excellent book *Catching Salmon and Sea-Trout,* did not
appear to agree. He argued that, in his opinion, there was
*never* the need to scrape the bottom; and that fish taken on
a sunk line could be hooked well above the bottom. All experienced writers seem to agree on the necessity of long casting,
however, in order to get the fly down to a worth-while depth,
and the manipulation of it into a position to which the fish
would not have to travel a great distance in order to take it.
Personally, in really cold water, I like my fly to be well
down. If, on the odd cast, I scrape a rock or some protrusion
on the bottom I feel that bit more confident of success. There
is, of course, a real danger of foul-hooking a fish when
manipulating the lure in this way; but salmon have to be
pretty thick on the ground for such an occurrence. On some
waters, with well-stocked pools, weights of fly and hook sizes
are limited to prevent the unscrupulous angler from the dis-
tasteful practice of foul-hooking; but for legitimate fishing in
cold water, if the fly is at the right depth to foul-hook a fish,
then it is also at the right depth to hook it in the mouth on a
genuine take.

In order to be at full potential for all types of sunk-line
fishing the angler would require lines of differing weights,
so that he could cope with high or low water conditions during
his visit. Flies would also have to vary in weight but not very
much in size. Judging from practical experience, Waddington
was right when he said that for early and late season fishing
there is little point in using a fly less than 2-ins in length. In
days of old, flies were tied almost exclusively on single hooks;
and those of over 2-ins in length were not very good in hook-
holding quality. There was a good deal of leverage with these
big flies, which made it easy to lose a fish once it had been
hooked. Nowadays the tube-fly, or an adaptation of this dressing is more practical since the triangle of hooks at the end
are articulated to prevent loss of fish from leverage.

My tackle for sunk-line fishing consists of three distinct outfits. The first is comprised of a strong 15-ft tournament-type, fibre-glass rod; and approximately 36-ft of GAAG (DT11) WetCel line, spliced to 27-lb test monofilament backing. This is my 'big-gun' and is brought into action when the Tweed is running a foot or two above normal level. There are, of course, a wide range of WetCel lines. The 'Fisherman' (neutral density), WetCel 1, WetCel 2, and the Hi-D, all have different rates of sinking. Some experiment may be necessary to find the best to suit your own conditions. Flies tied on brass tubes, with possible addition of lead, are the order of the day. The weight of the above length of WetCel is approximately $1\frac{1}{3}$-oz; and as some of the heavy leaded tube-flies can weigh up to 160 grains it will be seen that the total weight outside the rod-tip is getting on towards 2-oz. Casting with such tackle is a back-breaking business, and unless the river is exceptionally high, with consequential necessity to get the fly well down, I resort to a slightly more manageable fly, which weighs about 60 grains. My basic technique for heavy fishing is to work out the shooting head until it is beyond the

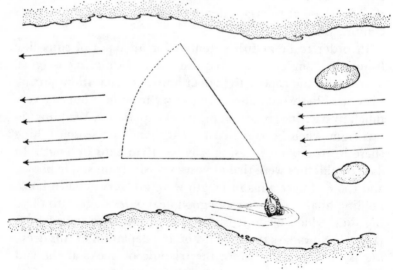

FIG. 1

rod tip. With the length I have mentioned and a suitable rod, it is just possible to lift this weight of line and fly and aerialize it. The great feature of having a short length of fly line attached to monofilament backing is that it takes a lot of hard work out of distance casting; and enables a great deal of backing to be shot. Reservoir trout anglers use this technique a great deal and it is a very effective method of fishing the sunk fly. The main feature is to have just the correct amount of fly line, which the rod can comfortably aerialize, spliced to the backing. Some experiment may be necessary to find this ideal length for your rod. Casting techniques have to be altered slightly to cope with what is still a very heavy fly; and a distinct pause must be made on the back cast. The new rhythm is soon mastered, however. A great deal of the mono-filament backing may then be shot, in order to achieve a worthwhile distance. It is even possible to make a quick mend in the line in order to take some of the downstream belly out of it, before it has sunk too far. The rod point should be held well up to get the shooting head *and fly* well down; and the rod should be held well out, at right angles to the current, to prevent the fly coming round too quickly (see Fig. 1). Leading the fly round by altering the angle of the rod is to be discouraged since it is likely to make the fly move too quickly. Once the cast is fished out the backing is hand-lined in, and a further cast made. As much of this type of fishing may well be done from a boat, the boatman will determine the distance between consecutive casts. Boat fishing in this style is also much easier, since the bottom of the boat makes a handy platform to hold the coils of monofilament backing until they are shot out in the final fore-cast. This method of fly-fishing is a tedious business. But for the regulation require-ments on Tweed during the fly-only period, one feels that spinning would be a much more sensible way of doing things. Necessity, however, is the mother of invention; and if you must fish the fly on a big river in February or November, the described method is the most effective I know.

The sunk-fly fisherman will not, of course, always find a high river at such times. Hard February frosts quickly lower the water levels. Once the river is down to normal height, the tackle I have described would be far too heavy; and the angler would get snarled up on the bottom as every cast came round. In these circumstances, there is an inclination to put on a *smaller* fly. This should be resisted! Obviously, you will need a much lighter fly; 36-ft of GAAG (DT11) WetCel can be replaced with the same length of GAG (DT10) WetCel line, or equivalent ungreased silk line. On such occasions I discard the flies on brass tubes, and resort to flies of the same length on aluminium tubes, these designs weighing somewhere around 25 grains. Rod strength can also be reduced. My 13½-ft Hardy 'Wye' or a 14-ft 'LRH' seem to cope quite adequately. Technique remains basically the same; but it should begin to feel a little more like fly-fishing in the full sense, and the fly will not bang you on the head while casting, as frequently as the heavy one does! The lower water should also ensure that the fish are more settled in their lies, since they are unlikely to run very fast during a cold spell.

There are occasions when really low water greets the early and late season angler. Under such conditions the outfits I have described would be too heavy, and the lure would snarl up on the bottom. However, I have only encountered really low water on two occasions; and on those occasions I was glad to have a terylene GAAF (FT9) line on hand. This line sinks more slowly than the WetCel lines. It seems ideal for really low water conditions. There are, of course, many other lines with slow sinking qualities which would serve equally well, but to reach full potential the sunk-fly fisherman, ideally, should have at least two line alternatives. One should have fast sinking qualities; and the other, slow sinking. A little experience will teach the angler, by a glance at the river, which outfit is likely to be the most effective for presentation.

In the main, I have so far dealt with circumstances which force the angler to use a sunk-fly, out of sheer necessity. In many of the conditions I have described the angler would have been better advised to spin. It could be argued, however, that a fly can be fished more slowly than a spinner, and thus be more effective. A skilful angler should have no difficulty in fishing both lures at the same speed; but I have never changed my earlier opinion that on a high water in the spring or late autumn, spinning is more productive. To illustrate this we need only consider the recorded catches on a well known beat of the Tweed, where as I have said, the fly is mandatory until 15 February. Then, when the regulation is relaxed, all anglers put away their fly-rods, and come out with their spinning tackle. In a general year, this change doubles the number of salmon caught. There is no certainty, of course, that this is due to the spinner being more effective at all times. It may well be that preference is pure fancy; and that the salmon are only responding to a change of lure because, for the past fifteen days, they have seen nothing but flies. My own private feeling is that it may well be nothing more than the fact that the bulk of anglers are more skilful with their spinning tackle than they are with their fly tackle. I well recall one instance, however, after we had been spinning for about a week with diminishing catches, when I reasoned that the fish might well show some interest in the fly again. I had spun down a pool twice with different baits and had taken nothing. 'Let's go down it with the fly,' said I to the gillie. The fly promptly took two fish from that same pool. Admittedly, this does not prove anything. The fish were fresh-run, and might well have crept into the pool while we were changing to fly. They might well have taken the spinner had I gone down with it a third time. But, at least, we knew there had been fish there all the time; and as they had refused the spinner on two occasions, it seemed reasonable to show them something else. It could also be reasonable to assume that it was the change that brought the required reaction; although there were complex possibilities. For instance, the conditions might simply have changed for the better during those minutes I was using the fly. Most salmon anglers are well aware of the fickleness of salmon; and the blank day up to, say, 3 p.m. may suddenly

B

turn into a halycon one, without change of method or style.

We have already assumed that salmon in fresh water require nothing more than a peaceful lie in which to idle their time away, until the inclination to spawn comes upon them. We have speculated upon the various reasons why a salmon will take a fly, spinner or bait; but we are still no nearer any worth-while solution. Some writers on salmon hold the belief that fish will not take until they are settled in a pool; others, that the fish must become unsettled before they will take. I have sufficient evidence, from my own experience, to show that both cannot be either right or wrong. If salmon take when they are both settled and unsettled, we should catch a lot more of them. There must be some other factor which influences their taking habits; and I am convinced that both settled and unsettled fish will take on occasions. The oxygen theory was one which my good friend Reg Righyni speculated upon in his book *Salmon Taking Times*. The book is well worth examination, even if it leaves the reader in some doubt about the extent to which he should recognize these suggested taking times; but it will at least give some clue to help the identification of good conditions, to give a reasonable guide to selection of suitable tackle and lures. If we had sure knowledge of a definite taking time, there would be little point in fishing until this came. As it is, most anglers are well aware that the salmon have not read our books! They have an awkward habit of pleasing themselves. The angler who fishes longest, in a skilful fashion, is generally the angler who will catch the most fish. He will catch them, at times, when he considers that taking inclination will be most unlikely; and he will fail at times when conditions look most promising. Only the salmon are likely to know when they are going to take. It would require a field-laboratory to predict reactions. Nonetheless, the reading of *Salmon Taking Times* is very worth-while; and may help the angler to recognize some of the conditions under which he may, or may not, expect sport. Many of the experiments now being conducted on fish passes, where temperatures, pH values, barometric pressures and several other factors are assessed, indicate that Righyni's arguments are well founded when it comes to his prediction about running salmon. He is a skilful angler and seems to have acquired the knack of only wetting a line when there are fish to be caught. Most experienced salmon anglers have, quite unconsciously perhaps, learned to recognize times when to fish hard – and when to sit and watch. Many of these times are difficult to predict or determine, and it is virtually impossible to lay down any sound formula.

As a general rule, it is reasonable to assume that we shall not catch many salmon when they are running hard and fast. Experiences on the Awe during an early season, when the Orchy fish are running through, indicate that few tarry long enough to succumb to the angler's lure. Again, fish which have become settled in a pool seem to become more uncatchable the longer they stay there. So, it seems reasonable to assume that the best taking conditions occur somewhere near the point when settled fish become unsettled, or vice versa. The height of the water will have a great bearing on these factors. I shall deal with this in a separate chapter. Doubtless there is something in the oxygen theory propounded by Righyni; and conditions of light, temperature and barometric pressure must all play an important part.

Having said that much of our early season fishing would be better done with a spinner than a fly, I must now go on to say that there are a few occasions when I would back the sunk-fly against any other method; but not with the back-breaking tackle used in the early spring. Just as the early season trout angler is keen to change from wet-dry to dry-fly, I am quite sure that many anglers make the change from sunk-line to greased-line before greased-line conditions have reached their best. Let's face the fact that greased-line fishing is less tedious than any form of sunk-line fishing; since a floating line is very easily lifted off the water, whereas the sunk-line has to be brought to the surface of the water before it can be lifted. Attempting to lift a drowned line, for a backward cast, is one of the surest ways I know of smashing a good rod. A simple roll-cast downstream should bring the line to the surface. It can then be picked up for the backcast before it has time to sink. It is sometimes wise to make a false cast, in order to get a clean pick-up before the final cast is made. This method, however, is not very advisable on quiet, gliding water; since it can well disturb the fish the angler is hoping to tempt.

For general sunk-line fishing (not the early and late season techniques I have already discussed) I use a rod of some 12-ft to 13-ft in length, with a GBG (DT9) or HCH (DT8) Wet-Cel line, and monofilament leaders of around 12-lb test. I see little point in using tapered leaders. They might give fractionally better turn-over of the fly; but thanks to the convenience of cutting the required length of level nylon monofilament from a spool, I rarely bother with anything else. Tapered leaders, with knotted sections, are an abomination for greased-line fishing; but are satisfactory for the sunk-line. If you must use a tapered leader for all your fishing, I recommend the knot-less taper variety. They are a little more costly, but are worth the difference. The trouble is that they are rarely made in adequate lengths. There are many occasions when I have a distinct preference for a leader longer than the standard 9-ft, and certainly when using a white or lightly coloured line. Fly sizes may be varied quite widely with this sort of outfit; but, of course, we shall rarely be using the monstrosities we used back in the early spring.

Let us think, perhaps, of a late March or April day; or a similar period at the end of the season. The fish will already have seen a variety of big spinners and flies. There may even be a few who have already succumbed to the small fly on the greased-line. The water temperature may be hovering around the 50° mark. One day it may be 46°; and a day or so later it may be up to 52°; and a day or two after that it may be down to 48°. Things will be in a state of flux; and on top of this, the water may be rising or falling, settled or otherwise. Days may be cloudy or sunny, with air temperatures higher or lower than the water. The angler may well be uncertain, as we all frequently are, of just what to do for the best. He may well

have tried spinning or fishing the fly on the floating line to
no avail. It is at such times that I go for the sunk-fly. Fly sizes
may well be pretty much the same as those of the ones I use
on my greased-line outfit. I recall one occasion when I had
spent an entire morning one late September, with both
spinner and the fly on the floating line. The pools were full
of fish, and I felt that at least something ought to take. Following lunch, I put on the sinking line, and the same No. 6
double Blue Charm I had been using on the floating line. In
the short space of forty-five minutes I took three fish weighing
18-lb, 15-lb and 12-lb – and lost a fourth. Who knows? Conditions might have changed after lunch. I might have got these
fish on the floating line. This is one of the mysteries of the
game. I do not pretend to be able to tell you rhyme or reason
for it. The fact is I *did* make a change; and I *did* catch three
fish; and again it would seem reasonable to assume that the
change had some connection with my success. There are so
many things in salmon fishing that one can only assume; and
as assumption is frequently more entertaining than reality,
we sometimes assume so much that we confuse it with facts.
The greatest bulk of salmon fishing literature has been based
on assumptions. So it leaves us with no alternatives.

In the type of mid season sunk-line fishing under discussion,
the depth at which the fly fishes does not seem so important
as it does during the early or late season. Indeed, if Balfour-
Kinnear had confined his comment about fly depths to this
type of fishing, I should agree with him that the fly only needs
to be a foot or so under the surface for it to be effective. We
can only presume that now the large sunk-fly and heavy
spinner are too easily seen, and have ceased to interest the fish.
The fly on the greased-line is too near the surface; and its taking requires too much effort on the part of the fish. The small
sunk-fly is an elusive thing; something that vibrates in mid
water, and may be taken easily with little effort. All these
may be assumptions, I know; but assumptions are born from
experience. In the days before the discovery of greased-line
fishing, nearly all fishing was done with a line that sank.

Plenty of fish were caught in those far-off days. Why should they not be caught thus now? What has changed? Certainly not the salmon, only the angler's fashions. This is not to decry the great sport of greased-line fishing; but to re-establish a place for traditional methods at a time when everything is either new or brighter than white.

Times to try the sunk-line with small flies are difficult to predict. But if the fish are fairly settled, and have seen a variety of spinners or small flies on the floating line, a trial with the sunk-line may do the trick. There are times when such tactics will pay dividends during what look like ideal greased-line conditions: high summer, even, when the water is low, and fish lie sullen and comatose on the river bed. Techniques are basically the same as for all other methods of fly-fishing and the fly should be cast out, to give adequate cover to the stream being fished, and then allowed to swing round to the angler's own bank. There may not be the same urgency to make the fly move as slowly as one would do in very cold water conditions; and it is often good tactics to speed up the pace of the fly by either downstream mends, or hand lining. Alternatively, I have seen occasions when I have literally 'hung' the fly over a known lie for periods up to several minutes, to have it taken when I least expected. Try whatever you fancy; but do not become stereotyped in style.

A worth-while alternative to true sunk-line fishing has presented itself with the advent of a floating line, with a sinking tip. These lines are currenly on the market and consist of a main body of floating line, with approximately a 9-ft head of sinking line. They are easier to lift off the water than a fully sunk-line, and enable the fly to be presented at a slightly lower depth than would be possible with a complete surface floating line. In a really strong current they may be used for the greased-line method, since they prevent the fly from skating on the surface; something which occasionally happens with a fully floating line. For general sunk-line purposes, however, they do not quite fill the bill, but I should rarely go fishing nowadays without one in my tackle bag.

Sunk-line fishing forms a basis for our tactics with salmon; traditionally so, and, still worthy of its place today. In some respects it is tedious, and there are times when spinning is not only easier, but quite likely to be more productive. There are times, however, when the sunk-line really comes into its own and its use should never be discarded as old-fashioned. Let us now take a brief look at the wide variety of flies which may be used with this method.

AUTHOR'S NOTE:—*Although the rods described are perfectly adequate for the tasks involved there has been a dramatic improvement in rods of fibre-glass construction. Bruce & Walker's 'Bruce Major' is an excellent rod for early-season sunk-line fishing, as is Hardy's 14-ft 'Jet'.*

# 4
## Fly Fishing Techniques

---

*No. 2.   Flies for sunk-line fishing*

HAVING dealt with the vast potential which sunk-line fly-fishing for salmon can offer the angler throughout a season, let us now turn our attention to the wide variety of flies which may be used.

I have already expressed the opinion that much of the early season fishing would be better suited for spinning. It would certainly involve less work; but because of certain bye-laws, there are some rivers – notably Tweed – where the fly is compulsory for the few opening weeks. It is not surprising, therefore, that the flies which have been evolved for this type of fishing bear a strong resemblance to the 2½-ins or 3-ins Devon Minnow. The Yellow Belly and Black and Gold are favourites with early season spinners; and so flies have been constructed to look vaguely like these, a play of sorts to design a lure to resemble a silver or golden sprat. There are few professional makers of such flies; but Forrest's of Kelso, market a range; as do Jewson's of 1 Westgate, Halifax, Yorkshire. Many anglers prefer to dress their own, and over the years, I have tried varying methods, from Waddington-type mounts to the plain brass or polythene-lined aluminium tubes. The trouble with the former is that if the hooks become damaged it is virtually impossible to replace them, and the entire fly has to be discarded; whereas with the latter, the hooks are separated from the fly and may be replaced as necessary. Most of my flies are now tied on standard tubes, which are obtainable from W. T. Humphries & Sons Limited, of Poughill, Bude, Cornwall. I have a stock in both brass and aluminium, in sizes ranging from 2-ins to 3-ins. Dyed bucktail is generally used; but care must be taken to ensure that the bucktails are of the best quality. Goat hair has straighter properties. It is largely a matter of choice which is used. I rarely bother to tie in any body materials these days; and the flies are easily and quickly constructed with varying shades of colour. It is a good plan to have a wide variety of fly colours, with a ration of garish-looking creations for high and coloured water conditions. Yellow and hot-orange are popular, with one or two streaks of black or dark brown; and for really low water conditions, much more sombre colours seem effective with plenty of black and brown. Some anglers prefer to use a keel fly. This is constructed with a small lead keel. Because it always swims keel down, the top part of the fly should be constructed with dark fibres and an underbelly of lighter fibres. The object is, of course, to make it resemble a small fish. Illustrated in the plates are a few examples. It will be seen that there are many variables and the permutations are endless. Some anglers prefer to use aluminium tubes entirely; and to have additional lead wiring round the body so that they may have a wider range of weights. I have already made the point that there is little sense in using a fly shorter than 2-ins for this type of fishing; and so, in order to cope with the varying river conditions likely to be encountered, the weight and colouring are the paramount factors.

Having built up or obtained our stock of tube flies, it is a simple matter to thread the leader through the tube and tie on a triangle of hooks. At this stage a half-inch piece of polythene tubing or rubber valve-tubing should be fitted to the rear end of the tube to keep the hook tight and held in line with the tube. This effective control of the triangle hook was devised by Thomas Clegg, an outstanding professional fly-dresser who works in West Calder; and is very material, as will be indicated later, to the very light tube-fly. Care must be taken when dressing the fly to ensure that the fibres will flow far enough backwards to just cover the hooks. They should not extend too far beyond, to avoid the risk of their presenting incomplete entry of the hooks into the jaws of the taking fish.

Some years ago I conducted a series of experiments with flies held on line to swim in a glass tank constructed to hold running water pumped through. The outcome of these experiments was an article in *The Field* (29 June 1961 – see Chapter 16). The main disclosure of my trials was a noticeable lack of lifelikeness in most of the old fashioned, heavily-feathered flies. They were inanimate in the water. More modern dressing designs, to the contrary, with either heron, goat hair, or bucktail winging, looked much more lively and could easily give the impression of a natural life in the artificial creation. In this respect, therefore, I think it safe to assume that the modern tube-dressing is a definite improvement on the old heavily dressed, meat-hook types; and I think that this could well be a useful advance in lure design.

As we have already seen, in Chapter 3, the flies mentioned are basically for those cold early or late-season days when the temperature is unlikely to exceed the low 40s. There are, however, other conditions when the sunk-line is worth a trial where these flies would be far too big and cumbersome for manipulation. These conditions are those suggested as the period of flux, before the fish show inclination to take the small fly on the greased-line; or times when they appear to be uninterested in everything, later in the season. Here our flies need differ little from those we should use for true greased-line fishing; but there are a few alternatives worthy of mention. Before we do this, however, it might be well to speculate upon the effectiveness of colour in our designs.

It is my fancy, and purely a fancy, that the smaller we make our flies, the less important the colour seems to be. The design of big flies has been suggested in a variety of colours—some garish. The intent of these designs is to cope with differing heights and clarity of the water. Above all else we have made them so that the salmon should have no difficulty in seeing them, and have designed them to fish at a depth where the salmon will have little difficulty in taking them should there be the slightest inclination to do so. As soon as water temperatures climb towards the 50° mark, however, the big fly loses its effectiveness. True I have caught fish with them, even in greased-line conditions; but I think the takes were exceptions. The fish are now content to take a much smaller fly; and it will be the illusion of life, and not the startling colours which draw their attention. As the fish should now be prepared to move out of their lies more frequently to take them, the colour seems less important. Nevertheless, I think that the angler should have an eye for colour; and the fly should be dangled in the water, and inspected against the river bed, so that the angler can assess its appearance and decide whether it appears to fall in line with its new environment. Several well-known writers have commented upon the value of pattern; but they have been referring principally to fly selection in greased-line fishing. We shall examine some comments in a later chapter. For sunk-line fishing, however, I do not think that pattern is of paramount importance; but it is perhaps a little more so than in greased-line fishing. With the sunk-line, the fly is being presented so that the fish may take a more critical look at it than they would if they inclined to take a fly just under the surface. Here, they see the fly more in silhouette; and usually decide to take it long before they are near enough to it for critical examination. We are well aware, of course, that on occasions the head-and-tail rise to the greased-line fly appears to result in a touch of the fly. In such cases, the fish may have seen some alarming feature, as it came close to it. It seems reasonable to assume that pattern will be more important in the sunk-fly, even if only slightly so. We do not know, as yet, why the salmon takes our flies at all; so there can be no *known* influence by so-called exact imitation as in dry-fly fishing for trout. In that case the angler tries to put on his leader the nearest fly-dressing creation possible, to the natural fly upon which he assumes the trout are feeding. Choice of salmon fly is largely a matter of fancy; and in many cases the fancy of one angler is just as likely to be effective as that of another. A great deal of mumbo-jumbo is talked and written about fly selection for salmon. Few factors assist the novice to make his own selection.

The basic influence on my decision which fly to use, is the overall colour of the river bed. On most rivers this is predominantly brown; but the water may vary in hues, dependent upon the colour of any suspended matter. Sometimes the water will look a faint green colour, following a thick spate; at others it will show a strong blue tinge from the *ultra-violet* of the sun's rays. It is advisable to pay attention to the effect of sunlight, since the fish are likely to see the fly in greater detail in the absence of sunlight than they can under full sunlight. There are certain conditions when the fish may well be virtually dazzled; and if they see the fly at all, it will be as an elusive silhouette. Fly colour, in such circumstances, will be of minimum importance. We cannot, of course, predict the influence of light at the precise moment of a take; but the old contention that it is undesirable to be fishing when the sun is shining straight down the pool from upstream, is sound common-sense. On most of our easterly-flowing rivers the sun, therefore, does not present any problems until evening time; whereas westerly-flowing rivers present a morning problem. The sunlight over southerly-flowing rivers may well be troublesome during early morning or late evening; but daytime fishing rarely presents a problem. Personally I dislike a very sunny day for salmon fishing; and dislike it particularly during the hot months of June, July and August. Earlier and later, a certain amount of sunshine may be advantageous; but even so, I like the sense of humidity in the air; and try to avoid those days when the whole landscape is visible for miles in sharp relief. Such days are better for photography or sunbathing – anything rather than salmon fishing! They are, of course, associated with high-pressure meteorological conditions; but can occur when a cold-front is approaching or going through. Wind direction, also has some influence. Winds from the west are inclined to be damp after their long passage over the Atlantic, and are generally favourable; so are some winds from the south. East winds are notoriously bad; but not nearly as bad over western, as over eastern, rivers.

So much for speculations on the general water and overhead conditions in their influence on fishing. Once again, may I repeat that there must be no *never* and *always* about these things; but the successful salmon fisherman quickly learns that weather and water conditions are among the most paramount considerations the angler must learn to take into account. Once he has decided that fishing is worth-while the next problem facing him is his choice of fly.

The smaller sizes of tube flies are all worth consideration; but because of their limited size, their slow turn-over tends to make them catch on the leader unless steps are taken to eliminate this risk. The solving of this problem, to a large extent, is the device of Thomas Clegg, mentioned earlier, of using a small piece of light rubber valve-tubing at the end of the tube. This keeps the hook and tube in line. It will also release the tube from the hook when a fish takes, and removes the risk of leverage by the complete fly causing the hook to come free from the jaws of the fish. Much of mid-season sunk-line fishing is done with these flies; and I have them tied to such patterns as the Logie, Thunder and Lightning and Stoats Tail. The sizes range from $1\frac{1}{2}$-ins to $\frac{1}{2}$-in. The small sizes even make quite good dressings for the greased-line. I prefer, however, to have all flies for sunk-line fishing rather more heavily dressed than those for normal greased-line fishing. A major advantage of the tube is that it lends itself to a good amount of flowing fibres; and some very life-like patterns can be made. I like to inspect all my flies in the tank of flowing water, paying little attention to their colour and more to their action. Tube weights may also be varied, as we do with those for the big flies; and some very effective mid-season flies have been tied on short brass or copper tubes (see Chapter 10) barely a $\frac{1}{2}$-in in length.

If the river is of sufficient height to warrant the use of a $1\frac{1}{2}$-ins or 2-ins spinner, there appears to be good reason for putting on a fly which is only slightly smaller than the spinner length, for sunk-line fishing. We may assume, I think, that the fly will fish a little more slowly than the spinner, and therefore, does not need to be quite as large. Much will depend on the presentation ability of the angler; and here again there can be no hard-and-fast rule. I dress many of my sunk-line flies on low-water doubles from hooks size 4 to 6. The reason for the low-water hooks is that they have a slightly longer shank than the normal hooks; and this may be used to continue the body-dressing further than would be desirable for greased-line fishing. Occasionally I under-wind fine wire to add to the fly weight. It is my opinion that the whole secret of good sunk-line technique is availability of a wide range of flies for weight and size variation, so that the angler can adjust his tactics as water conditions dictate. I am not, as I have said, very concerned with patterns; and as flies get smaller, the colours need be no more than the browny-black suggestion with, perhaps, a tinge of blue or orange at the throat as directed by the overall *colour* of the water. Many of the flies I use would not even possess a name. They are made up at the fly-tying bench with the materials on hand; and whilst they catch fish, I suspect that they would not catch many fishermen! Illustrated in the plates are some examples of the smaller sizes of flies used for sunk-line and greased-line fishing. We have now dealt briefly with the various fly requirements for all types of sunk-line fishing. Let us now examine two vastly different fishing days, and analyse the methods used.

AUTHOR'S NOTE:—*During the past few years I have developed a strong affection for treble-hooked flies, as tied on hooks supplied by Esmond Drury, for both sunk and greased-line fishing.*

# 5
## Sunk-Fly Fishing Tactics

*A day with the big sunk-fly*

It was a cold November morning on the last day of the season. The watery sun struggled vainly to push through the early mists; but there was a sense of urgency awake in the river, as first one salmon and then another flung itself into the air with that gay abandon so characteristic of the salmon in their quest for the spawning grounds.

'Howaryer feelin' this morning Sorr?' greeted Wattie Lauder, my Tweed gillie. 'Bit woolly,' I answered, 'Drank too much of your wine of Scotland last night. Anyway, how's the fishing going to be today?' 'Well Sorr – if you and the other gentleman will fish hard, there are fresh run fish to be caught.' The other gentleman, incidentally, looking just as woolly as I did was my old chum Colin Bell. A Scot by birth, he had spent the previous evening, as is the custom of many exiled Scots, in toasting absent friends. Despite his Scottish birth he was destined to be exiled in rural England at an early age, and had never caught a salmon. He was perhaps keener than I to take advantage of the good conditions, and was not long in making ready with his tackle.

Being a novice and a newcomer to the water I gave him first choice. He rightly elected to go off in the boat, with the gillie; leaving me to fend for myself, fishing from the bank. To be fair, however, it was a piece of water which I had known and fished for years. I knew many of the likely places suitable for fishing from the bank. As he would need the gillie's careful guidance, if he were to have any chance at all, I did not mind. The river was running about a foot above normal – a good height for our beat – and as water temperatures were in the low 40s, I reckoned I would need my big outfit and a 2½-ins brass-tubed fly. A 10-ft length of 18-lb test monofilament was utilized as leader; and a fairly garish-looking yellow bucktail fly was tied on.

I had not been fishing for more than ten minutes when I heard a shout from upstream and turned to watch Colin playing his first salmon. Down the river I overheard odd snatches of the conversation as Wattie gave Colin chapter-and-verse on how to play the fish. Some fifteen minutes later it was safely netted. A shout brought the news that it was a fresh-run 18-lb fish – and 'What the blazes are *you* doing, messing about?' I felt delighted for Colin and continued casting in silence; but, by that time, was beginning to scrape the bottom a little too frequently. I was fishing a long line and casting the 36-ft of shooting head, and about 60-ft of monofilament backing. Since I did not want to shorten the length of my cast, I wound in and tied on the same size and colour of fly; but on a lighter tube. This had the desired effect. I felt confident that it was moving sufficiently near the bottom to interest any fish which it happened to pass – but not so deep that it would scrape the bottom. I fished the pool down carefully, to no avail; and on my way back upstream, half an hour later, I saw Colin's rod up in the air once again as he was playing his second fish. He really was enjoying himself, and dealt with this one in a much more masterly fashion than he had dealt with the first. It was soon on the bank. A grinning Colin looked up, as much as to say, 'Now who's the novice?'

Unlike some anglers who cannot bear the sight of someone else catching a salmon, I was thrilled with his success; but felt that little bit of humility which I think does us all good at times. I started in at the top of my pool once again, with a determination to concentrate every inch of the way. I even changed my fly yet again, and selected a slightly less garish

one of the same size and weight. I was just about to break off
for lunch when I felt the determined tug of a taking fish. It
was a dour, heavy pull, and within seconds line was screaming
from my reel as the fish made a heavy run against the current.
Salmon in cold water seem to fight much more slowly than
summer fish; but they still use all their weight and power in
attempts to shake the hook. This lively fellow used every
dodge in the book to try and out-wit me. He did not expend
his energy in long, determined runs. Instead, he bored relent-
lessly, shaking his head like an angry dog; and although I had
now confined him to a small piece of quiet water, he had no
intention of giving up without a stout battle. The minutes
seemed to tick by very slowly as the contest continued. Some
twenty minutes elapsed before he laid on his side and let me
lift him out by the tail. He weighed 22-lbs, and was gleaming
silver, with the sea lice still on him.

At lunchtime, then, Colin had the advantage over me by
one fish; and as November days in Scotland are short if not
always sweet, I was anxious to have my turn with the gillie
and the boat before the best of the day had passed. The day,
however, was rapidly deteriorating. Any trace of the sun had
gone and a fine, cold drizzle added to the discomfort. My
chances, I felt – even with the boat and the gillie – were fast
diminishing. It would be dark by 4 p.m., and I should have to
work very hard and pull out all the stops of experience if I
were to avoid a hiding on my own water.

Lunch quickly finished, Wattie and I made our way to the
top pool of the beat. He quickly boated me into position
where my casts would cover the likely lies. I still had on the
fly which had brought the earlier success, and had not been
fishing for more than five minutes before I felt the heavy pull
of another fish. Cold water or not, this one definitely resented
any notions of coming gracefully as he set off on a screaming
run upstream. I thought, at first, that I must have foul-hooked
him, since I was on to my backing in no time as Wattie sculled
the boat after him as quickly as he could. A ding-dong battle
ensued before I could subdue him; but Wattie's big net was

under him suddenly and my biggest Tweed fish, to that date, a 23-pounder, was on the bank. He was well hooked in the mouth and had fought valiantly to gain his freedom.

The part of the pool we were fishing, however, was not quite so deep as the pool I had fished during the morning; so I made yet another change of fly to reduce the terminal weight slightly, although I did not alter the size or the style of dressing. We were soon afloat again and lengthening out the casts. Five minutes later I was into another lively fish; and then another, and another – and at the end of that short afternoon we trudged back in the failing light, with our burden of five prime salmon. A more than adequate reward for perseverence and experience was to find that Colin had drawn blank; but was already toasting his earlier success with many fellow anglers. Between us, we had accounted for eight fine salmon from a small stretch of water, on a day when less hardy types would have been huddled round a fire.

Conclusions? I am not sure there are any. The six fish to my rod, and the two to Colin's, give little clue to the relative merits between a novice and an experienced angler. I like to fancy, however, that my knowledge of the water and the ability to change my tactics was responsible, in some measure, for my better catch. I may be fooling myself, of course; if Colin had been in the boat that afternoon, with the gillie's help, he might have done equally well. The day, however, did demonstrate the effectiveness of the big tube-flies; and that they are a very worth-while substitute for a spinner when legal requirements make some form of fly obligatory – and, maybe, of even greater value in their own right.

### A day with the small sunk-fly

It was one of those exasperating June days when I didn't know what to do. There were plenty of fish in the beat; some of which were already so coloured that they might well have been there since the opening day. Other fish, however, showed every indication of having arrived only recently; and as the river was fining off after a nice rise, it seemed reasonable to suppose that a percentage of the fish could be absolutely fresh-run.

During the morning the river had been high enough to make spinning worth-while; but I had tried both the small spinner and the greased-line to no avail. The day had dawned bright and sunny with a fresh, but light, breeze from the south. There was, however, a slow build up of some fair weather cumulus cloud; and following lunch, the sky consisted of a higher percentage of cloud than blue sky. Fishing wise, therefore, the day was improving. During the morning I had evidence of a little interest in both the spinner and the fly. A 1½-ins Black and Gold Devon Minnow had received a vicious pull; and I had noticed a nice head-and-tail rise to a No. 6 Blue Charm on the floating line. Following the first occasion, I tried both smaller and larger spinners. I tried fishing them fast and slow, upstream and across, and downstream. None of these tactics were of any avail. Despite the fact that the day was not quite right – to my liking anyway – I felt that with only a slight change of tactics, there were fish to be caught. It was an occasion long before the advent of the salmon disease (since which any form of taking prediction is virtually impossible) and I felt that it only required a slight tactical change to ensure a chance of catching a fish. The movement to the fly had suggested some willingness on the part of the salmon to have a go; but although I tried further fly variations, I was still fishless.

It was while having my lunch that I pondered over these problems. 'High time to take a bit of your own advice,' I thought. 'You are always telling people not to discard the sunk-fly too lightly. Is this not one of those times when it might pay off?' My lunch finished quickly, I replaced my floating line with a GBG (DT9) WetCel line; and put up the same leader and No. 6 Blue Charm which had been on the floating line. The cloud cover continued to increase; but the air temperature remained roughly the same and, as far as I could detect, the masking of the sunlight was the only variable factor involved. Doubtless there were many others of which I was not aware; but as I waded into a favourite pool I began to get a vague feeling of confidence. The better feel of the day for fishing brought expectancy; however indefinable, this is something the angler feels rather than measures. There is certainly no formula for it, other than the sense created by the hard and bitter school of experience, which somehow tells you when things appear to be promising. I had not been fishing for more than ten minutes before I felt the determined take of a good fish. There were no doubts about this one; the fish took the fly firmly and made sure the take was no light touch. He came up immediately, made a splashy boil and set off on a screaming run upstream. I was on to the line backing in no time; but followed him quickly and soon had all the backing on the reel again. As soon as I got opposite, the fish ran again and was soon wallowing about in the white water at the head of the pool. Once he was here, I eased the pressure in the sure knowledge that this was the best place to tire him. There were a few anxious moments as he jigged and bored among the rocks and obstructions on the bed of the river. After five minutes of this, however, he began to move downstream. His slower movement showed that the bulk of the steam had been taken out of him and it was not long before I caught glimpses of his glinting sides. I was quite surprised to see that, far from being one of the fresh-run fish, he was somewhat coloured and had obviously been in the river for a fair period. After a few more panicky rushes, he lay still and on his side. It was a simple matter to tail him and ease him up the bank. At 2.30 p.m. it was my first of the day; a fine though slightly coloured 19-lb cock fish, safely on the bank.

The greased-line pundits would inform me, no doubt, that this fish could have been taken on the greased-line; and for all I know, they may be correct. The fish might even have taken the spinner that I had been using during the morning. The point is I just don't *know* – nor I suspect, could anyone else *know*. The fact was that such methods had failed, but the sunk-line had succeeded. What was even more confusing was that I went on to take another two fish on the same sunk-fly, and had three further offers with which I failed to connect. By 4.30 p.m. I had fished the most likely water and could not maintain further interest. I was more than satisfied with three fish; but there was still plenty of daylight left, and even the chance of some sea-trout from dusk onwards.

It was about this time that I thought that a quiet break at the local pub would make a pleasant interlude. I spent the next hour with a quiet dram, and some bright chit-chat with the landlord and the locals. Back at the river once again, my entire experience shrieked greased-line to me. Fish were head-and-tailing all over the river. The light was soft and the breeze had dropped to a mere zephyr. The sun could be seen like a transparent globe with its light filtered through the high layers of alto-stratus and wispy cumulus. There were several layers of fine clouds which cast a yellow glow over the scene through their transparency. Apart from the bubble and sparkle of the streamy runs, all was tranquil. I knew, instinctively, that I should really be using the small fly on the greased-line; but the fact was that I felt too lazy to change! Instead, I compromised. Throughout the day, the river had fallen a good two inches. If my No. 6 Blue Charm had caught fish at 2.30 p.m., would it not be sensible to now try a No. 8? Then, possibly, go back to the No. 6 as the light failed, or even a No. 4 as it got darker still? This was the way my primary reasoning worked. I put on a No. 8 Logie – don't ask me why the Logie, I suspect that it was the only No. 8 that was handy – which is no reason at all. I started once again at the top of the favourite run. There was a slight eddy at the top of the pool; and although it had always looked to me like a good resting place, I had never moved a fish in this particular place before. I unhitched my fly from the rod butt and let it fall on the water in preparation for casting. Instantly, to my complete surprise, a salmon swirled at it; then moved back to its lie. Incredible! The salmon was lying not more than 9-ft from where I was standing, and yet he had the cheek to make a pass at my fly! If he could do it once, he might well do it again. I cast carefully with the mere rod length of line, so that the fly would pass again over the precise spot. The resulting action was like a slow-motion drama. The fly was within inches of my feet when, out of the depths, came a big mouth which slowly turned upon the fly and, seemingly, swallowed it whole. The tension was terrific. I had to restrain all my trout-fishing impulses to refrain from striking. After what seemed an age, the fish turned; and as he did so, I raised the rod tip and was fast into what appeared to be a more silvery fresh fish than any I had seen that day. I will not bore you with details of the prolonged and hair-raising battle; but he turned the scale at 16-lb, and was covered in sea-lice. Number four went safely into the bag.

From then on followed a chapter of mysterious incidents. By 7.30 p.m. I had changed back to my No. 6 Blue Charm; and in quick succession, I had four offers with which I failed to connect. They could, possibly, have been trout or sea-trout; but such takes are detectable after experience of them and I felt pretty confident that they were all offers from salmon. I did not quite know what course to adopt. Had the change from the No. 8 to the No. 6 been made too prematurely? Or should I really have changed already to the No. 4? I decided to go for the latter, tied on a No. 4 Logie and started fishing it. There was no doubt about the next offer and I was soon playing a lively fish which was quickly beached. It was the smallest fish of the day, barely up to 8-lb, and was colouring up a little.

By any standards, to take five salmon in a day must be considered a good catch. I had enjoyed a wonderful day of sport; and, for the moment, I was content with my catch. As the light failed, the air turned cooler and as I was fully content I decided to give the sea-trout a miss and wend my way home. Quite a few days elapsed before I began to reflect on that outing. Why was I so complacent? What was there to be really satisfied with? It had been a day when I had received no less than fourteen offers to the various spinners and flies, and of those fourteen offers I had only succeeded in hooking five fish.

Surely, upon reflection, this was a poor showing? Where had
I gone wrong? What variable permutations could possibly
have given fourteen instead of five? The plain fact is: I don't
*know*; nor, I suspect, does anyone else. It is quite feasible that
some experienced angler would have adopted different tactics,
and might have taken more than I did. On the other hand an
equally experienced angler could have done things in a
slightly different way and finished with a blank day. He
would, no doubt, have come back with great tales of the offers
which had come his way; and his diagnosis might well have
been that the fish were not properly on the take. Having tried
greased-line and spinner during the morning. I think that my
tactical decision to change to the sunk-fly was the right one.
Apart from anything else, it did secure five fish for me. I may
have been too lazy to change back to greased-line after tea,
when conditions looked good for that method; but who can
tell me that it would have been more successful than the sunk-
line, which took the two fish during that period? Such factors
are, in my opinion, impossible to assess. I should need the
perception of the Almighty to be able to predict exactly what
to do during any one minute of the day. The odd fish might
have responded better, with a firmer take, to a 2-ins Black
and Gold Devon Minnow at, say, four minutes past three,
despite the fact that the same fish might take a No. 8 Logie
quite firmly at ten minutes past six. How can we predict such
acute changes in reaction to fly or spinner behaviour? The
fact is we cannot! This doubtless provides one of the irritating imponderables in salmon fishing; and gives power to
the elbows of some who incline to scorn salmon fishing as
purely a game of luck. This, however, is not quite the way I
see it; for the fish present a constant challenge to the angler.
He cannot, and will *never* find a suitable formula for *all*
occasions; but, being the questing soul, he will continue his
attempts to find one. Herein, perhaps, lies the greatest fasci-
nation in salmon fishing; its inducement of a search for a
formula which the angler suspects does not exist; and *never*
(I use this word with reserve) will exist.

The sunk-fly secured me five fish during a day which was half-spent with other methods which had been unsuccessful. Can there be any more justification for using the sunk-fly at such times? Possibly, had I persisted, I could have taken more on the greased-line. This is a fascinating form of fishing which we should now consider in greater detail.

# 6

## Fly Fishing Techniques

*No. 3.   The floating or greased line*

PRESENT day techniques for greased-line fishing stem directly
from the methods which were developed and practised by the
late A. H. E. Wood; and a brief discussion of their origin
might be interesting. On page 69 of Jock Scott's book *Greased-
Line Fishing for Salmon – The Methods of A. H. E. Wood, of
Glassel,* Wood gives details of the birth of his idea on an Irish
river during July 1903. Apparently the river was very low,
and the fish were all lying close to the sill of an eel weir.
Traditional methods had failed; but Wood detected that the
fish were rising occasionally, and apparently taking a small
white moth from the surface. Eventually Wood put a small
artificial on his leader and dapped it over them. It evoked
such interest from the fish that in the short space of a few
hours he succeeded in landing six. He lost others and pricked
more than he cared to count. Following this experience, he
found himself fishing as near to the surface as he could make
his flies fish, and started greasing his line to facilitate this.
Wood goes on to say that from then on, he became convinced
that salmon either wanted the fly well down near the bottom;
or wanted it as near to the surface as he could make it swim.
He forsook his mid-water tactics from that day onwards. As I
have said in my earlier chapter, however, I do not agree fully;
although, on the waters that Wood fished, he may well have
had reason for his confined tactics. The Cairnton beat of the

Dee where he spent most of his time has always been one of
the most prolific beats on that river.

From a brief description of the birth of this method, therefore, it would seem that instead of making a case for greased-
line fishing as we know it today, Wood succeeded in showing
that, in fact, what those salmon really wanted, that July afternoon in 1903, was a dry-fly dapped over them. There is no
indication that present day greased-line methods would have
worked any better for him on that occasion, than the traditional methods to which he was so accustomed. Further
reading of this chapter also seems to give the indication that
his technique was akin to dry-fly fishing, since he claims that
he did not like any drag to be imparted to the fly.

I find it difficult to reconcile Wood's comment with the
type of greased-line fishing practised today. It would appear
that Wood liked his fly to float down, inert. Just how he would
expect it to move across the pool, from the far bank to his own,
without some form of drag, is a mystery. Greased-line tactics
today are entirely dependent upon some form of controlled
drag being imparted to the fly; otherwise, how could it possibly have the illusion of life? If the fly were carried down by
the current in an inert fashion, it would look like nothing
more than a piece of old flotsam; and unless it represented
some form of floating insect and brought a similar response
from the fish, as one gets in dry-fly fishing for trout, then it
could hardly be termed greased-line fishing as we know it
today.

There is, of course, quite a deal of evidence that salmon will
take a dry fly on occasion. The method is in common practice
on the Atlantic salmon rivers of the Eastern seaboard of
Canada, and has been tried with limited success on such
lovely rivers as the Scottish Dee. American expert, Lee Wulff,
rarely fishes in any other style; and has developed his ultra
fine tackle to the utmost limits of lightness, and catches many
fish with it. Further reading of Wood's comments, however,
indicates that his method did, in fact, induce some drag; but
that, after making what he termed a slack cast, he liked to

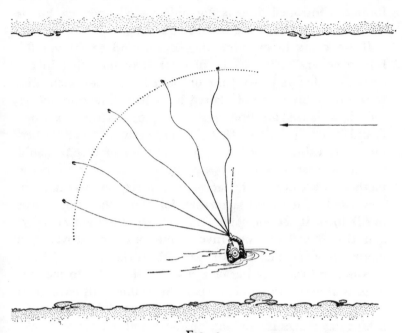

FIG. 2

Wood's method of leading the fly

lead the fly round so that it did not describe a true semi-circle. In this sense, therefore, whilst dragging to some extent, it was not dragging completely; but at a compromise speed somewhere between full drag and the speed of the current. If the water speed were five miles per hour, it could be assumed that fly speed, for part of the period against the current would be in the region of $2\frac{1}{2}$ m.p.h. This is still drag; and as such, forms the basis for all our thinking in modern greased-line techniques. Wood's flies were constructed so that they had to drag, to some extent, before they would resemble any sort of lure. They did not look even remotely like a dry fly; and, for the most part, were sparsely dressed on long-shanked single hooks. He even went to the extreme, on occasion, of painting the shank only. Such a 'fly' has to drag in order to evoke interest; and we must assume that some form of controlled drag is not only forced upon us, but is essential in all forms of greased-line fishing.

If we come to examine the background to salmon fly-fishing generally, it may be of interest to note that in the early days, before general use of plaited silk lines, such lines were invariably made of plaited horse-hair. The question is, did those horse-hair lines sink as rapidly as the silk line? Could it not be, in fact, that the very early salmon-fly fishermen were using methods very akin to those of Wood? Could it not be that Wood only succeeded in re-discovering the method by accident? The facts are very hazy on this question. Nevertheless, it would seem that, following the change over to silk lines, it became common practice to fish the fly deeply; and that Wood did not invent, but only re-discovered, a method to make the fly move nearer the surface.

Nowadays the greasing of a silk line, in order to make it float, is almost a thing of the past. Such lines still have great merit; but the continued greasing necessary throughout a fishing day makes it a tedious business; and so most of us take the easy way and use the modern floating lines. Such lines do not always float as perfectly as the makers would have us believe; but they are very convenient, and eliminate the possibility of getting some of the line grease on the cast or leader (something which inevitably happened to me in the old days) which caused the fly to skate on the surface of the water.

Modern floating lines are made in a variety of weights and sizes. It is a simple matter to find the one best suited to your rod. Whether you decide on a line with forward-taper design, or the standard double-taper, is largely a matter of choice. You will certainly be able to shoot more line with the forward-taper; but you will find it virtually impossible to execute any worth-while form of Spey cast. I like to have both on hand, so that I may choose a line best suited to the conditions of the day.

My greased-line outfits consist of a 12½-ft Hardy 'Hollolight' rod or a 13-ft 4-in 'Cordon Bleu' (the 12½-ft 'Wye' is very similar in action) and a GAAF (WF9) or GAAG (DT9) AirCel

line. Line colour has been a subject which has brought much
controversy; but white lines are very much in vogue today, on
the basis that the under-belly of a fish is white, and that this
colour is least likely to be seen by fish swimming underneath.
This seems a perfectly logical assessment, but it must be
borne in mind that, whatever the colour of the line, it will
still cast as great a shadow as any other, since it is no more
transparent. The white line is certainly a joy to fish with.
The angler sees it plainly and knows, at all times, the precise
placing of his fly. There are times, however, when the short-
tapered portion of the line sinks slightly below the surface.
In these circumstances, I am not certain that white line is the
ideal.

I recall a favourite pool on the Lune. The pool is known as
the 'Groynes', and is labelled thus because of the number of
man-made groynes put there to prevent bank erosion. In a
good year, the pool holds a fantastic number of fish. But it is,
in the main, a difficult pool to fish correctly; and consists of
smooth, gliding water with many swirls and eddies. Vision for
the fish must be superb through that mirror-like unbroken
surface; and the fish are frequently seen moving off their lies
as the pool is fished down. Fishing this pool with a white line
has never produced more than the odd fish for me. Yet a similar line, in brown or green, has frequently produced good
bags. This, of course, proves nothing; it is merely a fancy. But
a fancy so long held, as far as this particular pool is concerned,
that I rarely bother to fish it nowadays with my white line;
preferring the same line of mahogany colour. On the clear
waters of Norway, many gillies shake their heads sadly when
they see a white line. 'White line – no gutt,' they say. Such a
remark may be born out of prejudice, but I fancy there is
something in it.

Having commented on the foregoing, I do not wish my
reader to think that I am condemning the white line out of
hand. Most of my greased-line fishing has, in fact, been done
with a white line; and I have also used one in Norway with
equally good effect. The fact is that if nature invested fish

with white bellies then it is more than reasonable to suppose
that a white line is less easily seen than one of any other
colour; always provided, of course, that the entire line floats
on the water and is viewed from directly underneath. Normally the fish should not see the line at all. The length of the
leader should eliminate any possibility of this. But if a small
portion of the head of the line sinks below the surface, it is
possible that it may be more visible than a line of more subdued colouring. On gliding water, where a certain amount of
tip submergence is likely, I have felt some conviction that
green or brown is a better colour. When we come to discuss
the question of fishing on streamy, popply water, we immediately find an ally in the fact that such water can hide a multitude of sins; and camouflage even the most garish looking
tackle. Much of our salmon fishing will take place in streamy
water, however, and the visual help of a white line far out-
weighs any other consideration. There may, of course, still be
a certain amount of tip submergence; but this fine detail is
lost in the streamy water.

I have never been able to determine, to my own satisfaction,
the exact depth at which a greased-line fly should fish; and to
some extent I feel that it is a factor over which the angler has
little control. There are those, I know, who feel strongly about
this topic. They argue that the depth at which the fly fishes is
paramount to success. My good friend Reg Righyni argues in
this fashion and his record of fish caught on the greased-line
makes it difficult to disregard his contention. The plain fact
is, however, that we are again dealing with fancies. Fancy
born of experience is always worth a hearing and when fancy
has stood the test of many years of fishing it can almost be said
to have become a fact. The trouble comes when we examine
the differing circumstances while fishing one single pool of a
river.

Perhaps the first consideration we should make in our
greased-line fishing is the length of our cast or leader. If our
line is floating and we rub down our leader with Fuller's Earth
paste (a mixture of glycerine and Fuller's Earth powder) to

make it sink, the length of the leader will have some bearing
on the depth below the surface at which the fly fishes. Bear in
mind that we are dealing with mere inches or fractions of an
inch. If we incline to fish the fly deeper still, we should have
to resort to a line with a sink-tip or even a fully sinking line.
The strength of the current will also have a great bearing on
the depth of our fly; and it can quite easily be seen that our fly
will fish higher in the water in a strong, streamy run than the
same fly would fish in a slacker portion of the pool. Whatever
the circumstances, however, I have no hesitation in putting
up the longest leader I can use comfortably (generally some
2-ft shorter than the rod I am using). As with sunk-line fishing,
I rarely bother with a tapered leader; and certainly avoid the
knotted variety as an abomination. If there is any tendency
for the fly to skate on the water, there may well be a series
of 'wake forms' from each knot on the leader; and I know of
nothing more likely to put fish off the take. The simple
fact is, however, that no two consecutive casts could ever make
the fly fish at precisely the same depth. There may be a
certain amount of line-tip submergence on one cast, that is
not apparent on the next. One cast may result in the fly skating
on or near the surface, while the next gets a better entry and
fishes correctly. Generally speaking, a skating fly is to be
avoided at all costs. I know of instances, however, when
deliberate skating has taken a fish, for such is the unpre-
dictability of salmon fishing. The Americans sometimes deliberately put in a 'riffling hitch' in order to make the fly skate.
This consists of a half-hitch around the fly, after it has been
tied onto the leader, so that it hangs at right angles from the
leader. There may, therefore, be advantage in trying this
method, if only for experiment. The ideal situation for most
forms of greased-line fishing, however, is that the fly should
be just under the surface of the water; and one of the best ways
I know of controlling fly depth is in the choice of the fly itself
for a particular set of circumstances.

It was Anthony Crossley, in his excellent little book *The*

*Floating Line for Salmon and Sea Trout,* who suggested correctly that if you need a No. 6 fly for the head of the pool it
would be logical to put on a No. 8 for the quieter water downstream. Doubtless, he was referring to the visual impact of
the fly on the fish; but there is also the question of the differing weights of the two flies, and the alternate depths at which
each would fish. Normally, however, weight of fly in greased-
line fishing is of little consequence; and a factor of greater
importance is the amount of dressing the fly contains and
whether it is dressed on single or double hooks. Contrary to
popular belief, the double-hooked fly (because of its extra
weight) does not always swim at a lower depth than a single
of similar size. The double-hooked fly, due to its extra bulk,
causes much more drag in the water than a single-hooked fly;
and on strong gliding sections of the river it is often difficult
to avoid the undesirable element of skating on the surface.
Under such circumstances the only solution seems to be to put
up a slimly dressed single offering the minimum drag in the
water. There are, of course, other occasions when the extra
weight of the double-hooked fly makes it fish slightly lower
in the water than the single. Only long experience on a particular stretch of water will tell the angler precisely what to
do under the conditions of the day. For normal fishing we
have to be content with the knowledge that our fly is somewhere, just underneath the surface; not skating, and not fishing too deep. The precise depth is almost impossible to determine, since depth will alter as the fly moves in the varying
strengths of current. If the fly has a tendency to skate, the
simple act of feeding a little line will often effect a cure; but
failing that, the leader may be rubbed down liberally with
Fuller's Earth paste. This, incidentally, has advantage if done
at the commencement of a day's greased-line fishing. It is more
than likely that the trouble will not be remedied until a
change of fly has been made; or the angler has moved down
the pool to flows of different type from those at the top of the
pool.

Having determined the length of leader, I cut off a level

section of monofilament nylon line of around 10-lb test. The strength of leader is normally determined by the height and strength of the water; or by the weight of fish likely to be encountered. Over low water on the Lune, for instance, I may well use 7-lb or 8-lb strength; but would rarely use less than 11-lb test on the Spey, or 15-lb test on Norway's Vosso river. Apart from any other consideration, it is not a good plan to fish with small flies and thick leaders; nor is it common-sense to fish with big flies on fine leaders. There is always the danger of cracking off the big fly while casting, and the small fly on a thick leader never seems to swim in a lifelike manner.

Let us presume that we have already decided that conditions are right for greased-line fishing. The water is at the right height and colour; water temperatures are in the 50s; and the air is warmer than the water. It might well be the month of May, with pools already full of recently run fish. The odd sign of a fish doing a porpoise-like head-and-tail rise will lend strength to our decision to fish with the floating line. We tie on our fly accordingly, and start fishing.

It is really amazing how an angler, when he goes trout fishing, will take every care to conceal his presence and stalk his fish. Yet the same angler, on a salmon river, throws caution to the wind, and barges in without a thought for stealth or river-craft. Salmon are just as shy as the wiliest trout. The fact that they do not always scurry out of their lie does not mean they have not been alarmed into non-taking mood. In all types of salmon-fishing, therefore, and particularly greased-line fishing, approach your chosen spot cautiously. On at least three occasions I have taken fish whilst the fly was literally dangling from my rod tip while preparing to cast. Had I bull-dozed my way to the river bank beforehand, the fish would either have fled or moved away slowly.

Having approached the chosen spot where you are to commence fishing, don't be in too much of a hurry to cast to the other side of the river. First let the fly dangle in the water. Make sure that the fly has life and movement in the current; and that the leader is straight, and free of wind knots or any

c

tendency to coil. The stretching of the nylon is the best primary method of rendering it straight and limp; and rubbing
down with Fuller's Earth paste, clay or soil will remove any
traces of grease imparted previously by handling. The nylon
monofilament should sink readily, and the fly should swim
in a hook-down position. When you have satisfied yourself on
these small points, start casting. Keep the casts short initially;
and be careful to watch the area you know your fly to be in,
to see any response from the fish. The first casts should be
made roughly at right-angles to the current, with the rod also
held well out at right-angles. Any tendency to bring the rod
round to a position parallel with the current should be
deferred until the fly swings round to the angler's own bank.
It is a common mistake among novice anglers to disregard
these points; but, if you think about it, you will appreciate
that any tendency to disregard them will only result in your
leading the fly round more quickly than it would travel otherwise despite the fact that, at this stage, you will wish your fly
to travel as slowly as possible. The principal cause of trouble,
as in all types of across and downstream fishing, is the 'belly'
formation in the line caused by the strong central current.
If a cast is made as in figure 3A, a to b, it will not be long
before the line has assumed the shape shown at a to c. If
this were to go uncorrected, the fly would soon start moving
at a faster pace than that desirable and, for the first part of its
journey, in a downstream direction. As we lengthen our casts,
therefore, we have to adopt a method of removing or prevent-
ing this belly from forming as in 3b. This is best achieved by
'mending' the line, as it is termed; and is simply done by a
slow-lifting upstream action just as the fly touches the water.
There are also other aids to good presentation which will be
discussed in a chapter on casting. It may well be necessary,
however, to make further mends in the line as the fly moves
round in the current. The central current will always tend to
form this downstream belly; and in order to make the fly fish
correctly, the line really should be smoothed out as the belly
forms. When the fly has reached a point at roughly 45° down-

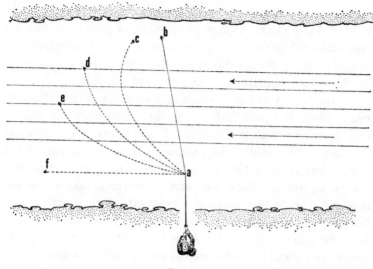

FIG. 3a

If the fly is cast (as in a) some excessive line belly will be caused.
Every attempt should be made to mend the line (as in b) so that
the fly will travel more slowly

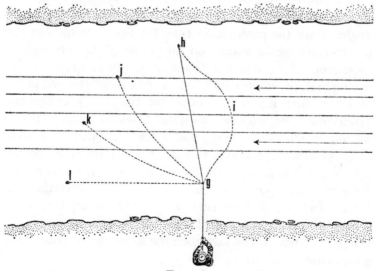

FIG. 3b

stream of the angler, tradition suggests that this is the most
likely taking place. A large proportion of fish, certainly, are
hooked in this area; but it pays to concentrate throughout the
entire time the fly is fishing, and even make a few slow pulls
on the fly before lifting for the next cast.

By the time you have extended your casts so that they virtually cover the pool, it is quite likely that you will wish to
cast more line than you can aerialize comfortably. The extra
distance is best achieved by shooting line. At the end of the
cast, a few coils of line are handlined in. The line is then
picked up for the back-cast; and as power is applied in the
fore-cast, the hand-held line is released. With practice, it is
possible to shoot quite remarkable lengths of line; but care
must be taken not to fish a long line just to show off. Long-
line tactics should only be used as river conditions dictate.

Generally speaking, therefore, the foregoing tactics form
a basis for all our greased-line fishing. We continue casting
down the pool, trying all the time to cast the same length and
in the same direction as at the start. We move down the pool
slowly or quickly as we wish. Personally I should rather fish a
a pool down twice, quickly, than once, slowly; and there are
some who argue that they would prefer to be the second
angler down the pool, rather than the first. I think that this
preference depends mainly on the nature of the pool and the
experience of the angler in fishing it. I have no qualms about
fishing first, second or third; but in the two latter cases, prefer
to know that my predecessors are reasonably competent.
Under ideal greased-line conditions, I would prefer to follow
an angler who is spinning, rather than another competent
fly-fisherman. It would be doubtful whether the spinner
would take fish; and it would be my hope that it would merely
serve to wake up the fish and act as a sort of advertisement
for my fly! There have been a few times when I have fly-
fished behind an army of spinners, on hard-fished association
waters, and have taken fish when the spinning fraternity have
gone home clean.

One of the greatest controversial questions is exactly what

to do when a salmon takes the greased-line fly. Some writers argue that all the time one is fishing, a yard of slack line should be held between the reel and the butt-ring. When resistance is felt, the slack is allowed to slide through the rings; and the rod point is then drawn sideways towards the angler's own bank. Some say that the perfect greased-line take is when the line stops and the point slowly sinks. A one-two-three count is made; then the rod point is raised slowly to drive the hook home. Other writers think that the perfect take is when they see a porpoise-like head-and-tail rise at their fly, and they raise the rod slowly as in chalk-stream dry-fly fishing. My own experience and that of the late Captain T. L. Edwards (who, incidentally, caught over 300 fish in one month alone on the greased-line fly) is that it matters little what you do. Perhaps also I could have no greater support for my argument than that of one of the greatest salmon fishers of our time, G. P. R. Balfour-Kinnear. In Chapter 3 of his book *Catching Salmon and Sea Trout,* he gives a very reasoned argument for *not* feeding slack line. Referring to the *fact* that the fly may be easily disengaged from a salmon's mouth, he says: 'If you do not want to hook the fish, then be as gentle as you can – even to the extent of throwing loose line at it . . . You may well say that all this is nonsense and that you catch fish this way. Of course you do. You would find that if you threw the rod into the water whenever you saw a boil and picked it up five minutes later, you would catch fish; but not so many as if you were more orthodox. I contend that throwing line to a fish has mistakenly become orthodox because so many fishermen follow a false teaching.'

In most instances, therefore, the fish is hooked – or it is not. There should not, of course, be any attempt to strike at the rise; but after a fish has been felt, then it has either hooked itself or has merely pulled the fly. My own technique is to fish without any slack line at the reel, holding the line lightly between my forefinger and second finger. If a fish head-and-tails at the fly, I wait for the pull; and under slight resistance, to set the hook, let it pull a few coils of line off my reel. For this reason I frequently fish with a very light rachet on the reel. There are many times, of course, when hooking fails; but I cannot see, for the life of me, how any other tactics would work better. When the fish takes without the promising head-and-tail rise, the first thing we usually know about it is a determined pull. Before we have time to do anything else about it, the fish is either hooked – or not.

All the above comments, of course, refer to normal streamy or gliding water. There are occasions, during low water periods, when there will be very little flow in the river; yet fishing the greased-line will be worth-while. Because of lack of flow, the fly may sink deeper than in a normal current strength; and a stoppage of the line may well be the first indication that a fish has taken the fly. With very small flies, however, the fly may still be sufficiently near the surface for the angler to see the head-and-tail rise, or a bulge in the water. Under these latter circumstances it would not be sensible to strike until the fish is felt; since, in most instances, a salmon will hang on to the fly for a lot longer period, rather than make a sharp grab and rejection like a darting moorland trout. Even then, grilse as well as some salmon have a habit of taking quite quickly at certain times of the season; and the angler who dallies too long may not even feel the pull. There can be no hard and fast rule. Certainly, salmon may be given more time than one would normally give to trout; but once the fish is actually felt, I see no rhyme or reason for delaying the strike. Perhaps the word 'strike' is misleading. There should be no need to strike in the full sense of the word. If the angler has been fishing diligently, his line should at all times be under control; and there should be no 'S-bends', coils of line floating on the water, or slack line to be taken up before contact is made. The literal meaning of the word 'strike' should not, in fact, be applied to salmon fly-fishing!

If we assess the point at which an angler stands on the river bank to be 6 o'clock (provided he is fishing from the left bank); directly upstream will be 3 o'clock; and directly downstream, 9 o'clock. Immediately opposite him, on the far bank,

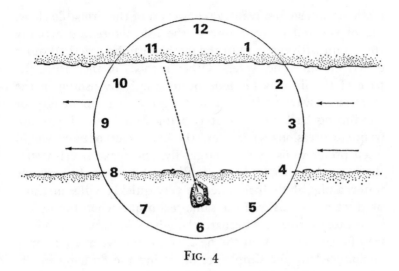

FIG. 4

will be 12 o'clock. For my normal greased-line fishing I like
to commence with a cast to 11 o'clock, followed by a quick
mend to bring the fly slowly through 10 o'clock – the point
where fish are likely to take. Then to 9 o'clock, before the line
retrieve is started, and a fresh cast made. In slacker water, I
may well make a cast to 12 o'clock, followed by several downstream mends before the retrieve at 9 o'clock. In very strong
water, however, it might pay to concentrate on fishing the
portion between 10 o'clock and 9 o'clock as effectively as
possible when, by wading out a little, the angler is able to
make the fly fish very slowly through this narrow arc. It all
depends upon the angler's assessment of the best tactics to
adopt. Only practical angling experience will reveal this.

There are times when, in very low water, hardly any movement by the current will be imparted to the fly. Casting upstream to 1 or 2 o'clock and handlining the fly back will sometimes work; as will the technique of what is termed 'backing-
up a pool'. In the latter instance the angler starts fishing at
the bottom of the pool; and, following each cast, he takes a
pace or two upstream in order to drag the fly over the lies
more quickly than a stationary position would permit. The

method has the disadvantage, however, of the probable showing of yourself or your line to the fish before you actually
cover him with the fly; but the method can be practised quite
effectively on some waters. Other mehods of increasing the
pace of the fly may be done quite simply by fishing in the
traditional way; and either making downstream mends, or
handlining back as the cast is being fished out. There are
frequent occasions when I use the latter method; and would
often prefer to fish with a larger fly, and make it fish faster,
than fish a smaller fly in the traditional manner. In very low
water, a biggish fly hand-lined in very quickly will sometimes
produce a take, as will the same technique when the fly has
been cast upstream. Alternatively, I have known occasions in
very fast water – say, at the head of a run – when a take may
be induced by the simple act of letting the fly hang in the
current and be made to move slowly downstream by paying
line off the reel. There are many variable permutations to all
these tactics; and when in doubt, a bit of experimenting often
produces a surprising result. Don't be fooled into thinking
that you have suddenly found an answer! On one day, the fly
dropped downstream may work; but it may thereafter be
completely ineffective for several seasons. Much the same
applies to the fly thrown upstream, and quickly retrieved.
There is still no formula; but the experienced angler knows
when best to try these tactics. They are, at best, only a poor
alternative to traditional greased-line methods; but they sometimes have the advantage of saving an otherwise fruitless day.

Provided that the angler can recognize good greased-line
conditions, and can cast to a reasonable level of competence
with tackle suited to the job, greased or floating-line fishing
is possibly the easiest form of salmon fishing available.
Perhaps the most difficult task is that of deciding which fly to
use. We shall move on to discuss some aspects of fly selection,
in our next chapter.

AUTHOR'S NOTE:—*I have done some re-thinking about spinning under
good fly fishing conditions and have more comments in Chapter 9.*

# 7
## Fly Fishing Techniques

*No. 4.   Flies for greased-line fishing*

I HAVE already discussed the various techniques the angler may adopt in order to take salmon on the greased-line fly; and have pointed out the necessity for the angler to carry a wide range of flies if he is to be able to meet all the varying conditions likely to be encountered throughout a season's fishing with the floating line. In Chapter 4, when discussing the question of colour in salmon flies, I made the point that it was my fancy that the smaller we make our flies, the less important colour seems to be. Let me begin, therefore, with a brief examination of this colour question by referring to some of the well-known authorities of the past.

On page 41 of Jock Scott's book (referred to in Chapter 6) Wood is reported as having commented, 'As regards pattern I do not believe that this matters at all. Blue Charm and Silver Blue are my stock, simply on the principle that one is more or less black and the other white and so give me a choice.' Again, on page 144 of the same book, we read 'I do not believe in the colour flash theory at all; in my opinion it is simply a case of the fly travelling – accidently or otherwise – at such an angle that it arouses the curiosity of the stiff fish. No fisherman could make his fly travel in exactly the same way at each cast; and although he may *believe* that a different colour would flash and attract the fish, my idea is that it is the different way in which the fly is presented.' Yet again, on page 164, when comparing his methods with those of Crossfield,

Wood comments 'Except for a fly out of the ordinary, just for experiment, I see no object in changing unless you can convince me that fish are particular as to certain colours. I should be quite happy with one fly only – in various sizes; in fact, if I started all over again I should use just Black Doctor and Silver Doctor, the one dark and the other light.' Mr Crossfield replied to this with 'I am in absolute agreement with you about particular shades of colour just being so much nonsense; but I do like to have a dark fly and also a light one.'

So far as is possible I have not quoted out of context; and I would not like it to be thought that, because of these quotes, such eminent anglers would have used gaudy flies in order to prove their point about the lack of importance of colour. I have already mentioned the importance of colour, to my mind, in big sunk-flies; but am firmly of the opinion that the smaller our flies become, the more subtle and elusive the colours should be. The question of colour has caused a rage of controversy throughout the years. Richard Waddington, one of our leading authorities, gave it a great deal of coverage in his excellent book *Salmon Fishing*. In my opinion, Waddington gave more thought to the entire problems of salmon fishing than were ever undertaken since books on the subject were first written. The fact that his book was written twenty years ago, and that advance in factual knowledge has proved him wrong on some counts, in no way detracts from the value of his perceptive thinking. Every theory put forward waits for destruction. On the question of colour, however, there seems to be a little confusion; and a fine distinction must be made between the words colour and pattern. On page 112 of his book, Waddington comments, 'The question of the value of various colours and patterns of salmon flies is one that is constantly recurrent and one on which widely divergent views are held. I think that most fishermen have felt that to suppose that the salmon could differentiate between say a Black Doctor and a Thunder and Lightning was faintly ridiculous; and the more modern school of thought is tending all the time, largely as a result of the experience of greased-line fishing, to the belief that colour is of little importance in the salmon fly.' Continuing to the bottom of page 115 we read 'Colour then, can have little effect, for it is the tone of the fly that is important' etc. etc.

The foregoing remarks were made to support Waddington's argument for his own particular design of fly. Such flies have made a great contribution to any worth-while advancement in salmon-fly design since the salmon fly was first invented. Personally, while using this design for much of my sunk-line fishing, I prefer the more traditional double or single for the floating line; but still find occasions for using the smaller type of Waddington's fly. When we turn to page 211 of Waddington's book, we find what appears to be a minor contradiction. He says, 'In greased-line fishing in the standard manner matters are very different. Probably as much as 50 per cent of one's luck depends on using the right size and *pattern* of fly in the right place.' Of course, 'size of fly' and 'being in the right place' are paramount considerations; but how can Waddington differentiate between pattern and colour? Surely, of necessity, these two are inter-related? On page 223 he goes on to say, 'I used to think that the *pattern* [my italics] of the greased-line fly was of no importance and that anyone who fished for a whole season with but one pattern, chosen at random and tied in the various necessary sizes, would be every bit as successful as the angler who gave himself several choices. . . . I am no longer of the opinion that the pattern does not matter. On the other hand, I am equally certain that small differences between one pattern, and another very like it, are both unnoticed and unnoticeable by the fish. . . . I do not think that colour, except in so far as it affects tone, is of the slightest importance.'

For the greatest confusion, we must turn to page 269 of Waddington's book where he states, 'Nor do I personally very much mind what pattern of fly I use. I have known the time when nothing but the Blue Charm would do. . . . I have seen seasons when the Silver Blue was the first choice – or a Logie or a Jeannie. Today it appears to be the Hairy Mary. All

these, and many other patterns, catch fish equally well and it
is only wishful thinking that invests any pattern with magic
qualities.'

To my mind, a pattern is a mixture of colours; and 'a tone
is the result of such blending. We could so arrange our
patterns of colours to give us a red tone; a sky-blue tone; or
even the most garish green, if thought desirable. So, along the
line, colour has some importance; and, in my opinion, the
emphasis should not be laid on colour alone; but, to my fancy,
that colours should become more subdued and elusive as our
flies become smaller. Presumably, it is in this respect that
colour is regarded as having no importance. If, for one fleeting
moment, we had some vague idea of what the salmon take our
greased-line flies for, we should have some cause for pedantry
in this vexed question of colour or pattern. As I have stated
in earlier chapters, we are still no nearer any such knowledge.
Any guesses we make are mere speculation. Over the years,
however, certain greased-line patterns have emerged which
find more than general usage; and a few fancies have stood
the test of time for so long now that they have factually established themselves as regular taking patterns. Such of these
flies as come to mind include the Blue Charm, Logie,
Thunder and Lightning, Black Doctor or even a Silver Blue
– the latter being a fly I rarely use. One of our greatest
catchers of salmon today, Major the Hon. J. Ashley Cooper,
stated in a recent article, concerning greased-line fishing, 'As
to pattern of fly this appears to matter little, provided the
dressing is sparse.'

If we agree, therefore, that colour or pattern in the least
defined sense of these words have little bearing on our fly
selection, what are the paramount considerations we should
make before deciding which fly to use for a given set of circumstances? We have already discussed the effects of slimly
dressed singles, heavier dressed doubles etc., in varying types
of water currents; and, to a large extent, I let my choice of fly
be dictated by these considerations. My favourite flies may be
difficult to name, since they are now tied by either my wife or

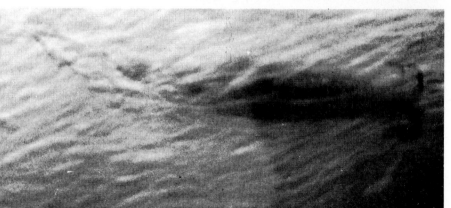

Top left: The late Oliver Kite with two salmon taken from the River Lune

Top right: An 8 lb salmon taken by team work. Arthur Oglesby being filmed by BBC *Look North* cameras

Bottom: Waddington-type fly, seen in current of moving water. Camera exposure 1/15th second

Above: Ken Morritt tailing a salmon from the River Dee, Scotland

Left: Arthur Oglesby with his biggest salmon of 49½-lb taken from the River Vosso, Norway, on June 17, 1973

Above: Odd Haraldsen gaffs a nice fish of 23 lb from the Vosso

Left: The world record for 1965. Odd Haraldsen with a fish of 60 lb from the River Vosso at Bolstad, Norway

Below: Eager to be upriver. Salmon leaping at a foss pool on the River Tengs, S.W. Norway

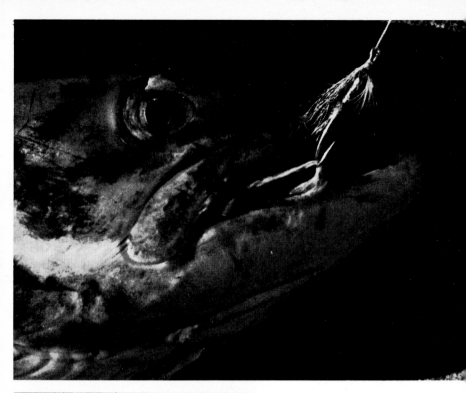

Above: A fly-caught fish of 30 l[b]
The fly is held by a thread of fles[h]
River Vosso, Norway

Left: Arthur Oglesby with a fish o[f]
33½-lb taken from the River Vosso i[n]
Norway

Below: Odd Haraldsen fishing o[n]
the River Laerdal, Norway

Above: Odd Haraldsen playing a fish of 33-lb on the River Vosso in Norway

Left: A diseased salmon lying in a Tweed backwater, November 1968

Below: Commercial netting off Carleto-sur-Mer, Gaspe, Canada

*Atlantic Salmon Association*

Above: Arthur Oglesby instructing at Grantown on Spey

Left: The late Captain T. L. Edwards demonstrating the roll cast

Right: Arthur Oglesby tailing out a fish of over 20 lb from the River Vosso at Bolstadoyri, Norway

*Ken Pettinger*

Top: The River Sella at Cangas de Onis, Asturias in Spain

Bottom: The famous Restigouche river, New Brunswick, Canada

*Atlantic Salmon Association*

myself; and, as neither of us are very expert, tend to be of the simplest design and construction. I shudder to think of them ever acquiring such names as Oglesby's 'Orrer, Artful Arthur, Grey Grace, or Gracie's Glory. Having a pattern of fly named after me is definitely something to which I do not aspire. In general, however, my favourite patterns follow a rough facsimile of such well-known flies as Blue Charm, Logie, Thunder and Lightning, Stoat's Tail and Hairy Mary. Perhaps my favourite consists of nothing more than a black silk body with fine tinsel ribbing, a touch of orange cock hackle at the throat, and some black squirrel tail for winging. I make these in a variety of sizes; and with varying amounts of dressing on both single and double hooks. As it is, it vaguely resembles the Thunder and Lightning; and for an alternative I should substitute the orange cock hackle for one of blue, to give me a type of Blue Charm. My so-called Logie would have a touch of yellow silk at the tail followed by a main body of claret silk, and fine tinsel ribbing, a mixed blue and ginger throat hackle, with dark brown squirrel tail for winging. Another favourite would be all black base with only the fine tinsel ribbing to make the contrast. These, with the possible addition of some flies with an all-tinsel body, constitute my stock. I have already said in Chapter 4, when writing of sunk-line selections, that I like to choose a pattern of fly which blends in with the overall colour of the water and the river bed. It should not stick out like a sore thumb; and should, therefore, be of subdued colouring and tone. Indeed, its design might suggest that I did not want the fish to see it too easily! Bear in mind, always, that the angler will be looking *down* at his fly when the salmon will be looking *upwards* at it; and, dependent on the actinic value of the light and its direction, could see the fly either in bold relief or as an elusive silhouette.

As I have already stated, it is my opinion that size of the fly and the amount of dressing it contains are paramount considerations; and, as a general rule, there is nothing much wrong with the old formula that the higher the water temperature, the smaller the fly should be; but it is essential that this be related to river height, strength of the current, and colour of the water. Water temperature, by itself, is no guide; and must be equated with these other factors. In my early days of greased-line fishing, I took water temperatures religiously. It is, of course, very important that the air should be warmer than the water; but actual knowledge of water temperatures is only a small consideration in making an assessment of the fly to use. Wood argued, and I would not quarrel with him, that a No. 6 should be regarded as the basic size for greased-line fishing. However, a No. 6 heavily dressed fly is a vastly different proposition from a fly of the same size that is lightly dressed. In fact, a heavily dressed No. 6 may well look larger than a lightly dressed No. 4.

My plan, therefore, is to concentrate on a range of sizes between 4 and 8, with the odd 10 for occasional use; and have one set of flies lightly dressed against the second set, heavily dressed. I tie these on both singles and doubles; and thus finish up with around twelve alternatives of any one pattern in sizes 4, 6 and 8. On a normal height of water, under good greased-line conditions, I should normally select a lightly dressed No. 6 as the fly to start with. Choice of pattern would be dictated by such considerations as overhead light, colour of the water or river bed, pure fancy, or the fly that was most convenient in my fly box! If the day were bright, with a good sprinkling of blue sky and white clouds, then I should almost automatically select a Blue Charm. If the day were grey, with a tinge of peat in the water, then it would almost certainly be the Thunder and Lightning or the Logie – or even the all-black Stoat's Tail. A really bright day with low water might induce me to put up a Silver Blue instead of the Blue Charm. The bulk of my selection would be based on fancy – and on nothing else; since, in the final analysis, there is little other basis for selection.

If conditions remained the same, I should persist for quite a while with the fly of my choice; but if no response were forthcoming from the fish, I should ultimately change to a fly of the same size with heavier dressing. I cannot tell you why I should do this; nor give any rhyme or reason for doing it. If the river were dropping slightly throughout the day, as it does most times when sport is to be at its best, then it would seem logical to put on a smaller fly. I might well do this at a later stage; but not without an exploratory cast or two with the heavier dressed fly. What I should really hope for would be some response from the fish; but not necessarily a take. Fish will sometimes move to a fly that is more easily seen, without actually taking it; and if I did get some sort of response, and failed to connect, I should promptly fish that same cast again with a sparsely dressed No. 8, in the hope of secure hooking next time. Just to add to the confusion, there are times when fish will make a pass at a fly because it is too small. The real answer then lies in putting on a larger or more heavily dressed fly. Such are the fascinating variables in a day's greased-line fishing. Only rarely should I take into consideration the question of pattern, for with the patterns I have named, the colour differential could hardly be discerned by the salmon; and, in my opinion, is of little consequence, particularly if basic selection is followed in the first place.

My most productive days with greased-line have frequently commenced with a good spinning water. Rain in the hills has brought a rise of water and some fresh fish into the pools. As the river fines off, spinning becomes the order of the day; and undoubtedly a few fish are taken. Suddenly the fish go off the spinner; and if I have my wits about me, I realize that it is high time I fish with the floating line and a lightly dressed No. 4 fly. As the river falls, so does my size of fly until, finally, I am using lightly dressed No. 8s. There may come a time when even a No. 10 should be the better size; and I carry a small stock in this size for such contingencies. As I have said earlier, however, I tend to regard a No. 10 as too small for general fishing. I prefer to fish a No. 8 at a slightly faster pace than normal. My choice of a single or double hook would be entirely dependent upon the character of the water, and not on the consideration that the double might give me better

hooking qualities, which they may possibly do! I have outlined the circumstances, in the preceding chapter, which
induce me to put up the double or the single. I rarely bother
to take into account any other factor than that of making the
fly fish in a manner which is correct to meet a given set of
circumstances.

To sum up this chapter, I think that too much emphasis is
placed upon pattern, and not enough on the amount of
dressing a particular chosen pattern contains. We have seen
the importance of fly size; but have come to realize that a
lightly dressed No. 4 offers a similar sized illusion to that of a
heavily dressed No. 6. We have seen that a heavily dressed fly
on the double hook offers greater resistance to the water than
a lightly dressed fly on a single hook; and therefore, in most
circumstances, does not necessarily fish at a lower depth. In
fact, because of its bulk, it may well skate in strong gliding
water. There are, of course, a thousand and one permutations
one can make in the construction of greased-line flies. Treble-
hooked flies have merit on occasions; and those designed by
Lt. Col. Esmond Drury have found great favour with some
devotees. There is not a fly made that does not have a use at
some stage in the game. The great problem is largely a personal one; and only experience will yield the secrets of the
tactics to adopt on a chosen piece of water, at the time of the
year you are to fish it – coupled with the whims of the
elements, and of your chosen quarry – the salmon!

AUTHOR'S NOTE:—*As I commented earlier. I have now come to have a
strong affection for flies tied on Esmond Drury hooks and I have also learned
some wisdom about ultra-small tube flies with trebles as small as size 16.
These new thoughts are aired in Chapter 9.*

# 8
## Greased-Line Fishing Tactics

*Days with the greased line*

MOST salmon anglers regard the taking of salmon on the greased-line fly as the epitome of angling sport. I am not quite sure that I agree. Certainly I rate it very highly; but it is comparatively easy when compared with sunk-line fishing. The angler has little need to think of that third dimension, the depth of the water, which is so paramount in its influence on sunk-line tactics. Naturally the angler has either to know his water, or have the services of a reliable gillie available. A good gillie can be a gem during a day's greased-line fishing, for he can position himself where he can watch the movement of the fly and the reactions of the fish. On other, smaller, rivers, the angler may well be able to see these reactions for himself and my mind instantly goes back to one of many tantalizing visits to the Argyllshire Awe. Fly-only is the rule; and I had access to a middle beat of the river during the early part of August. The best of the fishing was over and August is a notoriously difficult month anywhere. The pools, however, were full of fish but the river had an irritating habit of going up and down like a yo-yo as the Hydro-Electric boys, further upstream, diverted or halted the river flow. I was to have access to the beat for three alternate days during that week and at 5.30 a.m. I was down at the top pool on the first day. I started off with a good old standby, a No. 6 Blue Charm, and had not been fishing for very long when I detected a salmon rising to it out of the depths of that gin-clear water.

At the last moment he shied away and despite further casts showed no more interest. Following my basic tactics I changed to a heavier dressed No. 6, whereupon two salmon moved out of their lies but made no attempt to take. Further fishing seemed useless for the moment so I sat down to rest the pool for five minutes. I really did not have a clue what to do next. Eventually I put on a No. 8 Blue Charm and after five minutes had elapsed I cast again over the lie. A fish promptly came for it boldly; but I felt nothing more than the slightest pluck as my fly swung free. After a further five minutes I tried again with a No. 10, but from then on no fish would look at anything I put over them. It was time to move to another pool.

Down at the next pool I could see the fish plainly in their lies, but although the No. 10 was cast most carefully over them I could get no response whatever. One of the fish was head-and-tailing very persistently; but he showed not the slightest response to my fly and despite further fly changes I could do nothing there. At the tail of the pool, however, the water looked quite interesting and although I could not see any fish, due to the water turbulence, I reckoned it was worth a cast. By this time I was back with a lightly dressed No. 8 and I cast this across the pool to cover the most likely looking water. The fly was half-way across when I felt a pull. The fly was left free. Then another pull came, but the fly was still swinging round. At the end of the swing, and just as I was about to retrieve, I got the third pull. This time the fish was hooked. 'At last,' I thought, 'I've got one.' It fought with all the dash and verve of a little game fish, leaping and twisting in that gin-clear water; but before thirty seconds had elapsed it threw the hook, and left me with a slack line and a mental inquest into what had gone wrong. A little reflection convinced me that it was no use fishing that pool any longer; so I went down to the next pool. There the result was pretty much the same as that over the first pool.

By this time the sun was up, and it would not be long before the best of the fishing ceased until dusk. In the three days I fished that water I rose or hooked thirty fish. I played one gallant fish, well over 20-lb, for more than twenty minutes before he gained his freedom. Another was tailed and on the bank before he slipped out of my hands and back into the water as the fly fell out of his mouth. Yet another ran me down two pools before he, too, regained his freedom; and one unlucky, solitary 7-lb fish was the only one I knocked on the head to take home. Some of the fish merely boiled at the fly; others gave it a cheeky pull and some stayed on for varying periods. Doubtless the experts would tell me that I should have fed them line; or, alternatively, I should have been quicker on the strike. I don't *know* – and I suspect that they would not *know*, despite firm personal convictions! Some would doubtless tell me that the fly was the wrong pattern; or that my choice of size was all to blame. If this were so, then it is my greatest regret that they were not there at the time to show me how to do it!

During July 1969 I had an opportunity of a return visit to the Awe. The river was lower than I had ever seen it. I was informed that, since the Hydro-Electric Board had com- menced regular operations, the river was now kept at a constant level. The river seemed to hold a good head of fish; but they were all, in the main, running grilse. The main salmon lies seemed untenanted and the only fish being caught were being taken from the tails of pools where they might tarry awhile before continuing their upstream pilgrim- age. It was difficult fishing during the heat of the day and the bulk of the sport was confined to early mornings or late evenings. By August the fish had become almost uncatchable; but I still have high hopes of really conquering the Awe one of these years.

Days with the greased-line fly are not always as tantalizing as the ones I have described and anyone fortunate enough to be on some of the middle beats of the Dee or Tweed during May can make greased-line fishing seem like child's play. At this time of the year, and in good conditions, the fish are not greatly concerned whether the fly is a lightly dressed No. 6

or a heavily dressed No. 8. Fly selection factors are still important; but when fish are really on the greased-line fly, this
factor diminishes and the angler who can make a reasonable
selection, and can cast and cover the lies competently, is
generally assured of some sport. We cannot, however, all be on
such classic beats at the peak of the season. We have to make
do with what is available. Many rivers during this peak
greased-line month may still be waiting for their first runs of
the season. Over on the Lune we have a theory that if the
fish are not there in March, there will be nothing of any consequence until the first floods of July; a time when the peak
of the greased-line fishing is passed. Although May sees the
peak of this type of fishing on a lot of rivers, therefore, it does
not mean that there will not be many other months when
conditions will be good, even if only for short periods.
September is frequently a good month but is spoilt by the
fact that most salmon, at this time of the year, are well past
their best. They are full of eggs and milt, and colouring up
considerably. There may well be, of course, some fresh fish
entering the river all the time; and anyone who catches a
fresh-run Tweed fish at the back end of November will
marvel at its lovely silver colouring.

As I have said earlier, however, August is a notoriously
difficult month; but is frequently a time when we get heavy
rains and good runs of grilse and salmon into our rivers. Good
greased-line conditions may only come for a precise and short
period as the river fines off and before it gets too low; or,
worse still, there is another rise in the water. An unsettled
river is about the most difficult to fish. I have frequently
timed a visit to a river to coincide with good greased-line conditions, but have found that overnight rain has thwarted me.
One such occasion which comes to mind was when I planned
to take a guest over to the Newton water of the Lune. The
river was enjoying one of its best seasons for many a year. The
pools were full of fish and a three foot rise, two days previously, had brought the river into fine trim. 'With anything
like luck,' I told my friend, 'it should be right for tomorrow

and you are certain to catch a fish.' During this particular season, catching fish had become the accepted thing. It was practically unheard of for my friends or myself to visit the river without catching something; and as I drove the winding miles to Lunesdale I was full of optimism. On arrival I was due for a shock. A thunderstorm had hit the valley the previous evening and the river was four feet above normal height, with most of the good lies unfishable. Conditions were such that, normally, I should not have bothered to put up a rod. My guest, however, who had done only a little salmon fishing before, was anxious to make the best of a bad job. Who was I, then, to dampen his spirits and tell him it was useless? So, suggesting that he spun with a large Toby spoon, I left him to his endeavour.

We fished all morning without an offer, slinging out our Toby spoons in the faint hope that something would hang on. By lunch time I was despondent and decided to try for the sea-trout with a small fly on a floating line. When our water is slightly coloured, the sea-trout will often take the fly during daytime; and I felt that fishing the quiet tails and slack corners would offer the best chance. Further, I had received a new Hardy rod the day before. It was a 10½-ft split cane, single handed 'Crown Houghton' fly rod, designed for sea-trout fishing; and I was anxious to give it a trial. I was delighted with its action; but, after an hour of abortive fishing, I was soon back to slinging the ironmongery around. Coming to the tail of a pool, I was startled to see a salmon do a head-and-tail rise within a few feet of the bank. Within seconds he repeated the act. I quickly dropped the bait rod and grabbed the sea-trout rod. A short cast, and the small Invicta I had on for the sea-trout, was floating over him. Up from the depths he came, like a fat, chalk-stream trout rising to a lightly placed dun, with a perfect head-and-tail rise. Then followed the awful suspense until the pull; and, suddenly, he was on, fighting for his life in that turbulent river. Pretty soon my rod was being subjected to treatment it was never designed to receive. By judicious walking up I managed to contain the fish within the pool. Any thoughts of beaching it, as I do with most of my fish nowadays, were out of the question since I was having a full time job to keep him within the pool. With such slender tackle, I should probably have had to say goodbye to him had he taken me downstream. Eventually he began to tire and I was pleased to accept my friend's gaff. The final moments were tense and I really had to bend that rod to keep him from going down. Then the gaff went home and out came a 10-lb salmon.

On reflection, it was one of the most satisfying fish I have ever caught. It was a triumph over adversity. It initiated a new rod in a manner by which few rods are initiated (it is still perfectly straight) and it turned a depressing day into a victorious one. My main problem, however, remains unsolved. Why does a salmon rise to take a small fly? Why did *that* salmon take a small sea-trout fly in flood conditions? We shall never know the answers. Herein, for me, lies the challenge of salmon fishing.

There have been quite a few occasions when the use of the greased-line fly has, short of worming or prawning etc., brought me the only chance of fish. Its use on days such as the one recalled can be effective when conditions have been hopeless; and for want of something better to do, I have played about with a fly rod. There was such an occasion on the '£1-a-week' association water at Grantown on Spey. It was during the month of May; but the water was so cold that all the locals were still spinning; and though dozens of anglers were fishing this water, there were days when no fish were being taken. When fishing a relatively strange piece of water I am greatly influenced by what the locals are doing. They live on the water, they know its every mood and whim; they know the lies for varying heights and the successes and failures they have had under diverse conditions throughout the years. For the first part of the week, therefore, I joined them in their spinning but met with no success.

On my last day there I pondered upon the problem of how I was to get a fish to take home. That there were a few fish

in the beat was a certainty; but consistent spinning had failed
to bring a successful conclusion and it occurred to me that it
was just possible that the fish had seen too much of the spinner, on that hard fished water, and that they might respond
to a change. That morning I put up my 12½-ft Hardy 'Hollolight', a GAAG (DT9) Air-Cel line (white this time), 10-ft
leader of 11-lb test nylon, and a double-hooked No. 6 Thunder and Lightning. I had little confidence that this would
work any miracle for me – but at least it would be a change!
Had I been a resident of the district, I doubt if I should have
fished. It was one of those days that did not inspire confidence; but I was prepared to fish for the simple reason that
I had nothing better to do.

I dillied and dallied for quite a while. It was noon before I
had put on my breast-waders and got up to my armpits in a
favourite pool. I knew the pool fairly well and knew where
the best lies were likely to be. I started casting, taking pains
to present my fly neatly. Slowly, I became conscious of the
fact that I was fishing with greater concentration. There was
an air of expectation, even. I don't really believe in a sixth
sense, but if there is such a thing – I became conscious of it!
Suddenly there was a vicious pull at the fly, and seconds later
a salmon was thrashing on the surface of the water and my
fly came back to me. When I examined the fly I found that
the leader had fouled the fly between the double-hooks while
casting; and at the moment that salmon had taken me, the
fly must have been reversed. This was a tragic happening
when I had striven so hard all week for the chance of a fish.
The fish, however, had meant to have that fly; and if *one*
could take it so boldly, why not another one? I straightened
my leader, re-tied the fly and was soon back in the water again
and covering the exact spot where the fish had taken me.
Then I detected a lovely head-and-tail rise, with a firm pull
coming some split-second afterwards. There was no doubt
about it this time. The salmon was firmly hooked and I bent
the rod to him. He fought strongly in the rapid current; but

before ten minutes had elapsed I led him down to a sandy bay and tailed him out. He was a fresh fish of 8-lb.

I sat down, lit a cigarette, and gazed at my hard earned prize. Was it the same fish that had taken the earlier fly? I should never know; but it was quite on the cards that there were other fish in the lie; so back I went and commenced casting again. I was getting towards the tail of the pool, and just beginning to realize that I had fished the best, when I saw my line straighten and I was into another fish. It fought just as strongly as my earlier fish and about the same time elapsed before I was able to lead it into the sandy bay and tail it out. It weighed $7\frac{1}{2}$-lb; and a handsome brace they made. I was back in time for lunch to learn that these were the only fish taken, so far, that day; and by the end of the day they were still the only fish of the day that between 50 and 80 rods, fishing the water, had taken.

Many anglers claim to have a sixth sense when it comes to fishing. I don't accept this as such; but do recall one instance when something on the verge of extra-sensory perception happened to me. I was once again on a favourite beat of the Lune and had a full quota of guests sharing the beat with me. My principal concern was to see that *they* caught fish; and I spent the bulk of my time gillieing for them and advising them how to fish the most likely places. By 4 p.m. we had not a single fish to show for our efforts. I picked up my fly-rod and started at the tail of the queue fishing down the main pool. We had done our best and my guests were all know-ledgeable anglers. They had combed the water with spinners and flies. What chance had I? I could not produce any magic; and I should be fishing over well-hammered water with no variation up my sleeve. I started casting. I don't even recall the fly I fished at the time; but it was obviously a standard pattern, and quite possibly one that the fish had already seen on quite a few occasions that day. I was coming to a likely part of the pool when suddenly I felt very tense and the whole of my senses tingled. I swear that there was no other visual evidence to make me thus; but the next four seconds seemed like hours and then I saw my line straighten, and I was fast into a fine fish of 11-lb. The details of playing and landing are immaterial; but what on earth (or in heaven) gave me that four second warning that *something* was imminent? I had fished that same likely place in the pool on hundreds of occasions before without feeling the slightest expectancy. I had even taken countless fish from the same lie without any evidence of fore-knowledge. It is doubtless true that one's concentration becomes more alive at those 'known' taking places; but the feeling I got was much more tense than mere speculative concentration.

For the reverse of the coin, I have many times had my fly or bait taken when I was least expecting it to happen; and perhaps the most remarkable example of this was an incident when my wife took two fish under near-miraculous circumstances. We had gone over to the Lune for a couple of days, mainly at her request, to get away from it all and not because conditions were promising. We arrived during the late afternoon to find the river running off a shade more quickly than I would have liked; but it was not so low that it would be impossible to fish the head of the streams. I was quick to take a fine fish of 13½-lb on fly, whilst my wife was busy spinning; and at the end of the day this had been the only offer either of us had received. The following morning gave us a brilliant sun in a cloudless sky. By 10 a.m. the heat was of tropical quality. I groaned 'We haven't a hope of catching fish today! But still, I expect you want to try?' 'Yes,' my wife replied, 'I want to practise with your fly-rod, so that I shall be able to cast with reasonable competence.' Up till then, my wife had few notches on her fishing rod, and the odd fish she had caught had been taken whilst spinning with a fixed-spool reel and a Toby spoon. She had yet to take her first Lune salmon – and her first fish on a fly. I made myself comfortable on the river bank and laid back in the sun in my shirt-sleeves. The curlews were circling and screeching high overhead. A flight of duck came our way and banked slightly to the right to keep just out of shotgun range. A small dipper alighted on

a rock and took in the pleasures of his environment; and just
then a lazy old salmon jumped awkwardly in mid-stream. My
wife had received sufficient instruction to know the basic
casting action with a fly-rod and I left her to her own devices.
She commenced at the head of the pool in her thigh waders,
casting a short line with reasonable competence. I watched
her fish the pool down until the water was lapping around the
tops of her waders, which required her to cast that extra bit
of line to cover the pool properly. Woman are nothing if not
persistent and for the next half-hour she almost lashed that
pool into foam! Some casts went moderately well, while others
fell in a heap. She stood in the same position for a further
half-hour; but her casting was improving slowly, even though
all the salmon in the vicinity must have seen the fly for the
past hour. By now, however, she was just content to cast. We
both knew that there was no chance whatever of taking fish.
The fly was prescribing the same arc for cast after cast. I was
nearly asleep when I heard 'HELP!' Thinking that my wife
must have fallen in, I jumped up. Her rod tip was jerking;
but I could only imagine that some small salmon parr had
seized the fly and given her a fright. Then the line screamed
from the reel, and I was astounded to realize that she must be
playing a salmon. Needless to say I was quickly by her side
and giving all the advice I could. She played it cautiously
and, despite all my entreaties to hurry things up a bit in case
the fish got free, she took her own time. Some twenty to
twenty-five minutes elapsed before I was able to tail it out
for her – a slightly coloured fish of 8-lb. She was over the
moon! She promptly grabbed the rod and went back to her
casting, and hammered away at the same old piece of water.
Another half-hour elapsed; then suddenly the same old cry,
and I looked up to see the rod tip jerking again. Stupid
woman! What on earth was she doing catching fish on such a
hopeless day? Could she not realize that conditions were
hopeless and that her constant casting was only frightening
the fish? What right had the fish to take the fly anyway?
Didn't the fish realize that some clumsy woman was on the

other end of the line and that he should be sheltering from the hot sun and lying sullen behind a rock, gasping for breath?

My wife was much more confident with this second fish and played it with greater expertise. Barely ten minutes elapsed before she had it ready for tailing and I was able to lift out another slightly coloured fish of 10-lb. I had to eat my humble pie that day and my wife is now convinced that, despite my long experience to the contrary, such a day is ideal for taking salmon on the greased-line fly.

As if to add insult to injury, there came another day when conditions were just as bad. I was sweltering in my office when the telephone rang. 'Can we go to the Lune this afternoon,' said my wife, 'It's such a nice day'. 'Nice day for sunbathing!' I answered; but, reluctantly, agreed to go. On arrival on the river, the sun was shimmering over the distant hills. I put up a fly-rod for my wife and despatched her across the river to do her best. There were a few salmon in the pools, I knew; but I felt no desire to fish, in the circumstances, so just lolled around the fishing hut. An hour elapsed before I began to feel slightly unsociable. My wife, as I could see in the distance, was having no joy. I had better put up another rod and go and join her. Because of the low water I put on my brown floating-line; and for no reason at all, tied on a small Stoat's Tail tube-fly. Then I made my way across the narrow neck of water at the head of the pool. The river was much too low for fishing anywhere but the head of the stream; but there were a few fish jumping lazily and awkwardly; and as an act of companionship, rather than a desire to fish, I started fishing the pool down behind my wife. Barely five minutes had elapsed before I felt the slightest resistance to the fly; and thinking that a floating leaf must have fouled it, I raised my rod point slowly to find that I was into a lively fish. I was using a very light leader of 7-lb test and had to play that fish with kid gloves before I was able to lead it into the bank and tail it out. It weighed 12½-lb; and although slightly coloured, could not have been in the river for more than a few weeks.

These incidents, therefore, pose some of the mysteries of salmon fishing; and to my mind emphasize the fancy that under the most difficult conditions, of low water and high temperature, the small greased-line fly will sometimes save an otherwise hopeless day – a day when other lures and baits might not stand a chance. Fly on the greased-line is also one of the most pleasant ways I know of taking fish; and has earned for itself a prime place in the sport of salmon fishing.

# 9
## New Thoughts on Fly Fishing

SINCE writing the bulk of the original text of the first edition of this book it has been my good fortune to fish on more of the classic beats of the Spey. It was not until 1968 that I took over from the late Captain T. L. Edwards as chief instructor on the angling courses at Grantown. Following this, however, and through the kind courtesy of the Strathspey Estates and the Seafield Sporting Club, much of their water has occasionally been made available to myself and members of the courses. I have been able to fish these waters during the peak season in May and have also had opportunities of fishing there in July – so often a difficult time anywhere. I am on record, in earlier chapters, of commenting that I rarely like to use flies smaller than size 10 and that I would rather fish a pool down behind a spin fisherman than another competent fly fisherman. Both of these statements, in the light of additional experience, now need some qualification.

I still incline to the view that so far as single-hooked flies are concerned the angler is best advised not to go much smaller than size 10. During May of 1972, however, the Spey was lower than I have ever seen it and having tried size 8 flies briefly it did not take me long to decide that 10's would be more likely to produce some offers. I caught the odd fish on size 10 flies, but through the grapevine I got reliable reports that other anglers were raising fish to 12's and 14's. When I asked the percentage of fish hooked to those risen; and of those hooked which were eventually landed, I got a pretty dismal reply. The offers were there in

93

quantity, but the number of fish hooked and landed was abysmally small. These findings led me to do some reappraisal of the
single-hooked fly – particularly in the smaller sizes. I had already
concluded, rightly in my opinion, that to expect a firm hooking
with a single-hooked fly smaller than size 10 was asking a lot.
Size 12 and 14 flies are frequently used for trout and to expect a
salmon to open its big mouth to one of these small flies and be
hooked every time did not seem to make sound sense. It was about
this time, however, that I was enjoying a new-found love affair
with flies dressed on the long-shanked trebles as supplied by
Esmond Drury. I do not know if he supplies them in size 14 but
most certainly they are available in 12's and having tied a few
12's for trial it was not long before I had one on my leader and
was giving it a swim. Although much of my time in Grantown is
given over to instructing I do get the odd hour when I can fish
and of the three fish I subsequently rose during that period of
exceptional low water, all were hooked and landed on size 12
trebles.

By July of 1972 I was once again in Strathspey and the river
was even lower than it had been during May. A chance meeting
with Mr. Hamish Burdon of Forres brought the news that he was
successfully using minute tube flies terminating with a size 16
silver treble hook. Invariably these small hooks took firm hold in
the tongue of a fish and it was not long before I had begged one
or two of these minute trebles from him. At that time these silver
trebles were more scarce than gold in Strathspey, but I understand that Tom Saville of Nottingham now stocks them as a
regular item. While not entirely contradicting my earlier opinion,
therefore, I have eaten a limited amount of humble pie on this
question and have come to see the wisdom of retaining an open
mind on anything to do with salmon.

On the question of spinning and fly fishing in marginal conditions I have also had to modify my opinions somewhat. Most of
our classic rivers are now subjected to higher fishing pressure than
ever before. Even the best beats of the Spey are fished every day
and every week – excepting Sundays. The fish get little respite

from enthusiastic anglers and as soon as one party are packing up for a week the new influx of anglers arrive full of their own brand of dedication. Beats are spun and fly fished according to the preferences or competence of the anglers fishing them. Odd fish are caught and, although it may sound pompous, I suspect that more are caught by accident than design.

During May of 1973 the Spey was again almost as low as it had been throughout 1972, but sharp snowstorms during early May found water temperatures lower than to be expected at that time of the year, with the bulk of visiting anglers content to spin. At the end of a hard day instructing on the casting platform I motored down to No. 2 beat of the Strathspey Estates' water to see how the anglers were coping. The gillie on this beat is an engaging young man by the name of Eric Robb. Not only is he a very competent and genial gillie, he is also one of the finest spey casters I have ever seen. Talking over the problems of the day with him, he complained bitterly about the amount of spinning, suggesting that if more of the anglers would fish a greased-line fly they would do better. Under the prevailing weather and water conditions at that time I found some difficulty in fully agreeing with him, and we continued to argue the point at some length. As an instance of his conviction, however, he suggested that if I got into my breast waders and waded out into the tail of the Manse pool – which incidentally had not been fished that day – I would take a fish on the fly. I must confess, here and now, that I did not share his optimism or enthusiasm, but suggested to him that he take a dose of his own medicine and show me how to do it. Without a second bidding he donned breast waders and got into the pool. His first casts took his fly over very sluggish water, but he continued to wade down quietly between each cast and was slowly getting near to the tail of the pool where the current would give a slightly increased pace to the fly. He was throwing a very long line and his spey casting was a delight to watch. At about his tenth cast, however, he made the comment that the pace of the fly was just about right and the words were barely out of his mouth before I saw the line tighten and he was fast into an 11-lb fish which was eventually safely landed.

On the following afternoon I again went down to see how the anglers were doing. The weather was even colder and as I recall not a single fish had been taken that day. Eric Robb was there, however, and in such confident mood that I nearly had a five-pound bet with him that he could not repeat his performance of the previous day. Most certainly I had no inclination to fish myself and I urged him to have another try. A strong, cold, north-west wind hampered his casting, but it was not long before he had a good length of line out and covering another likely lie – this time in the main Manse pool. Within a few more minutes I saw his line tighten, but that was all and when we examined the fly we saw the problem. The wind had caused the treble-hooked fly to loop over the end of the leader so that it was swimming in reverse; but had he been more fortunate in this respect he could, once again, have proved me so wrong in my own assessment.

Talking the matter over at some length, I had the sense to realise that I was talking with a man who is not only a very competent angler, but one who has the distinct advantage of knowing almost every stone in his beat. He has that indefinable quality of being able to assess all the factors and make a tactical appreciation of the situation. He could, at any time during the day, take a client's rod to try to catch a fish for him, and he has a rare ability to know when it pays to fish hard and when it seems preferable to sit and watch the others. He is like many other expert gillies on the Spey, as far as practical fishing is concerned once April has passed, as with the biblical lilies of the field – they toil not neither do they spin.

The general feeling among many Spey gillies is that when April has passed, unless there is exceptional high water, that fly fishing will not only offer the best chance of fish it will also be less disturbing to the water. The word 'spin' under these circumstances is classed with many other four-letter words. Spinning, they say, in comparatively low water, even though it may be cold, will not only put fish off the take, but it will also create upstream or downstream migrations of fish who seek nothing more than some respite from the ironmongery that flashes around them. If, therefore, the gillies can find a piece of water which has not been spun to a foam they feel very confident that, at a time of day of their own choosing, they will have every chance of taking fish on the fly.

I must confess that in the light of this experience I had some fresh thoughts on fly fishing and spinning. However, I am not going to give my reader the full satisfaction of a contradiction for I have successfully fly-fished in the wake of spin fishermen too many times not to see the full value of it. The technique, if that is the right label, can frequently be used to advantage on rivers that are not hard-fished. Conditions may be ideal for fly fishing, but a slight rise in the water brings anglers to the river when it may not have been fished at all for several days or weeks previously. The extra water may induce some anglers to start operations with a spinning rod and it is then that I like to fish the fly behind them. If the fish are fresh-run, which well they may be after a slight rise, then the spinner may take a few, but it will not be long before the fly will be in with a better chance as water levels fall. Following that, of course, prolonged spinning is likely to do more harm than good.

As an example of further humiliation I suffered on the Spey during 1973 let me cite another instance when I was fishing with one of the world's most eminent anglers. It was mid-May, the scene was Pollowick, and my companion was none other than Al McClane. Now Pollowick is one of those classic Spey pools which not only holds a vast number of fish throughout the season, but has several good taking lies. It joins with the Dunbar and March pools to form the bottom beat of the Castle Grant water. For many years this portion was retained by the late Countess of Seafield for her own private guests, but it is now under the control of the Seafield Sporting Club. If I had to choose one pool on the Spey as a favourite, I think it would be Pollowick, but it is not the most challenging pool I have ever fished and water temperatures have to reach a critical level before fish will take in the main stream. To introduce Al McClane fully would require more words than can be found. First as Fishing Editor and then as Executive

Editor of top American magazine *Field and Stream,* he has become a legend in the U.S. Not only has he fished his native
country from coast-to-coast, but he has fished all over the world.
Current rumour has it that he has just accepted an invitation to
fish in China as a guest of Mao Tse Tung – but then I digress.
He arrived at Pollowick one very cold May morning with
nothing more than a single-handed fly rod and a pair of light
thigh waders. Frankly I did not rate his chances too highly and
was quick to tell him so, but I offered to lend him a spinning rod
and a pair of breast waders so that he could shorten the odds.
The spinning rod was refused with scorn and I was politely told
that anyone who would spin would also steal. There was some
temptation to take the waders, but eventually he settled for his
own and made ready with his tackle. The rod was a fairly stiff-
actioned affair, some 8½-ft in length, and carrying a forward-
taper No. 9 floating line with a sinking tip; and the fly of his
choice was single-hooked No. 6 Jock Scott. Not knowing the pool
at all and being confined to thigh waders, he was most insistent
that I fish it down ahead of him so that he could see where I
waded and thus follow as best he could. Grabbing my 13-ft 4-in
'Cordon Bleu' rod with a treble-hooked fly of my own tying I
decided that the water was too cold for the head of the stream
and I waded out in to a portion known as the Green Bank. Some
long casts were required to cover the pool adequately, but I fished
it down carefully, pausing frequently to look back to see how
Al was coping. His casting was impeccable, but was made tedious
by the fact that he had to throw such a long line that the handlining of the backing took a long time. Several loops of hand-held
backing had to be shot in the forward cast, some loops were held
between his fingers and others between his teeth, but the final and
important cast went out like a bullet.

As I came to the tail of the pool without so much as an offer
I glanced upstream again to watch Al's fly as it swung round to
within a few yards of where I was deep-wading. Quite suddenly
the water bulged and I saw Al's line and rod tighten at the same
moment. The fish fought well on that short rod and it was not

long before he tailed-out a nice fish of 9-lb. I was really too de-lighted to be humiliated, but he had virtually taken that fish out of my pocket. Ah well! I had occasionally done it to others so I had to be prepared, like a good Christian, to have them do it unto me.

During the exceptionally low waters of 1972 and 1973 on the Spey, therefore, I added to my experience. I did catch my own fair share of fish, but the important thing was that I retained an open mind so that modified tactics could be absorbed and exploited.

## 10
## Fly Fishing – Conclusions

---

WE have seen in the foregoing chapters that the fly, fished in its varying forms, is quite capable of taking fish throughout a season. We have studied the conditions for the big sunk-fly; and the small, sparsely dressed fly on the floating line. We have discussed situations when a medium-sized fly may be fished to advantage on a floating line with a sinking tip; or even smaller or larger flies be fished on a sunk-line in the middle of the greased-line season. There is no end to the permutations in which the all-round fly-fishermen may indulge.

Over recent years, however, I have come to suspect that the number of times when conditions are perfect for true greased-line fishing are not so frequent as some writers would have us believe. The history of disease in our rivers (dealt with in a later chapter) has affected taking habits. Land drainage and mild forms of pollution have combined to make some of our rivers less pleasant for the salmon to live in than they were in days gone by. Fish do not respond in the same way as they did, even ten years ago. Doubtless, also, fish change their habits slightly from season to season, and from river to river. I can recall seasons when certain spinners were more productive than others and when different flies seemed to hit the jackpot. Current experience indicates, however, that there are few occasions when taking fish cannot be caught with some form of fly. But to work on the old contention that once the water temperature has reached 48° the only satisfactory method is to use the traditional greased-line tactics will severely restrict the angler's range of attack. The advent of the forward-taper line with a sinking tip, although unheralded by a fanfare of trumpets, is one of the latest things to improve the fly-fisherman's lot. The line has this disadvantage of not being quite so pleasant to cast as a fully floating line; and, of course, it is virtually impossible to do any worth-while Spey-cast with any forward-taper line. They are, however, marketed in the double-taper variety and I have both on hand for differing circumstances. During the 1969 season, however, I used such a line fairly extensively and surprised myself with the number of successes, and near successes, I achieved. My fly-box has also held some new patterns among its ranks, for I have found that a short, *heavy* tube-fly often moves fish that will not respond to traditional greased-line patterns.

Doctor George Bain, of Taynuilt in Argyllshire, has fished the river Awe for many years, and has evolved a fly (there is really nothing new in it) which has proved so successful on that river that other, visiting, anglers rarely bother to fish with anything else. The fly is tied on a short piece of *heavy* copper or brass tubing, rarely more than $\frac{1}{2}$-in long; and can be made in varying patterns to suit personal taste. His basic fly has nothing more than a bit of brown and blue squirrel tail for the winging, and the copper tube is painted black. These flies hit the water with a resounding plop, when cast, and I was quick to christen them 'Bain's Bullets'. I now have a wide variety of these flies and find that I use them more frequently than ever before. They have proved successful on many rivers, other than the Awe, and are worth-while aces to have up your sleeve for those days when you don't really know what to do for the best. I have taken fish on them when traditional greased-line methods have failed. I have had other successes when a small spinner has failed. This, of course, is not to infer that they will replace either of these methods; but they present a very worth-while alternative. They can, on occasion, be cast upstream, and handlined back as one would

do in upstream spinning; but it is a tedious business and by
no means a sure way of taking fish. Perhaps their greatest
feature is their ability to take fish in those marginal conditions (so difficult to detect) such as days when air temperature is slightly less than that of the water; times when fish are
running and normally unconcerned with settling in a lie for
more than a few brief minutes; or occasions when, due to
rain, the river level is regarded as ideal for the spinner despite
the fact that angling is in the middle of the accepted greased-
line season. These 'Bain's Bullets' will never show that the
effectiveness of the traditional methods has disappeared, but
are a worth-while extra to have on hand.

For many anglers the sight of a head-and-tail rise is sufficient inducement to persist with the greased-line fly. I refer,
of course, to the lazy and rolling motion that a settled salmon
sometimes makes, rather like an aldermanic trout sipping in
a floating dun; and do not refer to the bold forward leap – so
characteristic of a running fish; nor to the awkward, backward splash which is so typical of a resident fish that has been
chivvied out of its lie; nor to the move of a kelt making its
tedious way downstream. Surface-moving action of the salmon
tells us something, if not very much; but the persistent head-
and-tailer is worthy of attention, particularly if he moves in
the same lie for a number of occasions. Take care, however,
to ensure that the fish has not been disturbed by your presence, since many a salmon that has been pushed out of his lie
by the angler who has waded too deeply will head-and-tail his
way down a pool; and so, at times, will a running salmon
move in an upstream direction. Head-and-tailers at the head
or tail of a pool also, are almost invariably running fish. It is
also particularly interesting to note the behaviour of running
salmon at the foot of a weir. Invariably they do a head-and-
tail rise before commencing their leap. It would appear as
though they were taking a sneaking look at the obstacle before
tackling it in earnest.

As a general rule, I would prefer to see trifling surface

activity by the fish, rather than too much. Hectic leaping activity usually indicates a pool with too many fish in it for their individual comfort. In such conditions the salmon are all preoccupied with finding a comfortable lie, and constantly chivvy each other for the best position. Small wonder that they pay little or no attention to our offerings when they are so occupied! When in these conditions I have watched them, on countless occasions they deliberately back away from an approaching fly or bait.

Perhaps the greatest information that may be gleaned from the regular head-and-tail riser is that the fish is quite likely to be the sole resident of his current lie; and, as such, may well defend his lie against any and all intruders – even a minute No. 10 greased-line fly, or a thumping great spinner flashing past his nose. There can be no hard-and-fast rule; but tradition dies hard and, in general, the angler is better advised to follow basic rules and approach such a fish with the fly.

To sum up, therefore, we have seen the need for varying types of tackle for adequate cover during a season's fly-fishing. In the early and often bitter months of the season, a heavy fly rod is needed with a good sinking line and varying weights of flies in excess of 2-ins long. Colours may range from a garish yellow to subdued brown and black – depending on water height, temperature and clarity. The fly will be required to get down to the fish; certainly until the water warms up to the mid forties. Then will come a transition period; a time when, as water temperatures approach 50°, the greased-line may be effective; but more than likely the medium-sized fly (about No. 4) on a line with a sinking tip will save the situation. It is a good time to experiment with fly sizes and when fish are quite likely to show some indication of the wide range of sizes they are prepared to accept. By the time May comes, however, it is safe to say that a No. 6 will be the basic size with patterns such as the Blue Charm, Thunder and Lightning, Logie and Stoat's Tail worth trying.

Do not, however, become wedded to this style of fishing for the remainder of the summer; and be ever watchful for those marginal conditions when the use of the sunk-tip line, or fully sunk-line, will save an otherwise blank day.

AUTHOR'S NOTE:—*In this short chapter I comment on the comparative lack of good greased-line fishing days. Although some contrary views are expressed in Chapter 9, I am still basically convinced of this. There may be periods of a day good for greased-line fishing, but the number of days and times are still not so frequent as some writers would have us believe.*

# 11

## Spinning (General)

---

LET me begin this chapter by stating that by far the bulk of my salmon have been taken with a spinner. Of late years, however, I tend to favour fly-fishing in its varying forms; and consequently do not spin as much as I used to in my fish-hungry days. Up to 1966, however, if anyone had imposed a severe restriction on the techniques I could use, but had left me to name the method (with the catching of fish as my prime objective), I should have selected, without question, a medium spinning rod, a fixed-spool reel and a 2-ins Black and Gold Devon Minnow. This combination has undoubtedly accounted for the lion's share of the fish I have caught. I can rightfully claim, therefore, to know something about spinning; and to know from considerable experience that it is not always as simple as contended by those who scorn the method.

For the purposes of discussion, however, it is important that we deal with all the varying aspects of techniques separately, since there is much more to successful spinning than the mere hurling of a bait into the water and winding it back for the next cast. The Americans draw a distinct line between what they call bait-casting and spinning. A bait-casting reel is what we should call a multiplier; and a spinning reel is generally referred to by us as a fixed-spool or thread-line reel. Both methods, as we shall see, have distinct advantages and disadvantages; but by being versatile with either, we are able to cope with all the varying conditions to be found on a river throughout the season. It is generally accepted, however, that spinning in the early spring and late autumn, on fairly big rivers, is best accomplished with a double-handed rod and a multiplier reel. Then for small stream, late spring and summer fishing, we turn to a single-handed rod and the fixed-spool reel. After taking my spinning very seriously for several earlier years, however, I found that to be fully versatile I required at least three spinning outfits to see me through a season.

My principal outfit for early season fishing in Britain consists of a 9½-ft Hardy No. 1 L.R.H. rod, with a 6000C Ambassadeur reel and 15-lb test nylon line. There are those who argue that monofilament line is more liable to cause an overrun when casting, and prefer to use braided line. Some advantage may be gained by using such monofil as 'Platil Soft' or oval section monofilament. It is of little account which you choose; but the braided line is slightly more difficult to cast to maximum potential distance, although it does minimize over-runs. The above outfit will handle most of the heavier spoons and Devon Minnows, together with any additional lead weighting; but is not the most suitable outfit to use with terminal tackle weighing less than ⅝-oz.

For periods in beween the seasons I like to have a slightly lighter double-handed rod (there are several now made in fibre-glass between 8½-ft and 9½-ft) with a medium sized fixed-spool reel. Those reels that find a place in my tackle bag include the Intrepid 'Elite', Abu 'Cardinal 77' and the Garcia 'Mitchell 410'. The last named is particularly useful when rapid retrieve of the bait is required. A monofilament line of some 10-lb to 11-lb test completes the list; and such an outfit will handle a very wide range of weights. Indeed, if I were to be further limited to one specific spinning outfit throughout the year, this would be the one I should select.

For fishing in high summer or fishing a small river, my third outfit consists of a 7½-ft Hardly 'Wanless' rod (single-handed) and the Intrepid 'Elite' fixed-spool reel, loaded with

7-lb to 8-lb nylon monofilament. The entire outfit is delight-
fully light and easy to fish with; and has frequently shown
successful handling of a fish up to 20-lb in weight.

Before turning to spinning techniques, I would first like to
outline some of the advantages and disadvantages of the fixed-
spool reel and the multiplying reel. For some strange reason
the fixed-spool reel has, over the years, acquired a deal of
adverse publicity. It is thought to be too easy to fish with. Its
use became 'not quite the done thing', and was ranked with
downstream wet-fly fishing for trout on a chalk-stream, or
worming for salmon. The label 'Yo-Yo' was applied and stuck.
Die-hard salmon anglers turned their noses up at it and
stayed with their old fashioned centre-pin reels. Then the
modern multiplier came on the scene and suddenly, almost
overnight, it acquired a status of respectability. Quite apart
from its relative merits against the fixed-spool reel, it became
the reel to use. Anglers with their early beats on Tweed, Spey,
Tay and Dee, took to them quickly; and the multiplier became the tool of the angling aristocrats, and the fixed-spool
that of the artisans. This, as I saw it at the time, was the only
yardsick by which the merits of each reel were judged. It
might be interesting, therefore, to investigate some of the
known *facts* and assess the merits of each reel.

Because of, or in spite of, its aristocratic associations, the
multiplier has many commendable features: (1) it carries a
good length of heavy line; (2) it enables baits of terminal
weights over $\frac{5}{8}$-oz to be cast further than with the same line
on a fixed-spool reel; (3) it does not put any kink into the
line; (4) it is possibly more pleasant in operation when playing a fish; although this is dependent on the preference of the
angler and is something I personally do not accept.

The multiplier does, however, have features which, in my
opinion, outweigh many of the advantages: (1) it has a tendency to over-run, particularly when loaded with monofilament line and when the angler is pushing for distance; (2)
there is a general necessity to use heavy baits, since few multipliers will handle small baits effectively; (3) it encourages a

tendency to use lead at a time when, for practical fishing reasons, lead may not be desirable; (4) the multiplier usually necessitates use of a double-handed rod in order to get casting distance; (5) the multiplier often has incorporation of a level-wind device, which again restricts distance; (6) there is a serious risk of over-run when casting into wind.

Turning to the fixed-spool reel, its advantages are: (1) over-runs rarely occur, and casting into wind is no real problem; (2) it enables the angler to change his weight of bait at will, without severely restricting distance; (3) it enables the angler to fish with or without lead, as fishing conditions dictate; (4) it permits the use of a single-handed or double-handed rod, as preferred; (5) it eliminates the need to change hands after the cast has been made; (6) it has a quicker rate of retrieve than most multipliers.

The fixed-spool reel has, however, a few disadvantages: (1) its inability to carry heavy line without severely restricting distance; (2) it may, on occasion, put twist into the line when playing a fish; (3) there is a so-called 'awkward' feeling as the line is wound on to the fixed-spool at right angles. But this is greatly reduced if a roller bearing is incorporated into the bale arm.

On balance, therefore, it would seem that the fixed-spool reel is the more versatile outfit, which I sincerely believe it to be; and, if logic be applied to our fishing, we quickly see that there is a strong case for equipping oneself with both outfits. The multiplier has merit for the early spring fishing, when big baits are very much the order of the day; and the fixed-spool reel has merit for late spring fishing when the angler may be called upon to make drastic changes, throughout a fishing day, in the sizes and weights of bait he is likely to find effective.

It is fair to say that lines in excess of 12-lb test should not, normally, be used on the fixed-spool reel of average size. Such thickness of line would severely limit the potential of casting distance. On the other hand, there are few rivers where lines in excess of this strength are necessary; but I do like to feel a little more armour in early spring on Tweed, or the wild rivers of Norway. It is then that I go for lines of 15-lb and 20-lb test on the multiplier. If I had to restrict my fishing to one type of reel throughout the year, however, I should be with the artisans and not with the aristocrats!

There are, perhaps, a few finer points of tactics to be discussed. Most anglers are right-handed; and with the fixed-spool reel they can cast and commence the retrieve without changing hands. Much of my fishing is done from the left bank of a river (that is the side of the river looked at as one faces downstream) and thus, with a fixed-spool reel, I can hold my right hand well out over the river to eliminate much of the line belly caused by strong central currents; whereas with a multiplier I should need to transfer the rod into the left hand before the retrieve commenced, and then have the slight disadvantage of facing partially upstream in order to have my left hand over the river. These may well seem trivial points; but they matter to me and I suspect make a difference to the amount of fish I could catch during a spinning season. The angler who consistently fishes the right bank of a river, however, may well find that the multiplier has advantages for him. Maybe, as an American salesman said, 'It's largely a matter of preference.'

The fact is that there is a case for both reels; and the all-round spinner would be well advised to equip himself with both, so that the variable equipment gives him the means of coping adequately with the problems faced in varying conditions. Let us now examine, in detail, the various spinning techniques.

AUTHOR'S NOTE:—*At the time of writing this chapter the bulk of my salmon had been caught by spinning. Nowadays, however, I fish the fly a lot more and the ratio of fish caught by this method is now increasing.*

RODS. *With continued improvement in fibre-glass design, rods of split-cane construction are becoming things of the past. There are now a lot of excellent glass spinning rods.*

REELS. *The Intrepid 'Elite' is now out of production but the latest 'Super-Twin' is excellent in every respect.*

## 12

## Early Season Spinning on Big Rivers

I HAVE already outlined details of the tackle I use for heavy
spinning. There are occasions, notably in Norway, and dealt
with in a later chapter, when much heavier rods than the
No. 1 L.R.H. spinning rod are called for. The No. 2 or No. 3
L.R.H. may be necessary, or one of the worth-while range
now made by Bruce and Walker; but for most spring conditions in Britain I have found that my No. 1 L.R.H. or a
glass rod of similar action, is more than adequate. I am never
quite so concerned with rod action on a spinning rod as I am
with my fly rods; but it is nice to have a rod with action
through to the butt, and it is particularly important when
using a multiplying reel. Many fibre-glass rods have a tendency towards tippiness and these do not make an ideal
marriage with the multiplier.

We have already seen that, in order to get the utmost
advantage from our spinning rod and multiplying reel, baits
weighing in excess of $\frac{5}{8}$-oz are almost a 'must'. For general
usage I would go even further and say that I feel in greater
command of such an outfit when the terminal tackle is near
to 1-oz (30 gm) in weight. Throughout these chapters on
spinning, the reader will detect a keen awareness of the
weight of the bait. This is a paramount factor; and, therefore,
the choice of tackle and weight of bait must invariably be
dictated by the size of river, height of water and strength of
current.

Let us imagine a pool on the Tay or Tweed during the early months of the season. The river may well be running a few feet above normal summer level; the water temperature will doubtless be struggling to top the 40° mark; and the early run fish will be tending to hold up in the lower beats of the river. There will be little inclination, on their part, to take sub-surface lures or baits fished in mid-water. The angler will be obliged to get his bait well down in order that it will swing into the lies at an acceptable level. A touch of frost at night will slow down any tendency the fish may have to run at this time of the year; and, as I have already outlined in Chapter 3, spinning, with a big bait, is usually a more logical way of fishing unless the big sunk-fly is obligatory. Much of my comment concerning sunk-fly fishing in the early spring, and the correct assessment of fly weight in that chapter, is equally applicable to spinner selection and tactics; and as such forms a basis for all our thinking in the presentation of a lure, fly or bait to the salmon.

Having arrived at the water side we are now posed with the problem of bait selection. We know that the bait has to get well down to the fish and that to use our multiplier to its best advantage the terminal weight should be in excess of $\frac{5}{8}$-oz. We also know that early spring salmon like a good-sized bait; and that for clear water conditions there are few to beat a 3-ins Black and Gold Devon Minnow, or a Yellow Belly of the same size. The weight of these baits is very much a variable factor, depending on whether they have been constructed from wood, fibre-glass, plastic or metal. It is, therefore, quite possible to have a 3-ins Devon Minnow in varying weights, so that the correct weight of bait may be chosen to match river height and current strength. The use of additional lead weighting is something which I should like to discuss at greater length later on; but as a general rule I am opposed to its use, and feel that when weight is required it should be in the bait itself. It is, of course, essential to have an additional swivel (apart from the one on the bait) and this should be placed about two feet from the bait.

We have already outlined the river conditions likely to
appertain during the early weeks of the season and it is then
left to individual choice to make an assessment of the bait to
use. Rarely should I bother with a bait of less than $2\frac{1}{2}$-ins
long at this time of the year (January, February or early
March); and, as we have seen, it is more than likely that a
$2\frac{1}{2}$-ins metal Devon would weigh as much, if not more, than a
3-ins plastic Devon. The weight, therefore, is the paramount
factor. There may well be, of course, some need for practical
trial and error. If I feel that my chosen bait is not fishing as
near to the bottom as I should like, but am convinced that my
size selection is just about right, then I shall seek out the
same sized bait constructed from heavier material; or, as a
final resort, use additional lead weighting. There are, of
course, countless occasions when rivers, at this time of year,
will be at near-flood level, and water clarification may not be
all that is desirable. At such a time I have found the range of
Toby Spoon baits and those imported by Efgeeco (F. Goddard
& Co., Ltd) to be most effective. These are available in
various sizes and weights; and if the weight is stamped on the
base of the bait (as it should be, on all commercially-sold
spinning baits) it is an easy matter to decide which spinner to
use under the circumstances. Choice of colour is, again,
largely a matter of preference; but the water colour and
height is a great indication. Dirty water calls for a flashy,
easily seen bait; whereas low, clear water may call for more
subdued colouring. Don't be too concerned with colour or
size in these early months; but concentrate on getting the
right weight, so that the bait will fish at the effective depth in
the water. Of the baits I prefer for early fishing, the $2\frac{1}{2}$-ins to
3-ins Black and Gold, or the Yellow Belly, are among my
favourites; together with, in varying sizes, weights and colour,
the Toby spoons. Natural baits are always worth a try, with
golden and silver sprats heading the list; but due to their
comparative lightness they generally require the use of additional lead. There are, however, quite a few natural bait

tackles marketed with built-in lead weighting; and at this time of the year they are the best to use.

It is important to establish the likely lies of salmon on an early spring beat. In many instances the fish will take up different lies from those which they would take up in warmer water conditions. They will tend to lie in the deep and comparatively quiet water, or on the edges of the main runs. In order to induce them to take, the bait will, invariably, have to be spun slowly over the lies so that they can take it with little effort. The colder the water, the less is likely to be the inclination of the fish to move a long way, or at any speed, to intercept the bait. All spring spinning, therefore, should keep the bait moving as slowly as possible, and fluttering in the current; and as near to the bottom as is practically possible. Admittedly it is most infuriating to get hung up at every cast; and with a varying depth of river bed, some eventual compromise has to be reached. My aim when spinning for early salmon is to select a weight of bait that, when cast out to the required point, will swing round at the right depth without any turning of the reel handle. Turning of the reel handle speeds up the passage of the bait through the water; and as we have already seen, the great desirability is to keep the bait moving at its slowest possible pace. There are those, I know, who cry, 'If I don't wind the reel handle, I get hung up on the bottom.' There are also those who, in order to simplify their casting (particularly with a multiplier), add additional lead weight where none is required, and have to wind in order to keep the bait from fouling the bottom. All these tactics militate against the successful presentation of a salmon bait. Sometimes, in really slack water, some winding does become necessary. But such conditions are rare on most spring rivers; and I feel fairly safe in saying that a weight of spinner should be selected so that it will revolve slowly in the current without any assistance by winding the reel.

The casual observer of spinning may regard the system as about the simplest form of angling in which it is possible to indulge. The angler merely throws out the spinner and

retrieves it slowly; then, taking a pace downstream, repeats
the process until a salmon takes hold. For many novices their
spinning is just as simple as that; and the fact that they
occasionally catch fish leads them to the belief that spinning
is easy. The plain fact is that to be really successful at spinning there is a great deal more skill required than is apparent
to the casual observer; and it is only when the basic elements
of spinning have been mastered that increased success will
come the way of the angler.

If we imagine ourselves to be on the left bank of a river;
(there is always some confusion as to which is the right and
left bank; but this is quickly assessed by looking downstream)
the approximate point to which we shall make our initial cast
will be 11 o'clock.

Although it seems perfectly elementary, it must be realized
that the spinner we throw out across the river will be greatly
influenced in its behaviour by the line connecting it to the
rod and reel. As soon as the cast is made, the bait slowly sinks;
but, unless you do something about it, the line, now extended
across the river, will be subjected to a heavy pull by the
central current across which it lies. It stands to reason, therefore, that whether you turn the reel handle or not, with a
downstream belly in the line, the bait will travel the first part
of its journey with its head pointing slightly downstream (Fig.
5). more important, it will also travel faster than is desirable
in order to have the best chance of taking a fish. At any rate,
certainly in the early spring months, I am frequently amazed
at many anglers who, after casting their baits in the manner
described, suddenly start to wind the reel handle as well. If
only they stopped to think, they would realize that such tactics
are not going to permit the bait to get down anywhere near
the fish; and, what is more, it will be moving so fast through
the water that none but the most foolhardy salmon will con-
descend to take it. Here again, if you dare challenge them, the
general retort would be, 'Well, if I don't wind it, the bait will
get stuck in the bottom.'

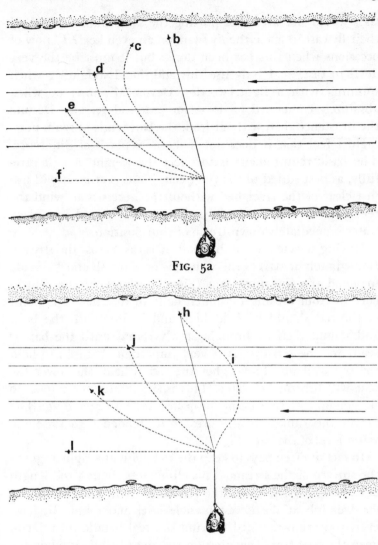

FIG. 5a

FIG. 5b

We have discussed, briefly, the use of additional lead. There are many anglers, I know, who advocate the use of additional lead weight. They say it makes the bait swim better and on an even keel. This is certainly a factor in their favour. But how do these same anglers explain the fact that they would not dream of putting the same hunk of lead on their fly cast to make the *fly* swim on an even keel? I know of occasions when this has been done; but it must be the very devil to cast. So I only use this additional weighting when spinning with a light, wooden Devon Minnow; or when absolutely compelled to do so for practical reasons. Despite the insistence that, without lead, the bait tends to swim nose-high. I feel that it does not make a ha'porth of difference. The basic requirement is to select the weight of bait carefully, as best suited to the river conditions, so that it will fish just clear of the river bed without the necessity to wind the reel handle at all until the bait has come round into slack water immediately downstream of your position.

Having selected a suitable bait, it is cast across the stream. Immediately it strikes the water every effort should be made to mend the line upstream (Fig. 5) to prevent the central current from causing too much belly in the line. The point of the rod should be held high and in line with the bait; and should then be brought slowly round until the bait is ready for the retrieve. It is very important, I think, to hold the rod well up. The higher the rod is held, the lower the bait will fish in the water. This is simply due, of course, to the amount of line being subjected to the water drag. The longer the sunk-line, the greater its tendency to raise the water level of the bait (Fig. 6).

In fact, it often pays to keep the rod point at a right-angle to the surface of the stream. This eliminates about a rod length of extra line belly, due to the central current; and thus makes the bait fish at the lowest possible level and speed. If, however, you are compelled to wind the reel handle in order to keep the bait from snagging on the river bed, it is advisable to change to a lighter bait; and I mean a lighter bait, not necessarily a smaller one.

On this basis it is quite understandable that a heavier bait will be required for the head of the stream; whereas, towards the tail of the pool, the current may only carry a lighter one. There is, I know, a tendency to put on a piece of lead for the

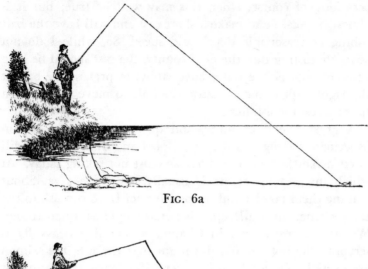

FIG. 6a

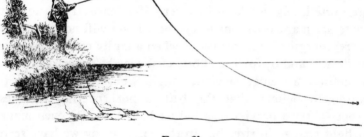

FIG. 6b

first part of the stream, and then take it off half way down the pool. In my lazier moments I even do this myself; but I am firmly convinced that a bait unfettered by additional lead weighting, and of just the right weight for the current in which it is fishing, is more successful in the long run. Certainly such baits are easier to cast since, with additional lead, the two separate weights at the end of the line tend to compete with each other during the cast, and this can kill a good deal of potential distance.

There are those who argue that distance casting is not important in salmon spinning. They say that, often, the fish are lying near the angler's own bank; and that long casting only serves to cover a lot of dead water. There are some occasions, of course, when this may well be true; but it is almost impossible to make a short cast and still have the bait fishing at reasonable depth and speed. So, while I do not advocate casting into the next county, the cast should be long enough to cover the water adequately; to present the bait at the right depth; and to cause the bait to move at the right speed across the fish-lies.

A great friend of mine, and quite a successful salmon fisherman, having fished down a pool and drawn blank, will often make the remark, 'They are just not taking today.' At which my prompt retort is usually, 'Well, let's set about making them take!'; and in spinning for fresh-run fish in the early spring, this philosophy is not as stupid as it may sound. We have already seen in Chapter 3 that if a heavy fly is scraping the bottom and down amongst the fish, the salmon are quite likely to take it in sheer self-defence. It is true that there are many occasions when the salmon will not take; but there are quite a few occasions when a faulty conclusion may be drawn; and by further effort, a fish may be induced to take. Sometimes a change of tactics might yield a fish. If there is reason to believe that the bait is not covering the lies properly, try a heavier or a lighter bait. You may even make a slight change in size; but in the early spring we have seen that this is often less important than the weight factor. Whatever else you do keep persisting. You may never know the moment when, due to some subtle and undetected change in atmospheric or water conditions, the fish will suddenly come into a taking mood. Then, at the umpteenth cast, you will suddenly feel an electrifying tug on the line – and a spring salmon is on!

I have mentioned nothing of fishing with plug baits for the simple reason that I have never used these baits. That they are effective on some waters I have no doubt. I believe that they are very popular on the Hampshire Avon; and indeed they may well be worth a try on other rivers of similar character. Anyone interested in plug fishing should read *Hampshire Avon Salmon* by Lt. Col. S. H. Crow.

On general summary, early spring fishing on big rivers usually requires long casting, and careful fishing through all the likely water; correct selection of the right weight of bait in order to spin the water at the slowest possible speed; and also to spin at the lowest depth without continually feeling the bait touching the bottom. There should be ability to make a reasonable assessment of the size and colour of the bait; and, above all, the persistence to fish hard through all the hours of daylight that come the angler's way during these early months. The fish, in the main, will be all fresh-run, and thus that bit easier to tempt. They do, however, require the angler to 'get down' to them; and this factor alone can make all the difference between success and failure.

AUTHOR'S NOTE:—*Another useful method of attaching extra lead to Devon Minnows is to wind lead wire around the trace between the hooks and swivel. My remarks about fibre-glass rods now seem unnecessary.*

# 13
## Mid-Season and Medium-Stream Spinning Tactics

THE season for the multiplier and double-handed rod is generally short-lived. Those anglers who persist with them throughout the year, either because of snob reasons or because they genuinely prefer them, are usually imposing limitations on their full potential. There may be a case for their continued use on Spey, Tweed or Tay when bait sizes and weights never seem to get too small; but as a general rule, and on the bulk of rivers, as late spring approaches the currents of the majority of rivers get too slack to warrant the use of big, heavy baits. We have already seen that the multiplier will not handle small baits effectively without the undesirable use of additional lead weighting; and thus, on a lower water, it is necessary to wind the reel handle. The most obvious course to take is to revert to the fixed-spool reel.

The fixed-spool reel is a very versatile piece of equipment. It has been much maligned in the past, but still emerges as the most popular reel in general use throughout the entire angling world. It is said that it is too easy to use; but watching the antics of some anglers when using such a reel shows that there are few who are really competent in exploiting its full potential. The simple act of casting, whether it be fly, bait or lure, is a subject I shall touch upon briefly in another chapter; but general standards are deplorably low and, as we shall see later, this factor alone is largely responsible for indifferent results in any type of fishing.

For general spinning, I load my fixed-spool reel with monofilament line between 10-lb and 11-lb test, perhaps the maximum line strength to be recommended for standard sized fixed-spool reels. For those who prefer a fixed-spool reel for all their fishing, there are larger models available (designed mainly for sea fishing) which are constructed to carry lines in excess of 20-lb test. Such a combination, however, will not handle a small bait adequately, and is to be likened to the multiplier in that respect. Loaded with such heavy lines they are not capable of casting the distances that may be achieved with a multiplier with the same strength of line and terminal weights around 1-oz. This is a factor which clearly indicates a case for both types of reel.

The standard size fixed-spool reel is more than adequate for normal spinning, provided that the line is loaded to the lip of the reel (a very important factor in gaining full potential casting distance). Take care, however, not to overload the spool as this will have an equally restricting effect. It will hold more line than is ever likely to be required with the most playful fish. For the transition period, between the early spring fishing and the delicate days of upstream spinning in low water, I prefer a double-handed rod of some 8-ft to 9-ft in length; and am not greatly concerned if the rod has tippy action or is as stiff as a broom handle. The latter design, of course, would not provide the ideal weapon with which to play a fish; nor would it make the ideal casting tool. I am merely inferring that, in this instance, rod action is not of paramount importance; and that many of the tippy, fibreglass rods now on sale are quite adequate for the task.

Although the use of a swivel is important when using any type of spinning bait or reels, its use is far more important when using a fixed-spool reel in order to avoid serious line kink or twist. The swivel should be mounted not less than 2-ft from the terminal bait; and if a long overhang is to be avoided, it should not be a great deal more than this length.

The use of additional lead is again something which I deplore for general circumstances and the same factors would govern its use as in heavy spinning with a multiplier.

Perhaps the prime feature of this lighter type of spinning is the greater degree of accuracy that may be obtained in casting. With a little bit of practice it will soon be possible, literally, to hit a dust-bin lid at 15-yds; and the angler is thus able to place his bait in all the likely-looking places without the necessity of changing hands. He is, therefore, in immediate control of the bait the instant it touches the water; sometimes this is a very important factor.

The same basic rules for bait selection as we discussed in Chapter 12 will still apply; but the angler is now able to use a wider range of bait weights without seriously limiting potential casting distance. Obviously, a 1-oz Toby spoon may be thrown a lot further than a $1\frac{1}{2}$-ins, plastic Devon Minnow; but the latter may still be cast a worth-while distance, and certainly further and more comfortably than would be possible with the average multiplier tackle used in the early spring. A good spinning day, with such tackle as I have described, may well come after a rise in the water takes place; and may happen at any time during the salmon season. The angler may well have doubts about the relative merits of the medium-sized fly on a sinking-tip line; or that there is merit in the use of a medium-sized spinner on such an occasion. So we have to presume that he has made up his mind to spin; and that, with water temperatures approaching 50°, he has selected a $1\frac{1}{2}$-ins to 2-ins Devon Minnow of the correct weight to suit the prevailing water conditions. The technique of fishing will be virtually identical with that outlined in Chapter 12. At this stage there is little point in trying out low-water spinning tactics. The basic technique is just the same as for heavy spinning. The bait should still be selected on a weight basis, and still made to fish fairly deep in the water; but there is not quite the same urgency in scraping the bottom as in early spring fishing.

Fish will be prepared to move a little more freely for the

bait and will often accept it in mid-water, or even near the surface; but there should be little attempt to speed up the movement of the bait. Here again a movement of the bait through the water without winding the reel handle is the situation for which to aim. Doubtless there will now be many more occasions when some winding of the reel handle becomes necessary; and certainly it will be advisable when the river is fining down to a good fly height. Choice of size and colour of the spinner or lure at such time is largely dictated by the clarity of the water; and there are many days, following a dirty flood, when it pays to resort to the same flashy Toby spoon that the angler may have used way back in February. My own favourite bait for a clearing water in late spring is a 2-ins Black and Gold plastic Devon Minnow, marketed by Halifax Products Ltd of Halifax. I have taken too many fish on this bait to discard it lightly, and a stock accompanies me on any salmon fishing expedition. Under such water conditions as I have described, however, ideal spinning situations do not last for very long. The angler must be ever watchful for a lowering of the water when fish will shy off the spinner and seek a more elusive lure such as the mid-water fly, or the greased-line fly as suggested in Chapter 10. The reason is that the time may come quickly when salmon will see the bait too readily; and if the angler persists too long with the spinner he only succeeds in frightening the fish, and thus spoils his chances with the fly. It is at this period when I take a secret delight in fly-fishing behind a good bait fisherman. The fish are just about to go off the spinner and will often give me the sport for which *he* was hoping!

As late spring moves on to summer, and conditions still dictate the use of the spinner, it may well pay dividends to vary one's tactics. The fish will now be in a much more playful mood. They may well be prepared to come out of their lies much more readily to intercept a bait. Size, weight and colour of bait will still be determined by water conditions; but the angler may well find that there is less desirability in restricting his tactics to fishing the bait as slowly as possible.

It always pays, I think, to commence in the traditional
manner; but if success is not quickly forthcoming, it sometimes pays to speed up the passage of the bait – or even to
cast it upstream and wind back quickly. I well recall one
such occasion on the Lune when both fly and traditional
spinning had failed to produce an offer. I knew, however,
that there were plenty of fish in the beat; but was at a loss to
know just how to get them to take. The same 2-ins Black and
Gold Devon Minnow, which had been on my spinning rod
all morning, was still on the rod; but I was at the wrong side
of the river to fish it properly in the traditional manner. So,
casting upstream into well known lies, I reeled it back as fast
as I could. In the short space of an hour I hooked five fish;
but have to confess that not a single one of them was landed.
Man-made groynes, with steel mesh gabions, saw my downfall,
since every hooked fish ran me under these, and I was power-
less to avoid a break. One of the fish literally took the bait at
my feet. He was a good fish for the water and I was just as
open mouthed as he was at the instant he took the bait with a
bang! I reckoned he was all of 30-lb.

# 14
## Small Streams and Ultra-Light Spinning

In the past two chapters we have discussed the basic requirements of early-season and mid-season spinning. Under suitable conditions, of course, it is possible to fish throughout a
season with a medium spinning outfit. Inevitably, however,
there comes a time when waters are low, and current is
reduced to a mere trickle. At such a time the current may
become so slow that it makes any form of fly-fishing a great
trial. Then, unless the angler wishes to resort to prawn, worm
or shrimp, he has only his spinning outfit upon which to
rely. Following the first floods of summer, some of our smaller
rivers receive their first runs of fish. Sometimes, within a
matter of hours, the fish are lying in waters at summer level;
and the angler is confronted with the problem of how to
catch them.

Deep-holding pools may be almost stagnant. In such conditions, they obviously lend themselves to prawn or worm
fishing. It is at such a time that a small spinner, on very light
tackle, may produce results. Spinning baits should rarely be
more than 1in long, and it is under such conditions that a
small quill minnow comes into its own. There will be, of
course, a need to wind the reel handle continually; and in the
slack water, it will matter little whether the bait is cast upstream or down. The thing to do is to try all ways; that is, to
alternate the speed of the bait, and make it move at different
levels in the water. In such conditions, with plenty of fish in

the water, there is a real danger of foul-hooking fish; but if the bait is getting down to where the fish are lying there is also every opportunity for it to be taken properly. There are no rules at all for this type of fishing; and I know of many instances when the most remarkable things have happened. Fish have taken the bait while it was dancing on the water during the retrieve; and made passes at it while it dangled in the water prior to the next cast. I even recall one instance when a friend of mine was worm fishing for salmon. The worm flew off the hook as he was casting, but a salmon seized the bare hook, as it was being retrieved for re-baiting, and was duly landed. Such incidents, while not commonplace, do occur at times and may have induced the late A. H. E. Wood to try a hook with a painted shank in lieu of a fully dressed fly. The smaller the bait, sometimes, the more intriguing it is to the salmon; and in order to cast these minute baits, short rods and lines not exceeding 8-lb test are very necessary. It can be a fascinating form of fishing; and, moreover, if the water is reasonably clear, the angler is often able to witness the entire action of the fish as it takes the bait. Concealment, of course, plays a very important role; and in this respect it can resemble chalk-stream fishing for trout.

Apart from the quill minnows I have discussed, there are several other baits worth trying. The Mepp range of spoon baits, sizes 1 and 2 are often worth experiment. Small Devon Minnows, barely $\frac{3}{4}$-in long and of the heavyweight type marketed by Hardy Bros., have taken fish for me on many occasions. The most effective tactic may be to make the bait spin through the water at maximum possible speed. If the bait is spun slowly under such conditions, there is every chance that the fish will see it for what it is; whereas, if it seems a fleeting thing, the fish may take it before the appearance of the small moving object has caused any suspicious reaction on its senses.

There are, of course, many occasions, other than those I have described, when the use of ultra-light tackle has definite advantage. I well recall an incident when I was fishing the

Lune in the company of a past editor of *Trout and Salmon*, Mr Ian Wood. Both of us had achieved limited success with the fly; but the water was on the low side, and quite a few fish were concentrated in the rough, streamy shallow water at the head of a narrow run. We had tried our flies over them without success. I had even failed to get a take with traditional and upstream spinning tactics; and was sat on the bank, at the head of the run, wondering what on earth to do. As I sat there, I picked up the small spinning rod and dangled the tiny quill minnow in the water. The current was sufficiently strong to make the bait revolve, and I slowly let the bait drop downstream by paying line off the reel. Such tactics had occasionally worked successfully with the fly; why not with a spinner? Suddenly I was into a fish. I hustled it quickly downstream, and out of the way. After successfully playing it out, I went back and repeated the process. Within a few minutes I was fast into another fish; and then took a third before the rest of the shoal became aware of the tumult, and moved out of the stream. Later that night, in the pitch darkness, I even took a salmon of 10-lb while fishing for sea-trout with a small fly. That was an unexpected ending to an unusual day.

Light spinning, after such incidents, has brought me plenty of fun and little formula. In its strange way, it can be just as fascinating as any form of fly-fishing. The angler makes up his own rules as he goes along; and the best of long-held theories have been shattered time and time again. Nowadays, however, I tend to spend the bulk of my time with fly. In terms of fish to be caught, I am sure that I am imposing unnecessary limitations upon myself. I have to ask myself whether it is the method, or whether it is fish on the bank, that matters most. I don't really know the answer; but so long as any form of fishing remains a challenge, I suspect that I shall indulge in it from time to time.

# 15
## Days with the Spinner and a Camera

Much of my early spinning was done on such rivers as the Cumberland Eden, Tweed, Spey and Yorkshire Esk. During later years I also did a deal of spinning on the Lune; and in terms of fish caught, I had some very successful times. Some of the most memorable days, however, were those when it was a struggle to get even a single fish; days when fly, prawn, worm and shrimp had all failed – or because I was out of baits for the last named three. It was only persistent spinning that saved a blank day, or even a blank week. In those earlier days I had much more confidence in my ability with a spinner than with a fly; so, consequently, I tended to resort to the spinner more frequently when the going was tough. Nowadays, as I have outlined, it is doubtful if I should always persist with a spinner; but its use has got me out of some embarrassing situations, and still does to this day.

During the early sixties I became an angling reporter for Granada Television and then followed this with a two-year period of similar activity for Tyne-Tees Television. There was never a deal of angling coverage on television and even to this day, despite the fact that angling has higher participation by the public than any other sport in this country, it gets scant TV. time. There are, of course, several reasons for this, not least of which is the great difficulty in getting the co-operation of the fish when an expensive camera crew lurks on the river bank; or of making a film with sufficient interest to hold a general audience. In the end I resorted to making the films myself, and giving commentaries on them from the studio. The method worked. I could go unobtrusively along the waterside and film my friends as they caught fish. There were many blank days; and there were occasions when I had to do the fishing, and then hand the rod over to some chum while I made ready with the camera. At the end of every month, however, I had obtained a small item somehow; and we never had to resort to any faking in order to depict real live fish being caught.

One of my earliest salmon-fishing features was to depict activities on the river Tweed. There were to be two of us fishing, Ken Morritt and myself. Since Ken is no mean performer with a cine-camera it was agreed that whoever hooked a fish, the other would run up and take over the camera. Day upon day we tried to hook a salmon; but it was not until the latter part of the week that we detected a fresh run of fish going through. Surely on that day, we thought, we should get some fish? We fished hard; and all thoughts of the camera were put to one side. At the end of the day Ken had hooked and lost no less than seven fish; and I had one little Springer to show for my efforts. Tomorrow, I thought, I will concentrate on the camera!

The following day we made an early start and I fished close to Ken with the camera at the ready. We were spinning with Black and Gold Devon Minnows (it was the month of March) and these lures, we reckoned, would offer us the best chance of sport. It was not long before Ken hooked a fish. I gave my rod to the gillie and dashed off with the camera. Just as Ken was bringing his lively fish ashore, the gillie hooked a fish; and I was thus able to film continually away and come back with some worth-while footage of two salmon being caught and landed. No more fish came our way for the rest of that week – but I had got my film.

Other memories of days with a spinning rod and a camera bring to mind some of the very pleasant times I spent in the company of the late Oliver Kite. Oliver was one of the most delightful characters I have ever come across in the angling world and his death, in 1968, was untimely, robbing the angling fraternity of a truly wonderful character. In the early days of our friendship we fished together for trout. Salmon were things of which he was a little scornful and he frequently pulled my leg about my being just another trout fisherman who had gone to the dogs. In the end, however, Reg Righyni and I persuaded him to come north to the Lune, where he was to catch the first two salmon he had ever landed. I never did make a real salmon angler out of him; but in latter years he became more tolerant of me – and of salmon!

On many occasions, when he came north, he was accompanied by Southern Television camerman Ted Channell, constantly on the look-out for material for his programme 'Kite's Country'. Oliver would rove the banks in search of elusive bird-life or some aspect of nature not commonly found in his native Wessex. There was one notable occasion when Righyni and myself were to try and catch a salmon for the camera to record. As luck would have it we both hooked fish at the same time and the camera was able to pan from Reg to myself to witness us doing battle. My fish turned the scale at 19-lb and I quickly hooked another one which made the 11-lb mark. Doubtless southern TV. viewers would get the impression that salmon fishing was easy; but things did not always work out this way.

My most recent experience, when I was glad of a spinner and another angler, came in the autumn of 1969. We were just finishing one of the worst Lune seasons in history, with a grand total, for the season, of ten fish for the three-rod beat. Of these ten fish, my wife and I had accounted for four apiece. Mine had been taken with the fly, and hers with spinner. Her best only made $10\frac{1}{2}$-lb, whereas my smallest went to $12\frac{1}{2}$-lb. This induced her to be very keen to win on sheer numbers of fish caught; and we agreed to have a final fling on the last day of the season.

The day before that, however, I received a call from the B.B.C. Television 'Look North' team. Could they come and film me catching salmon? At least they could come and try, I said, but with a forecast of south-westerly gales it would be a near-miracle if anything was caught. We assembled in the bar of the Royal Hotel in Kirkby Lonsdale, and I was immediately impressed by the fact that they were only ten minutes late. This was a high rating for TV. camera crews. I could not recall any previous occasion when they had been there within at least two hours of the stipulated time. They turned out to be a very professional crew. We were quickly on the river bank and I was soon fitted up with a chest microphone and describing to the camera, the basic scene. With a short lead connecting me to the sound recordist, and a further connection to the cameraman and director, we were a pretty formidable team as we bull-dozed our way along the river bank. For my first attempts I tried the fly. It was, however, a back-breaking business to make the fly act effectively as the wind kept whipping it upstream. Eventually I changed to the spinner; and it was well turned 1 p.m. before we were successful in getting the introductory shots in the can.

As far as practical fishing was concerned I had not yet done any. My wife was still busy hammering away at the water further downstream, out of camera range, and was still fishless. I felt obliged to tell the director to uncouple me from the sound recordist and let me spend some time on my own, in order to have a better chance to get a fish. If I succeeded then there would be ample time to couple me up to camera again, and let me describe the fight. It was an anxious hour I spent in search of a taking fish. The day was deteriorating rapidly and I felt sure that my chances were getting slimmer by the minute.

There were a few fish in the beat; but their skittering leaps indicated only too plainly that many of them were in the early stages of being affected by the disease. I roved up and down the best pool on the beat, trying first a 2-ins Black and Gold Devon Minnow, and later a $\frac{5}{8}$-oz Toby spoon. It was all to no avail. Two companions were also on the river trying their hand at the game; but by 2.30 p.m. none of us had anything to show for our efforts. I could well imagine the director's feelings! 'What a load of mugs these anglers are! Flogging away all day for an elusive fish, and here I am with an expensive camera crew and no story to take back to the programme editor . . .' Throughout the day, however, I had given him constant reminders of the great difficulty in making an angling film. How could he expect any self-respecting fish to take my bait with four hefty blokes pounding around on the river bank? Fishing is basically a solitary game where, with the stealth of the hunter, the angler goes unobtrusively about his business. 'My wife,' I said, 'has a better chance of catching fish than I have.'

By mid afternoon the director was getting desperate. 'I'm afraid that we shall just have to wind up the film,' he said, 'and you will just have to say that this is typical of salmon fishing. We may be able to use some of your own film, showing fish being caught; but the programme editor will not be very happy about it!' Naturally I felt very disappointed, but had known from the start that under the circumstances (the worst season for twenty years, poor conditions on the day, and disease back in the river) it would have been a near miracle if full requirements had been achieved. The television boys would have to expect this sort of thing if they were to give a sane and sensible coverage of angling. These fish had not read the script and were darned if they were going to co-operate!

We were about to call it a day when a shout from my wife indicated, only too clearly, that the miracle had happened. She had hooked a fish! The elegant four thundered down the river bank, and, uncoupling my microphone, I quickly waded out and took the rod out of my wife's hands. Back on the bank again, the mike was plugged in and I opened with the comment 'The miracle has happened – I'm into a fish!' What I do for *Art*'s sake! With camera whirring, the fish was quickly played out and brought ashore. It was a small 8-lb cock salmon and was triumphantly held up in front of the camera. My wife was looking on with quiet satisfaction. Not for her the glory of the silver screen! But perhaps a far greater satisfaction that she had not only wiped my eye, but had brought me down to size in the most unassuming way possible! How could I be anything but grateful to her? As for myself, I feel a fraud. The film looked good and was quite convincing; but I have to tell someone. She beat me!

# 16

## The Illusion of Life

---

THE multitude of spinning baits and lures now on sale to the bewildered angling public, and the general gullibility of salmon anglers in these matters as they religiously keep changing their baits when fishing, led me some time ago to do some serious re-thinking on this vexed question.

There are lures and baits which the makers claim have 'sonic' qualities. I imagine that these baits play a piscatorial version of 'Come to the cookhouse door, boys!' on passing through a pool; and that every salmon in the locality suddenly senses 'Grub's up!' – and with a 'Come and get it!' attitude, they all swoop on the bait. Other baits and spinners are claimed to have vibrating qualities. Doubtless by shaking their sensual hips and emitting high frequency vibrations they lure the unsuspecting fish into trouble.

My own, and indeed general, experience, has proved that there is no such simple formula for the wholesale capture of salmon. As I have grave doubts about sonic and vibrating qualities, I felt that the main line of thought and experiment should be along the lines of the visual image that persuades a salmon to take a bait, spinner – or lure of any type, including the so-called 'salmon fly'.

We must presume that when a salmon takes a bait in fresh-water, we have awoken the urge to prey in that fish. It has been argued that the salmon takes a bait either out of anger or sheer boredom. The fact remains that in the case of the

worm (a natural bait) the fish will often swallow it; though
whether it can subsequently digest it is highly doubtful. It is
reasonable to suppose, however, that if a salmon found a
Yellow Belly to be soft, appetizing and unarrayed with hooks
when taken in the mouth, it would do precisely the same
thing – that is, it would swallow it. I have seen salmon pick
up a bunch of lobworms and appear to chew them for some
considerable time before spitting them out, finally. This is
an exception to the rule. Many well-known salmon anglers
who are experts at worming will confirm that if the strike is
delayed too long, the bait and hook are frequently found in
the stomach of the fish.

In my opinion, it is the appearance and movement of the
bait which persuades the salmon that here is something that
he can eat. Whether he seizes upon such a bait out of hunger,
or under the influence of some other motive, is irrelevant.
He would hardly be likely to attack anything which, at some
time in the past, has not represented food to him; unless, of
course, he imagined it was necessary to defend himself or his
mate against an enemy.

I have mentioned the movement of the bait. I think that
this is important. Modern salmon fly-dressing trends indicate
that a fly should give a greater semblance of life when fished
in an average stream. The old inanimate and overdressed
patterns are fast dying out; and in their place we get the more
logical designs, such as the Waddington range, constructed
with long, flowing hackles – usually of black heron fibres.
Buck-tail is also becoming a popular material; and hair wing
flies are rapidly gaining prestige.

Some years ago I had an opportunity of filming various
types of flies, moving in a current of water. A glass-sided tank
was used, to which was attached an ordinary hosepipe. The
flies were then submerged and left to flit and dance in the
current, in much the same way as they would do in the river
when attached to the end of a line and leader. The cine-
camera seemed the ideal instrument to record their
behaviour, since it conveys their true appearance as seen

when working. Such flies as the Waddington series showed an exceptional resemblance to a living thing. Experiments with the more conventional salmon flies showed less action, in the sense that they looked like – conventional salmon flies!

My next problem was to convey, by means of a still picture, the life-like quality of certain flies. For ordinary work my cine-camera is operated at 24 frames per second. In other words, the illusion of movement is created by projecting 24 progressive still pictures every second. The persistence of vision of the human eye, however, is capable of overcoming 'flicker' at 16 frames per second, or even slightly less. As projector speed moves below this, our eye tends to see a series of well defined still pictures once again and the persistence of vision is lost.

In order to take a moving picture, a cine-camera must move the film forward a frame before exposing it. Normally, for half the time of the operation, the shutter is closed and the camera mechanism is transporting the film. During the other half, the film is stationary; and with the shutter opening, exposure takes place. I apologize to cine-enthusiasts for being so elementary! I merely wish to explain why, when operating at 16 frames per second, the camera gives an effective shutter exposure of half this speed – that is 1/32-second.

If we assume that the salmon has the same persistence of vision as our own, it is reasonable to suppose that, in order to capture a still picture depicting a bait or a fly as the salmon momentarily sees it, we should utilize a shutter speed of 1/32 second (or more) on the still camera. As a keen photographer, I have always aimed at having a sharp, well-defined print. These can easily be obtained, of course, by using still cameras with high shutter speeds or in conjunction with electronic flash. In such operation, the fly or bait is completely 'frozen' into a well-defined photographic reproduction. But this is well within our persistence of vision limitations, and could not possibly convey the comparatively slow moment of time when a salmon sees a bait or fly.

Initial experiments were then tried using lower shutter

E

speeds, in the order of 1/30th second to 1/15th second. Blurred, uninspiring photographs were the result. It could be argued, nevertheless, that they represented the illusion which the salmon sees. What was very noticeable, in the case of a series of Devon spinners, filmed in colour, was their overall similarity in tone. Various colour combinations were tried, such as 'Black and Gold', 'Yellow Belly' and 'Blue and Silver'. When seen on the movie film, it was difficult to determine which spinner was which; in fact, when spinning at critical revolutions, certain colour combinations blended to form a tone on the 'grey scale'. Combinations which lacked a full range of colours took on much more delicate shades than the basic stationary colours.

I think that it is quite a true statement that more fishermen are caught with these multi-coloured baits, which now litter the tackle shops, than fish! The problem, therefore, comes once again to our adversary the salmon; and we shall never know his views on the matter. The main point is that, for some reason, he can be induced on occasion to take a bait *or* fly. I really think that the type of bait matters less than we imagine; provided, of course, that we make our choice of size and colour to conform with the colour and temperature of the water. Until we learn differently, it would seem that the old rules of 'bright for a bright day', and 'dull for a dull day', are fairly safe. It would also seem reasonable to match the colour of the water with the colour of the bait; but if we must keep changing our baits at the end of every quarter-hour of fruitless fishing, I suggest that the change should be a bold one from the colour standpoint.

The increasing use of spoon baits for salmon in coloured water is interesting. Under such conditions, latterly, I rarely use anything else; and in this respect, I have had marked success with the French made 'Mepps', and with the Toby spoon. When conditions are such that the angler would not normally consider fishing, these lures have consistently taken good bags of salmon and sea-trout. On one occasion, fishing a coloured spate stream with these baits, I caught no less than seven fish on one day and five on another.

I feel that it is very important, under these findings, to weigh up the water conditions, and present to the salmon something which can readily be seen in turbid water (though less readily seen in clear water) in a manner that looks reasonable and natural to the fish. The rest depends on the fish mood; and if it is inclined to take, all is well. If not, well, hundreds of thousands of words have been written on this subject by more erudite persons than myself. The main point is that, for our good fortune, salmon continue to run our rivers, and occasionally they take our flies and baits. This ensures, as Pritt wrote, 'this endless field for argument, speculation and experiment'.

# 17
# Worming

IT was a hot June morning when Ken Morritt and I met at breakfast. We were staying at a small hotel on Dee-side; and for the past few days had been fishing the famed Dinnet water for salmon. Throughout the week we had limited ourselves to flies and spinners, and by concentrated fishing had each managed to average a fish or two a day. This, however, was to be our last day; and as I, perhaps, had a slight edge on Ken in the numbers of fish caught, we agreed between ourselves to take the gloves off and fish with any legitimate style we happened to fancy. We even made a bet that the one with the lowest catch would pay for champagne that evening. I should have known before I started that I was doomed to lose, for when Ken condescends to gamble it is anybody's bet that he will win.

Our gillies arrived and we went our separate ways. I was to take the topmost pool of the beat (Pol Slache) for the first part of the day; and knowing this to be a good holding pool, I thought that the sensible thing to do would be to try the worm and get a fish. The gillie seemed reluctant to agree until I explained the bet; and as we both felt that under the conditions we only needed one fish to win the day, on went the worm!

I cannot pretend any great expertise with a worm; but it was not long before I felt a few light touches, and after due time the fish moved away with the bait and was firmly hooked. Shortly afterwards we tailed out a nice little fish of 8-lb, and duly knocked it on the head. 'That,' I thought secretly, 'should win the day.' I removed my worm tackle and went back to the fly and spinner, with not so much as a further offer all day. Back at the hotel that evening I was quick to tell Ken of my success. 'You've been very lucky,' he said, as he opened the boot of his car. And there, before my eyes, were eight prime salmon. 'All on worm,' he said, with a twinkle in his eye. 'Expect that you got yours on fly?' It was then that I had to admit that I, too, had taken my fish on worm; but, not realizing that he was an expert in this method, had thought that I should win the day with my one fish. We did drink a little champagne that evening; but I only paid for one bottle.

Worming is, therefore, at certain times and seasons, a very effective method of taking salmon. It is regarded by many as not quite the done thing; and comes in for a great deal of criticism from those who, I suspect, are not very competent in fishing it correctly. Quite apart from any ethical considerations I should say that on fast flowing rivers its effective use requires almost as much skill as any other type of salmon fishing. But, having said that, I must confess that it is not a method which has great appeal for me. If all my salmon fishing had to be limited to the use of worm bait, then I should sell my tackle and resort to playing marbles. I am no longer the fish-hungry youngster I was in my early days of salmon fishing; and if it is necessary to use the worm in order to catch fish nowadays – as far as I am concerned, the fish go uncaught. I would rather sit on the bank and drink the wine of Scotland, or watch the birds, or take pictures – or anything!

This chapter, however, is meant to relate – however briefly – some of the tactics to be used in fishing the worm. As I have already said, I claim no great expertise with this bait; but in my early days of salmon fishing I did catch quite a few fish with the method on waters which lent themselves to its use – and where worming was permitted. There are some rivers where it is less likely to do harm than indiscriminate prawn

Top: An Atlantic salmon. In salt water in the Bergen Aquarium, Norway

Middle: Two salmon kelts in fresh water in the Bergen Aquarium, (Note lean look)

Bottom: Terry Race (left) and the author with a day's catch from the Tweed

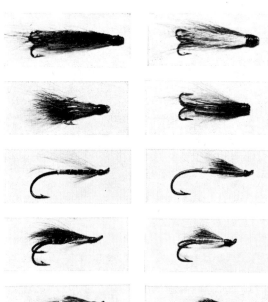

Top: Reg Righyni fly-fishin
for salmon at Upper Hendersyd
River Tweed

Above: Top left: Heavy kee
fly. Top right: Standard bras
tube-fly. Bottom left: Wad
dington-type fly. Bottom right
3 in brass tube-fly

Left: A selection of flies use
for sunk and greased-line fishing
Top: 2 flies, medium sized tube
2nd row: Fly on Esmond Drur
hook, and small tube fly. 3r
row: No. 4 Blue Charm and No
4 Logie. 4th row: No. 6 A.O.
special and No. 8 A.O. 5th row
No. 6 Blue Charm and No. 8

Right: Sea lice on a fresh-run salmon

Below: Grace Oglesby with an almost perfect back-cast. Fishing on the River Awe at Bonawe, Argyllshire

Above: The marked difference between a fresh salmon and a kelt. Kelts are not always as easy to recognize but look for ragged fins, distended vent and gill maggots to help you decide

Left: Arthur Oglesby with a 9 lb salmon tailed from the River Lune near Kirby Lonsdale

*Roy Shaw*

Right: Eric Robb spey casting the tail of the Manse pool on the River Spey

Above: Bunching at the butt-ring poses problems for users of the fixed-spool reel

Left: The curse of over-runs, ever present for users of the multiplying reel

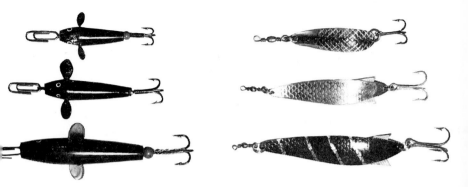

above : Salmon spinners and spoons

below : Eric Horsfall Turner playing a spirited fish. Upper Hendersyde, Tweed

Left: Gerry Barton playing a salmon on the Lune

Below: United States angler, Al McLane, plays a Spey salmon as the author looks on

fishing; and we have already seen how it can sometimes turn an apparently hopeless day into quite a bonanza.

There are, of course, some rivers where at certain times of the year, in order to be in with a chance of a fish, it is advisable to be able to use the worm. Small spate rivers such as the Yorkshire Esk, many Welsh rivers and those in the Isle of Man, all lend themselves to worming. The Esk is a river I know very well indeed; and in the late fifties and early sixties I fished it frequently. The river usually fished well following a dirty spate; but the bulk of salmon taken at that time fell to the worm fishers. By the time the water had cleared for successful fly and spinner fishing, the river was invariably too low for preference and the current insufficient to carry the fly or bait properly. The spinner could be used as the spate was clearing; but invariably it gave more success with the large sea-trout which run that river. There was a time when all migratory fish in this river were lumped under the heading of *salmon*; and there still remains a tendency to refer to them all as *fish*. One has then to inquire if the fish caught are in fact salmon or sea-trout. The invariable answer is that those taken on the worm, prawn or shrimp are salmon; and those on the spinner . . . sea-trout. This is not to infer that salmon are never taken on the spinner, since a good number are in fact taken this way; but these are at times when the river has fined down somewhat, and then the prawn, shrimp or worm are still likely to be more effective. Many of the pools will have a very sluggish current. The old hands at worming tend to sit on a box, put their rod in a rest and wait for the rod tip to start shaking. Such tactics with worm require no greater experience than knowledge of where the salmon are likely to lie; and I do not propose to elaborate any further on this style of fishing with worm.

On many of our classic rivers, however, there comes a time when salmon become almost uncatchable on flies and spinners. There are various reasons for this; and the period of inactivity may vary from the odd day to several weeks. Exceptionally low water conditions, with fish in the pools, but insufficient current to make effective the use of fly or spinner, may dictate the use of worm. A dirty spate followed by a period of turbid water often puts the fish off the take; and much the same applies to a period following good sport on fly or spinner, when stocks have not been replenished by a fresh-run of fish, and the uncaught fish are tending to get stale and potted. The shrimp or prawn may be effective on these occasions but to dedicated worm fishers, there is perhaps not quite the same skill required.

Generally speaking, although this is not paramount for success, the water temperature should at least have reached the 50° mark before worming should be contemplated. Another important factor, though often overlooked, is to know that all the main lies are tenanted with fish; and that they have consistently refused all efforts with fly or spinner. If, for your own reasons, you decide to fish the worm, the weight factor we have discussed throughout earlier chapters will be paramount in making the worm fish in the most effective manner. Ideally the worm, or worms (Fig. 7b), roll along the bottom of the river without getting hung up in rocks and snags. In practice, the angler too often selects too light or too heavy a weight; with the result that the worm either fails to reach the bottom or gets hung up after every cast. The correct selection of weight of lead to be used, therefore, requires some careful study; and for the angler trying out the method for the first time, there is inevitably a great deal of trial and error necessary before the weight selection is mastered. Even then the angler must be prepared to change the weight as he fishes down a pool, since pools vary in depth and strength of current. Watching the experts with the worm, such as Ken Morritt, Peter Anderson or Fred Taylor, is to realize the close attention they pay to lead selection before making a cast.

There is no doubt that for many forms of salmon fishing a thorough grounding in all the methods used by coarse fishermen is a great advantage. Many of the best salmon fishermen I have met served their apprenticeship with a float or a ledger; and thus have a decided advantage when it comes to thinking in that third dimension, the depth of the water and the strength of the current.

Choice of leads is largely a matter of opinion; and even among the experts there is little uniformity. Some go for a spiral of lead wire wound around the line, and so placed that it cannot get within two feet of the worm; If a salmon mouths the worm, the line will run freely through the lead spiral and no resistance will be felt by the fish. Then, when the angler is satisfied that the worm has been taken, he can make a firm strike to set the unusually large hook generally required for worming. A running lead, therefore, is almost a must. Leads which are fixed to the line tend to get caught in rocks; and then resistance is felt if the salmon mouths the bait. With all types of lead, however, there is the ever present trouble that it frequently gets wedged in the bottom; and it is advisable for the angler to devise some breakaway system that will spare the hook and worm should the lead get so jammed. One of the great advantages of a spiral of lead wire is that the angler may continually add weight, or take it off, as the strength of the current dictates. Ken Morritt even evolved a method of leaving the spiral ends free, and claimed that he got caught up less with this method (Fig. 7a). Running bullets are sometimes used; but the angler has to dismantle his tackle partially in order to add or take off weight. And, as we have already seen, it is very desirable to judge our weight of lead very critically, so this can become very tedious.

All the foregoing, of course, is dependent upon having a good stock of fresh lobworms. There are quite a few commercial wormeries and all charge roughly 15s. per 100 (post paid to the angler's address). If, however, you possess a reasonable garden it is an easy matter to extract and maintain a stock which will be ready when required. Lobworm hunting is quite a sport on its own, and I recall many dark nights, following a shower of rain, when I have gone out on the lawn with a torch to grab a few by the head. Even by torchlight they are very shy and the angler must tread wearily on the moist grass if he is not to send them scurrying back into their

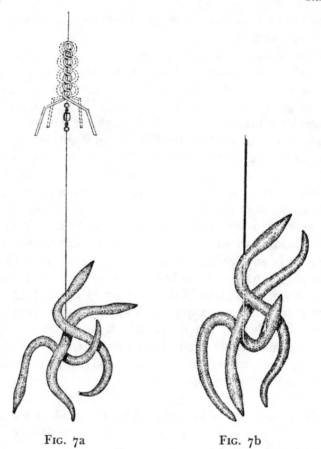

Fig. 7a                     Fig. 7b

holes. A firm grip is required, and care must be taken not to pull until the worm is losing its tenacity. Pulling too harshly will sometimes cause them to break in two; but once they slip out of your fingers they are down like a flash. If the worm collector averages fifty per cent success he is doing well.

Once collected, the worms should be kept in a cool, dark place. Damp moss is one of the finest things they can be kept in for reasonable periods, but damp, shredded newspaper is just as effective, and much easier to come by. If they are to be of best angling quality they require quite a few hours in the moss in order to scour themselves, and thus become tougher. Freshly caught worms are full of earth and quickly fall off the hook when subjected to the rough treatment they are likely to receive. Greatest care must also be taken to keep worms cool; and anyone who has left a tin of them in the boot of a car, under the hot sun, will have experienced the wonderful aroma they produce. Preferences for hook sizes vary; but I usually select about a No. 1 or 2. All hooks for worm fishing, when purchased, should be tied to a short length of strong monofilament line of approximately 12-ins in length. This may be looped or attached directly to a swivel, and then to the main reel line. Hooks with eyes are not ideal, since the worms should be threaded on the hook and well up the shank. Normally, about three lobworms are threaded in this way; and once the angler has made a correct assessment of the type and weight of lead to be used, he is ready to begin fishing. The best type of tackle to use is a medium-sized spinning rod, such as we discussed in Chapter 13, together with a fixed-spool or multiplying reel. Initially a cast should be made slightly upstream; and the rod point should be held well up as the angler feels the lead rolling over the bottom. As the bait trundles down, the angler can let line slip off the reel by either keeping the bale arm open on his fixed-spool reel or leaving the drum in a free-running state on his multiplier reel. Eventually the worm will come to rest downstream of the angler, at the edge of the current. It is in this situation that the angler should wait patiently in the hope that a salmon has followed the worm round, and is prepared to show some interest. Occasionally salmon will intercept a rolling worm; but they are, perhaps, more likely to follow it out of their lies, and may then be prepared to pay it some attention when it has come to rest. There will be many casts when, apart from frequent hang-ups, nothing happens; but the angler should always leave the bait in the resting position for a little while until he is satisfied that no salmon has followed it round, and there is the possibility that it will show interest. The reel should still be able to give immediate slack line; and the angler must be prepared to make many casts before the tell-tale twitching of the rod tip suggests that a salmon is interested. Of course it may well be a trout or, worse still, an eel that is mouthing the bait; but whatever happens, no attempt to strike should be made at this stage. Every time there is a good pull at the worm a little line should be slipped off the reel; and only when the angler is confident that a salmon has picked up the bait, and is firmly taking it back to his lie, should the reel be re-engaged and a firm strike made. The greatest mistake possible at this stage is to strike too early; and I have known many occasions when a full five minutes of twitches have had to be tolerated patiently before the fish has made off with a solid hold. Some anglers are prepared to wait interminable periods; and invariably, when the fish is landed, the hook is found a long way down the gullet. Short of a break, the fish would have little chance of escape.

As a method of taking difficult fish, therefore, worm fishing has much to offer the unfortunate fisherman who cannot combine a visit to the river with ideal conditions. Competent worming for salmon requires a type of skill, and a persistence, not very often found in the general run of salmon anglers. For me, personally, it is tedious; but I admit to a certain feeling of excitement once the tedium is over and there is a salmon twitching at the line. Will he take – or won't he? The seconds tick by slowly, full of suspense. Perhaps this is the greatest excitement that worm fishing has to offer.

# 18
## Prawning

---

JUST how salmon can differentiate between a shrimp and a prawn remains a mystery to me. But I have had ample evidence to show that they can differentiate; and that their manner of taking both these baits is vastly different. Both can be very effective baits for taking salmon; but it is not sufficient to think that a big prawn will be effective in a big water, and a small shrimp in a shrunken stream. This may well be the answer in some circumstances of course; but for those who enjoy this method of fishing, there is much to be said for an intelligent selection based on angling conditions.

Prawns come in various sizes. The best to purchase are those commercially packed in a good preservative. If they are too soft or two brittle, they will not stand the sustained punishment of continued casting. They should retain a good salty tang; and those with a cluster of spawn between their legs, known as berried prawns, are reputed to be the best. Dyes may be added to give them a rich red-colouring. Although most natural prawns are not seen in these vivid colours, there are several crustaceans that do, in fact, bear a rich red coat in their natural habitat, the depths of the ocean.

There can be no doubt that the prawn, on occasions, scares all the fish in a pool; whereas the shrimp rarely seems to have this effect. There are also times when salmon will take the prawn with such ferocity that the angler is inclined to think that it is the only bait worth using. It may be fished in several styles, and is another good ace for the salmon angler to have up his sleeve. But there are some waters and conditions of waters where its continued use will only make the salmon uncatchable. It must be used with a little forethought, there- fore, and not be fished persistently if there is any indication that it will scare the fish. On many Norwegian rivers the prawn gets continual use; and although it seems to account for many big fish, I have never been fully convinced that it has no adverse effect on some occasions – despite the fact that, given a choice, many Norwegian gillies will fish a prawn the season through. The bulk of my prawn-fishing in Britain has, like worming, taken place on the little Yorkshire Esk. I have taken my quota of fish with it on occasion; but have also seen a whole pool of salmon go completely berserk shortly after the prawn has entered the water, the fish leaping and skittering in all directions, and even running downstream and over the sill of a small weir, in order to get away from something that has obviously frightened them. I don't imagine that a seal or an otter in the pool could have caused more panic! This, however, was in a small stretch of water in which the salmon reaction was easy to see. How many times would there be the same reaction on a big river when the prawn had the same effect, but the effect was unnoticed by the angler? My regular Tweed boatman will not permit the use of the prawn during a normal season; and if he hears that rods fishing lower down the river are using the prawn, he is fully confident that we shall have some new fish in our beat before twenty-four hours have passed. Continued prawning, therefore, is likely to do more harm than good. Initial catches may be very encouraging; but the fish will slowly shy off the bait, and may well become uncatchable by any other legiti- mate means. They will become virtually useless for fly-fishing as long as they remain in a particular beat; and a further rise in the water, to lift the old stock upstream and bring a fresh batch in, will have to be awaited before prawning is likely to show success. At best, therefore, the prawn is a method of getting the odd fish in an otherwise difficult period. At worst, it will spoil the fishing for any type of lure; and will make an

angler very unpopular among those following on behind, or
fishing the beat during the week following his tactics!

Conditions under which to try the prawn vary a great deal;
but they are generally much the same as those under which
the angler would incline to try the worm. The general conditions are the crisp early mornings, with a suggestion of
moisture on the banks; days when, due to condensation, you
would get your boots thoroughly wet while walking through
the long grass to the riverside; days following overnight rain
or frost; and times when the salmon have had a good look at
everything else, and have refused all efforts to tempt them.

One of my favourite methods of fishing a prawn is the
sink-and-draw method. The prawn, suitably weighted to
match the current strength, is cast out with a normal spinning-
rod and reel suited to the water. The prawn is allowed to
sink, and is then slowly retrieved with a sink-and-draw motion
by winding a little line back on to the reel between each jerk
of the rod. The bait eventually swings out of the current, and
may be retrieved for the next cast. There may be many times
when the prawn will sink on to the bottom and get hung up;
but every bit of resistance should be treated as a take, and a
strike made. With this method, the take is usually firm and
decisive; but if a vast array of hooks is on the tackle there
should be little delay in giving the hard strike.

There are many ways of mounting a prawn; but in all cases
it should be mounted with its head and feelers at the bottom.
The choice of tackle is left to individual preference, or the
fashion for the water. On the Esk I used to favour a normal
triangle, about size 6. The prawn was straightened with a
baiting-needle and the line threaded through, and tied on to
the triangle. A straightened paper-clip was then placed
through the middle of the prawn along the same path taken
through the body with needle and line, in order to keep the
prawn straight. For extra weighting, a piece of fine lead-wire,
wound around the shank of the triangle, was generally sufficient for the sluggish current. On faster rivers, of course, the
shank may not be long enough to carry the required weight;

and the weight is then placed above the swivel, and some two feet from the prawn. Care must be taken to ensure that the prawn does not rotate when a sink-and-draw motion is applied to it; and for this reason it is often better to snip off the two pieces of tail, to prevent any likelihood of their acting as a propellor. A larger, single, worm-sized hook may well be used as an alternative to the triangle, but does not give quite such good hooking potential (Fig. 8). There are many commercial prawn tackles on the market, with a built-in straightening device. They have many advantages; but the prawn has to be tied down with red elastic thread to prevent it from falling off. The latter method is much used in Norway; and has the great advantage that many tackles may be mounted with prawns before commencing a day's fishing.

The array of hooks on these tackles usually ensures a good hook hold; and the elastic thread binding protects the prawn from many encounters on the river bottom.

As with all the other methods of salmon fishing we have discussed, the selection of the correct weight of lead to suit the current is equally important in fishing the prawn. Tactics in Norway, where a great deal of lead is used, will be discussed in a later chapter. For most British rivers, however, it is important to find the right balance of weight to keep the bait off the bottom, but not too high in the water; and the sink-and-draw action should not be done too quickly, and a slack line avoided by slow lowering of the rod during the

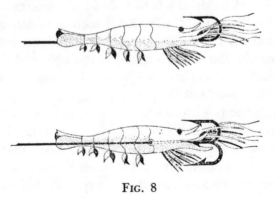

FIG. 8

period when the prawn sinks. If the line is allowed to go slack it is possible for the bait to be taken without the angler feeling the tell-tale pull; and as a salmon can eject a prawn very quickly this lack of feel of the take must be avoided at all costs.

In very sluggish water salmon will sometimes nip at the prawn; but they are, oddly enough, more likely to do this with a shrimp, as we shall see in the next chapter. Sink-and-draw, of course, is not the only method by which a prawn may be fished. The spinning prawn is often very effective, with the prawn mounted on a spinning flight, and fished in a similar manner to a Devon Minnow. Sometimes it may pay to trot the spinning prawn down a fast run, letting it drop down in a series of jerky actions; but the bulk of my success has been with the sink-and-draw method, and I have very little experience of successful prawn spinning.

On some rivers it is possible to fish a prawn from a fly rod. The prawn is simply lobbed out and allowed to swing round slowly in the current. This method lends itself to some waters; but not to most of the classic rivers of Scotland.

To sum up, therefore, the prawn should always be used as a last resort. It is a method of getting a few fish when all else has failed. Its use, however, should not be prolonged for too long since there will be a grave danger of making the resident fish almost uncatchable by you or by the angler following. On many Association waters the use of the prawn is rightly banned; but it has saved many a blank day for me, and in Norway gave me the largest salmon I have ever caught.

AUTHOR'S NOTE:—*The last sentence of this chapter is not now true for I have since caught a larger salmon by spinning. See Chapter 24.*

# 19
## Shrimp Fishing

WE have already discussed in the previous chapter how salmon seem to be able to distinguish between a prawn and a shrimp. We have seen how the prawn will sometimes frighten the fish, but on occasions will also serve as a very killing bait. It has been my experience that the shrimp does not have this frightening effect; and in the days when I did a lot of bait-fishing, I eventually came to have a distinct preference for the shrimp against the worm or prawn. It can be fished very delicately; and is perhaps one of the most killing baits for salmon that an angler can find.

Shrimps, of course, are smaller than prawns; but the same rules should be observed in their selection and preservation, and they may also be dyed in various colours to suit individual preferences. I have never been fully convinced that colour matters a great deal; and have caught the bulk of my fish on those of natural colouring, or merely dyed a dark scarlet. They may be mounted in a similar fashion to a prawn; but they are much smaller than the prawn, and do not show to their best advantage if mounted on prawn tackles. I frequently used the single-hook method, with a piece of paper-clip; and only with the larger shrimps have I bothered with the triangle. The shrimp may also be fished sink-and-draw; or, for that matter, in all the styles I have described for prawn fishing, although one of the most effective ways I know is fishing the shrimp with a float. For this type of fishing it is essential to know exactly where the salmon are lying. The

float is then adjusted so that the shrimp will trot along the
river bed, and the cast is made to a precise spot so that the
shrimp will pass within inches of the nose of the salmon.
Fairly quiet water is essential for this type of fishing; and
great care must be taken to ensure that the fish do not see you
before they see the bait. Deep holes and backwaters make
ideal spots and in clear-water conditions individual fish may
be stalked and cast over so that the shrimp approaches the
angler's selected fish. In many deep holes, however, it may
well be impossible to see the fish which you know to be there.
The first indication of fish interest you are likely to get is a
slight tremor of the float. The take of the shrimp is usually
very timid, and a slow dip of the float usually indicates that
the fish has taken it quietly into its mouth. Anything more
than a slight tremor, therefore, should be treated as a take,
and a prompt strike made in order to drive the hook home.
The bulk of fish hooked in this manner will generally be
found to have the hook in the roof of their mouths, which
rarely allows them to get free.

Smaller rivers seem to offer more opportunities for float-
fishing with a shrimp. It is fairly essential, I think, not to
pay out too much line; and, once again, the shrimp should
be so weighted that it will not only keep the float fishing in
an upright position; but also enables the bait to get down.
Little weight is required in a general way, since it is not prac-
ticable to fish in very fast water; and the method only lends
itself to quiet pools and backwaters. Care must be taken
when assessing the depth of the water; and the float should be
so adjusted that the shrimp will move slowly over the bed of
the river. To have it scraping the bottom would give too
many false alarms on the float; while to have it fishing too
high in the water would cause it to pass over the heads of the
fish. It is only when the fish get an eyeball confrontation that
they respond in the best way to the float-fished shrimp. Times
to try this method may be difficult to determine if the angler
is not fully conversant with the water. I well recall days on
the Esk when the shrimp sent me home with fish that seemed

uncatchable by any other method. On one occasion I had a guest accompanying me. The river, we knew, held a good stock of fish; but our continuous spinning up to 4 p.m. had not even produced an offer. 'Come on,' I said to my guest. 'We'll go up to the dam and try the shrimp.' He looked on in amazement as I put on a float, and a small shrimp mounted on a single hook. I adjusted the height of the float carefully to match the depth of the water; and quietly walked to the edge of the bank, and let the tackle swim slowly down in the deep water beneath my feet. The bait had barely travelled six yards before there was a slow submergence of the float. I struck hard and handed him my rod. 'My God!' said he as he felt the vicious tug of a fighting salmon, 'I would not have believed it possible!' As soon as it was played out, the fish was quickly brought ashore and knocked on the head. A fresh shrimp was mounted, and it was not long before he was play-ing number two. A third was finally brought to the bank before I called a halt. It would have been more than likely that we could have gone on catching fish for a further period by that method; but there were other anglers waiting to fish the water, and the taking of three prime fish ranging between 11-lb and 15-lb was more than satisfactory under the circumstances.

On yet another occasion I was on the river, barely an hour's drive from my home, by 6 a.m. The river was too low for the best spinning; and as this was in my fish-hungry days, I was quick to start fishing with the shrimp. It was destined to be one of those scorching-hot September days, and I had planned to be back in the office for 11 a.m. A two-mile walk got me down to some likely water; and in the next hour I took four prime fish on the float-fished shrimp, totalling about 57-lb in weight. The two-mile struggle back in the hot sun took the sharp edge off some of the enjoyment! But I was back in my office at the appointed time, with my colleagues quite confident that I must have got those salmon from the local fishmonger!

During those far-off fish-hungry days, it was inevitable that

I enjoyed a deal of unpopularity on that hard-fished Association water. In the end I got to the point where I concealed my catch so that fellow-members would not know how many I had caught. I then sneaked them away to the boot of my car, and quietly got on my way. On arrival at the river one morning I passed the time of day with a fellow angler. He was obviously a member of the same Association, but evidently did not know me nor did I know him. We did not trouble to introduce ourselves, but made brief inquiry from each other where we intended to fish. Upon telling him that I had thought of going downstream, he said, 'I wouldn't go there, if I were you. They tell me that that bloody Oglesby is down there . . .' I did not enlighten him about my identity, but said that I should go and join that very fine angler! I never did divulge the best day's catch I took from that water on the float-fished shrimp; and nothing will induce me to do it even now. It is something, in retrospect, of which I am not very proud.

Sometimes it may pay the angler to remove the float and just let the shrimp rove around in the water. It may be cast out and retrieved as slowly as possible. For this method, the shrimp should be practically weightless; and if the angler positions himself behind a tree, it is possible to drop the shrimp down amongst the semi-comatose salmon lying in a quiet backwater. Sometimes the shrimp is taken eagerly; but at other times the fish will only mouth the bait, without taking hold of it properly. I have watched salmon playing with a slowly retrieved shrimp; and have seen them come up to it to take it in their mouths. Before the pull has been transmitted up the line and to the rod, they have quickly blown it out of their mouths. Sometimes the salmon will attack the shrimp five or six times in this way before taking it firmly, or rejecting it altogether. It is a fascinating form of fishing in clear water, and enables the angler, who has carefully stalked up to the pool and remained quiet, to see a great deal of salmon reaction to the bait. Of all forms of natural-bait fishing, it is still the one that is most interesting to me.

## 20

# The Height of the Water

---

THE successful salmon angler could be said to be one who is thoroughly versed in all legitimate methods of fishing for them. He will know his greased-line techniques; will have mastered spinning under all conditions; and, if he is not content to go home fishless on occasions, he will have those three aces up his sleeve in the form of prawning, shrimping and worming. If he is like myself nowadays, he will only resort to the last mentioned tactics out of dire necessity when, for instance, a film cameraman lurks in the background and urgently wants footage of a fish being landed; or when unexpected guests want fresh salmon on the menu. While, therefore, I mainly restrict my salmon fishing to the fly and spinner, there have been occasions when I was glad of an alternative.

The experienced salmon angler will have extensive knowledge of the signs and seasons when a certain method is likely to bring him the best chance of sport; but if, like many salmon anglers, he has to book a beat in advance and travel some hundreds of miles for the fishing, he will never know ideal conditions for the particular stretch of water he is to fish. If the early months of February are his chosen time then, as we have seen, it is a fairly safe bet that the spinning bait, fished slow and deep, will be the wisest choice. Alternatively, a classic beat in May could well maintain nearly ideal conditions for the small fly on the floating line. But, even though

fish may be caught, there will never be the certainty that sport
is likely to be at its best.

From all this it may be argued that the nomadic salmon
angler, while having experienced the great variations of
different rivers, will never have that intimate knowledge
which would make him conscious of what is the paramount
question to answer correctly to ensure successful salmon fishing; that is, the height of the water. The angler who is fortunate enough, not only to live on the banks of a salmon
river, but to have access to the fishing, must have advantages
far outweighing any other considerations. After the continual
fishing of one stretch of water over the years, he will know
(perhaps quite unconsciously) when it will be worth putting
a line in the water; and when it will be more comfortable to
stay at home. The casual visitor has no such luck. He can
only fish diligently during his chosen time – in the *hope* of
sport. This very fact may well account for the reputed dourness of many Scottish gillies when they are dragged to the
bank of the river by enthusiastic tenants, in the full knowledge that if they (the gillies) could fish the river themselves
at that time, they would stay away. For this reason the finest
angler in the land would be hard put to compete with a local
expert on his own stretch of water. The native would know
the precise height when certain pools would fish best; and he
would also know the alternate lies under varying heights of
water; and the precise method most likely to achieve success.

For the non-resident angler, who consistently takes a beat
of a river at the same time every season, the odds get narrowed
down. He might well spend the first two years serving an
apprenticeship to the water; but if he persists, he will begin
to acquire some of the knowledge of the native and will
ultimately be in a position to exploit every favourable condition. There will be occasions when he is likely to find the
river either dead low or in roaring flood; but he will be able
to draw upon his experience to know whether fishing is
worth-while or not at any given height. Although it may seem
desirable, therefore, to fish a great variety of rivers, the

angler who persists with one specific beat will be able to fish
with greater potential than the roving angler.

In his excellent little book *Rod Fishing for Salmon on the
Wye,* J. Arthur Hutton states, quite categorically, that the
height of the water is, in his opinion, the most important
factor in successful salmon fishing. I endorse this comment;
but feel that temperature, overhead conditions and humidity
must also be taken into consideration to make the best assessment. With all these signs of the zodiac in their correct orbit,
and fish in the pools, the choice of a particular fly or bait is
comparatively simple. The late A. H. E. Wood was, perhaps,
the best example of 'one man – one beat' for season after
season, when he fished the Cairnton beat of the Dee. Wood
knew, no doubt, by a casual glance at the river, whether it
was worth fishing or not. With an annual catch of something
like three hundred fish, I suspect that he would not bother
too much with those doubtful days. Richard Waddington, to
my knowledge, did not actually live on a river; but he had
sufficient access to well known beats of the Spey to know the
water in all its moods, and how best to take advantage of
prevailing conditions.

Some of my earliest salmon fishing was done on the Argyllshire Awe; yet I fished that river for three seasons before I
caught my first Awe salmon. On subsequent visits successes
became more frequent; and although a gap of seven years
elapsed at one stage before I fished the river again, I now
have some idea of the best lies. Of late years I have tended to
concentrate my salmon fishing on two rivers – the Tweed and
the Lune. I take a beat on the Tweed for the same periods
each year; two weeks in the early part of February, and a
further two weeks at the end of November and I have now
been fishing that river for twelve years. I could not possibly
claim to have the intimate knowledge of that beat that the
local gillie has; but I know it pretty well; and from sheer
experience I know its varying moods at different heights of
water. I usually get my share, and more, of the fish caught.

The Lune, of course, is available to me throughout the

season; and if ever there were a stretch of water which is more influenced by its height, I have yet to see it. Unfortunately we have no measuring gauge on the river; but I have one small rock which, when it is just showing above the water surface, tells me that the river is at near-perfect height. For me, it is as good as a micrometer, since the water level assessment it gives usually informs me whether I can expect sport to be good or indifferent. A typical occasion which comes to mind was when I was to visit the river for a period of three days with another well known angler as my guest. We arrived one Thursday evening in late July 1966. I had heard that the river was in fine trim with plenty of fish about; but on arrival I was greatly dismayed to learn that there had been further rain and my tell-tale rock was nowhere to be seen. My companion, who had only fished the river on two previous occasions, thought it looked perfect. He quickly tackled up and was away before I had time to unload the car. For my part I was in no hurry. We were to spend a few nights living rough-shod in the fishing hut, and I spent the evening preparing the camp beds and generally tidying up the hut. When this was completed I relaxed lazily in a deckchair and watched the sun set in the west over a cosy glass of scotch. Darkness had fallen before my companion returned. He had seen several fish but had not touched one; nor had the sea-trout obliged in the failing light. Over a few more drams we discussed the prospects for the morning before turning into our sleeping bags for some quiet, peaceful sleep.

At 6 a.m. my companion was up and about, clambering into waders and generally disturbing the entire household. With one sleepy eye open I raised my head off the pillow to look out of the hut window and examine the water level as shown by my tell-tale rock. The top of the rock was still below the surface, although a faint wave line could now be detected from the water disturbance it caused. I slumped back on to my pillow and wished my companion the very best of British luck, 'tight-lines' and all that. By 10 a.m. he was back again, fishless, but hungry and keen to get at the bacon

and eggs I was frying over the cooker. This time he had seen
even more fish, and was completely mystified why at least
one of them had not taken his bait. Fully refreshed he was
soon back on the water, whilst I contented myself taking
photographs and generally relaxing. By nightfall on that
Friday evening he was still fishless; and was rapidly coming
to the conclusion that the fish were uncatchable. Before I
turned in, however, I had a last look at my rock and noticed
that a slight tip was now showing. With no more rain, the
river would be at perfect height for the morning.

At 6 a.m. it was I who was up and about, creating a com-
motion; and it was my friend who, between intermittent
snores, risked one sleepy eye at me with the news that he
would have breakfast ready by 8 a.m. Back at 8 a.m. I was too,
with three prime salmon, all covered in sea lice and all in the
'teens of pounds. This was too much for him. 'What had I
got them on?' 'A 2-ins Black and Gold Devon Minnow,' I
said. With that he was off, armed to the teeth with 2-ins Black
and Golds, while I completed my breakfast.

By 10 a.m. my rock was showing a little more; so I put the
spinning rod on one side, and got my fly tackle ready. A No.
6 heavily-dressed Blue Charm seemed about right for the
conditions. I waded across the river to join my friend to find
him still fishless. By midday I had a further two fish on the
fly; and it was not until 1 p.m. that my companion finally got
one to take his spinner. By 2 p.m. we had to be on our way to
join a further friend on another river; but I had mixed feelings about the move. It was my impression that if I had been
able to fish that day out, I should have broken the record for
the beat.

The height of the water, therefore, may be the paramount
factor as a guide to a successful day. Other factors, however,
must be combined with it to give the perfect day. But it is
only by the intimate knowledge of one piece of water that this
initial guide, the near-perfect height, can be estimated
accurately, and thereby a correct assessment made of the most
effective method to be used.

# 21

## The Lure of Norway

---

I INCLINE to the feeling that no salmon angler can consider his education to be complete until he has fished in all the Atlantic salmon-producing countries in the world. If this is the case, I still have some little way to go. I have not yet fished the famous rivers of the eastern sea-boards of Canada or Newfoundland; nor the rock-girt rivers of Iceland. I hope, however, that if the good Lord spares my bones for a short period following publication of this book, I shall have accepted invitations to visit both these fine salmon-producing countries; and to have wet my line over their prolific waters.

A hundred and fifty years ago salmon were commonplace in the rivers of Britain. Over the years, however, the number of rivers suited to maintain the salmon stocks has declined; and today, England cannot claim even double-figure numbers of worth-while salmon rivers. Scotland, Ireland and Wales still have their classic salmon waters, as yet unspoilt by the march of progress; but beats on Spey, Dee, Tweed and Tay are expensive and hard to come by, and the fifty-pounders of bygone days are very rarely caught.

At the turn of the century, British salmon anglers were those who had realized the vast potential of Norwegian fishing. Names like Laerdal, Namsen, Alta, Mals and Aarø gradually became the hall-mark of all the best in salmon fishing; and certainly all the rivers that held the biggest salmon. Perhaps the Aarø gained the most exotic reputation of all. It is a short and turbulent river, said to yield more fifty-pounders than any other salmon river in the world. The late L. R. Hardy fished there and was filmed catching monster fish. Richard Waddington achieved a lieftime ambition there by beaching unaided a fish of 51-lb, caught on a fly of his own tying. Charles Ritz in, *A Fly Fisher's Life*, referred to it as 'The Aarø – The Terrific!'; and mentions a fish of 76-lb, apart from twenty other fish over 50-lb. Thus, to the British salmon angler, the Aarø became the pinnacle, the ultimate of salmon rivers in the world.

Almost from childhood days, therefore, the lure of Norway has drawn me. By the spring of 1961 I could no longer resist the great temptation, and planned a family holiday to that country in the company of Ken Morritt and his family. We were to go there during August of that year, a time, I was to learn, when the bulk of the best fishing was over. It was not, however, to be essentially a fishing holiday. Most of our time was to be spent in sightseeing. Our chosen hotel was on the higher reaches of the Vosso river at Bulken, and within easy access of the town of Voss. The hotel had fishing rights on some of the upper Vosso water, and it was on this water that I first wet a line for the Norwegian salmon. To say the least, the hotel water looked magnificent; and a photograph of a visitor to that water, taken in June of the year and showing him holding a brace of fish weighing 64-lb and 55-lb respectively, did much to keep us on the ball! We fished in vain, however, but towards the end of our stay there we got access to some water at Geitle. There I managed to catch the largest and smallest salmon I had ever taken until then; a lovely fish of 27-lb and a mere tiddler of 4-lb. On our last day there we managed to arrange a further day on a beat of the river at Bolstadøyri; and on that beat, although I drew blank, Ken Morritt wiped my eye with a fish of 28-lb. I had no idea that the Bolstad beat of the Vosso was to see a great deal of me in the years that lay ahead; and that it would produce for me a salmon of large enough dimensions to fulfil my wildest dreams.

On my immediate return home, I must confess to a little disappointment. Where were all the fish? Why was such a magnificent river so desperately short of salmon? Doubtless, the many nets and traps I had seen throughout the river were taking more than their fair share and the angler was left with the 'odds and sods' that remained. A glance at the guide book revealed the following information on the Vosso: 'Here is one of the most remarkable rivers in the whole of Norway. Or perhaps one should say controversial, instead of remarkable; because there are people who have fished the Vosso for a fortnight without even seeing a fish, and there are also people who swear that they get fifty-pounders every summer. The Vosso is said to hold heavier salmon than any other river below the Arctic Circle; but it is equally true that they are few and far between. . . . There is too much indiscriminate fishing in the Vosso – both legally and illegally. So much netting is going on that visitors travelling by train from Bergen to Bulken may lose count of the number of nets they see from the train. One visitor reported three salmon traps in the space of exactly 150 yards. No bailiffs or river keepers, or any form of control, seem to be in being; and the river is practically a free-for-all. This is a great pity, because the locals are virtually killing the goose that lays the golden eggs. If the excessive netting and trapping were to be abolished, the Vosso could become the finest salmon river in the whole world; commanding fees that would put the river in the millionaire class.'

Anyway, I had been to Norway and I had caught a fish. There was no longer the same urgency to try conclusions with their salmon; and instead I renewed my efforts on the more prolific rivers of Britain. If they could not offer the monsters of Norway, or the magnificence of its scenery, they were at least full of smaller fish.

During the years which followed, tales of monster fish from Norway occasionally drifted across the North Sea. There was still a nudging desire to go back there again and to fish in what were, perhaps, more famed waters. The Norwegian bug

started to bite me again. By the end of 1965 I still had caught
nothing bigger than my fish of 27-lb in 1961. Let's face it,
there are not a great number of salmon anglers—even very
competent ones – who have caught fish over 30-lb; and naturally the 'size bug' was biting me hard. When was I going to
get a fish of 30-lb, or 40-lb, or even a heavier one? That great
salmon angler, the late Captain T. L. Edwards, in all his wide
experience of salmon fishing, had never taken a fish of 40-lb.
He had taken two of 39½-lb, admittedly; but the 40-lb tag
eluded him to his dying day.

It was in the early spring of 1966 that I received the first
intimation that I might be going back to Norway. It may be
interesting to relate on how a visit there again in June of
1966 became possible. A letter from one of our leading
angling journals indicated that a Norwegian travel agent was
keen to have a party of British anglers over to Norway to
sample some of their fishing. A list of six anglers was to be
submitted to him, from which he would choose two to go to
Norway at his expense. His objective was to show them the
full potential of Norwegian fishing, so that on their return
to Britain they could write of their experiences for the
national angling press. Naturally I was keen to have my name
on that list. Being a Yorkshireman with a certain amount of
Scottish background, if there's 'owt for nowt' I'm always
interested! My name was duly put on that list, along with
those of other salmon anglers with names more widely known
than my own. I did not stand a chance I thought; and except
for sheer coincidence, I doubt whether I should have been
considered.

There was, however, on that list the name of one angler
who was a personal friend of mine. I refer, of course, to Eric
Horsfall Turner. In his spare time Eric is the Town Clerk
of Scarborough! As luck would have it, and apart from earlier
angling in Norway, he had to go over to that country on
official duties during the early part of that year. While he
was there, he inquired in Oslo whether there was any trout
fishing available; whereupon he was told to call on Odd

Haraldsen, who was a travel agent in Oslo and had access to some fishing. During Eric's discussion with Odd, it transpired that he (Odd Haraldsen) was the self-same travel agent who had approached the British angling press for a party of anglers; and Eric was requested to give details of those nominated, all of whom he knew. The list was read through, and answered with factual brevity. Finally, the names of Oglesby and Horsfall Turner were mentioned for comments. 'Oglesby,' he said, 'is a good friend of mine and is a competent salmon angler, and also knows his angling photography.' 'What about Horsfall Turner?' The angler under question rose and bowed – with a broad grin! It appeared a sensible move, from Odd Haraldsen's standpoint, to put forward two invitations as a start; one to an angler he knew personally, and the other to an angler given a good recommendation.

In the weeks that followed I received full details of the tour that was to be arranged. We were to fish the River Jolstra; and, once again, the Bolstad beat of the Vosso. I was a bit dubious to say the least. Inquiries from friends who had fished the Jolstra revealed that this was a very fine river, with plenty of big fish. Even without this information, I should have accepted; but I must frankly admit that I was more keen on the idea of the Jolstra than I was on that of the Vosso. So on 15 June 1966 Eric and I took flight for Bergen, accompanied by a press photographer and film cameraman, Keith Massey. I was quite determined to enjoy myself, what-ever sneaking thoughts I had that the Vosso fishing would be mediocre.

Norway in June! The magnificence of it! Unless you have seen it, I am quite incapable of describing it to you. Mountains, lakes and fjords; tall pines; and the foaming torrents that rush, barely slowing, until they tumble into the sea. The impressive Jolstra river flowed beneath my hotel room. We had, behind us, the two-hour flight from Newcastle to Bergen; the overnight steamer trip from Bergen to Florø; and the fifty-mile car journey from Florø to Förde. The Förde Hotel proved to be very comfortable indeed and was within a few

minutes' drive of the Bruland beat we were to fish. Despite a
sleepless night on board the steamer and an 8 a.m. arrival at
the hotel, we could hardly wait for the arrival of our gillies at
9 a.m. and to start fishing. The Jolstra river is perhaps not
very well known to British salmon anglers but I had heard
such glowing tales of its monster fish that I was impatient to
try conclusions with them.

The sun was already high in the heavens. At this time of
the year, in these latitudes, it just does not become dark. The
shade temperature was in the region of 80° and the melting
snows maintained the river at a good level. In such bright
overhead conditions, on the face of it, our chances did not
appear good; but the melting snow kept the water temperature at a mercifully low level; and being only a few miles
from the salt-water fjord, we reasoned that we should have
fresh-run fish in their inclination to take – and ease our
chances of a catch.

Shooting the rapids in a small Norwegian boat is a bit
alarming at first; but after the first four pools I soon became
accustomed to the hectic ride through the foaming torrents
from pool to pool. Kjell, the gillie, advised me to use a large
spoon, since the water was a little too cold and heavy for
fly. At about the fifth pool down our beat, he put me ashore
on a small island and indicated the best salmon lies. At about
my third cast my bait stopped abruptly. On raising the rod
point I thrilled to the 'tug tug' of a heavy fish. As the fish
began taking line, Kjell pointed to the clutch mechanism
on my reel and shouted in broken English, 'More tight! More
tight!' I tightened as he suggested; but still the fish took line.
Again the command 'More tight – or he will go down the
rapids!' So, straining line and rod to a point where I felt the
tackle must break, I heaved all I dared. Slowly and log-like,
the fish moved inch by inch upstream from the lip of the
pool. The crisis, for the time being, was over. Occasionally
as I worked the fish back towards me, both Kjell and I caught
a glimpse of him in that gin-clear water. 'Big fisshe – 15
kilos!' he shouted. Quickly translating this into something

in excess of 30-lb, I knew that I had within my grasp a salmon larger than the fish of 27-lb that I had caught in Norway some years before. The salmon was one of the fittest I have ever played; and although I had put on a 17-lb test line instead of the more normal 12 or 15-lb test I use at home, I had to continue straining the tackle to the limit. Every time I tried to get the fish into the slack water he used his brute strength and weight to get back into the current; and after fifteen minutes of this I began to despair of even getting him within gaffing distance. I had reckoned without Kjell. As the fish came round for the umpteenth time, like a streak of lighning the gaff went out and my fish was on the bank; a beautiful 31-pounder, gleaming like a bar of silver, with the sea-lice still on him. That was to be the only fish of the day; and despite continued flogging of the water, we could not get into another. My enjoyment, however, was complete. Not only had I caught my largest-ever salmon, but press photographer Keith Massey had faithfully recorded the entire action on both still and movie film. If this was my only fish of the trip, it had been worth coming for!

Telephone calls that evening indicated that the Vosso was having a tremendous run of very big fish; fish that made my 31-pounder sound commonplace. Could it be possible that the Vosso I knew had been metamorphosed – or that something exceptional had taken place?

The following day we were on our travels once again. The steamer took us to Bergen; then an hour's train ride from there to Bolstadøyri. At last I should meet the man with whom I have developed a firm friendship – my host, Odd Haraldsen. We arrived at 11.30 p.m. in the twilight of a Norwegian midsummer evening. Odd commanded us to get quickly into the car as one of his other guests was playing a monster fish down on the fjord. We arrived just as the fish was being brought ashore. It was a magnificent fish of 37-lb, dripping sea-lice and as fresh as paint. It had been hooked in the river, but had fought so valiantly that the angler had been forced to follow it to the fjord in order to have a chance of getting it. All the excitement over, we retired to the fishing lodge. There we learned that this fish of 37-lb was nothing extraordinary. The records for this Bolstad beat from 24 May to 20 June that year showed that no less than eighty-seven salmon had been caught. Thirty-nine of these had been over 30-lb; eighteen over 40-lb; eight over 50-lb; and one over 60-lb. I hardly believed it! Where, in the entire world, was there such fishing? Could my dream river, the Aarø, even compete with such a record? My 31-pounder caught only the previous day paled into insignificance. I could not sleep a wink that night! I could not even imagine that this was the same river I had fished only five years previously. Yet the Vosso it was; and there we were – with an odds-on chance of getting a fish that would qualify for headline status back in Britain. I felt that the good Lord had indeed been very kind to me; for not only was the fishing 'fabulous', to use a much misquoted word, but the hospitality and friendliness of every-one left me deeply impressed.

The next day Nils, my gillie, arrived at 9 a.m. The day was even hotter than it had been on the Jolstra, with the mercury just short of the 90° mark. Fishing in high-breast waders, even in shirt-sleeves, is no easy task under such tropical con-ditions. During that morning I sweated and slaved, only to lose a good fish after playing it for a few minutes on a heavy Devon Minnow. The hook-hold just gave way; and I have no way of knowing whether it was a monster or not. With the heat of the afternoon fishing became impossible. I lay on my bed restlessly, waiting for the sun to lose some of its power.

By 8 p.m. we were back on the river, still in shirt-sleeves; but with most of the shocking heat now dissipated. Nils com-manded, 'Now we try the prawn.' Having indulged in a certain amount of prawn fishing some years earlier, I had more or less reserved its use for poor conditions; but if it meant a possibility of getting one of these Norwegian monsters, who was I to stick to principles? On went the prawn. I was soon to learn that the sink-and-draw methods used on these very powerful rivers were a lot more difficult than they

F

had been at home; and to work the prawn correctly required a certain amount of skill and knowledge of the river bed. Eventually, I got the hang of it again; and as Nils boated down the Upper Bolstad pool, things happened. The bait stopped. As I raised the rod and felt the heavy movement I leaned over to Nils and said, 'Fish!' At first I wondered if I had not in fact stuck on the bottom. Nothing moved. Then I felt the terrific weight of a heavy fish. For ten minutes I heaved and heaved, trying to get the fish out of the heavy current. The heaving had no effect. He stayed where he was, apparently oblivious of the fact that he was hooked. Doubtless the prawn and hooks in his mouth were nothing more than mere annoyance. After a further ten minutes of this tug-of-war game I asked Nils to boat me down to a position where I could impose some side-strain on him. Nils was very reluctant to do this, since it meant taking the boat dangerously near a point where he would be unable to row it up again. He kept repeating, 'Verra bigg fisshe – maybe twent-tree kilos!' Realizing that he meant something in the region of 50-lb, I paled at the prospect of ever getting a sight of the fish – let alone getting him ashore!

Eventually, however, I persuaded Nils to move down a little. The side-strain I was now able to impose on the fish began to have effect. Slowly it moved, and used its stupendous strength to fight upstream into the really heavy water of the main current. After five minutes of this he turned tail in a flash and rushed downstream. As my reel began to empty Nils shouted, 'He's going to the fjord!' He rowed the boat into the main draw of the current and we set off in pursuit. The great fish continued his headlong flight downstream. As we came to the rapids, with practically all my line gone, the fish moved violently into them. Down we plunged, fish and boat together. Foaming water splashed over the gunwales of the boat, which bobbed up and down like a cork in a storm. Within a brief period, all was quiet as we smoothed out on the placid waters of the fjord. Where was the fish? Winding the reel handle as fast as my hands would go, I took back the slack line; and to my great delight he was still on. Now in the quieter waters, I could at least get on better terms with him; terms that would perhaps be in my favour. By this time the entire village, it seemed, was on hand to watch – and offer *advice*! Then, some five minutes later, as the sun set behind the beautiful Norwegian mountains, Nil's gaff went home. Out came my biggest ever salmon of $46\frac{1}{2}$-lb weight. It was covered in sea-lice – and, to me, the most beautiful creature in the world.

After that, the rest of the trip was an anticlimax. I had caught my big fish; possibly the biggest fish I may ever catch! We continued the fishing and I hooked and played another monster for over an hour, without even seeing it. I never felt as though I had a chance of getting it. Eventually the tackle was strained almost to breaking point. Somehow, I felt he was not to be mine. Then I gave the rod to the gillie and took the line in my hand. Very slowly the fish moved. We won some line back on the reel. Then, suddenly and with a mighty rush he went downstream; and as he turned, the bait came out of his mouth. The game was over. I shall never know the weight of that fish, and to guess would be stupid. I had already caught my big fish; so that to expect fate to give me another of the same weight on the following day would have been asking too much! Quite apart from the fish, I again had the unique satisfaction of having the entire action being recorded on movie film. The film was subsequently shown on Tyne-Tees and American television, and I religiously guard the master negative.

It would seem that, as far as the Vosso was concerned, the prophecy of the guide-book was slowly coming true. This fishing is already commanding fees that keeps it in the 'millionaire-class'; and Odd Haraldsen has done much to control the netting, and improve the river.

AUTHOR'S NOTE:—*For further adventures in Norway see Chapter 24.*

## 22

## Salmon Through the Looking Glass

---

At the end of our short stay on the Vosso I strolled back to the superb anglers' lodge with my host, Odd Haraldsen. He is a salmon angler of great competence and experience, and our chat was about various points which showed during the play of my big fish. But behind this discussion, I had the feeling in my mind, 'This was the fish of my life. Now I shall be content forever . . .'

In a day or so my reactions had changed completely. As I have already said, during the three weeks before my catch eight salmon of over 50-lb had been taken from the same beat. One of them was over 60-lb. Why should a $46\frac{1}{2}$-lb fish, in these circumstances, be the fish of a lifetime? I am on the wrong side of forty-five, but if the good Lord spares my bones for another twenty years, must I spend those years with the thought, 'I have caught my largest salmon?' There have to be limits in this sort of thing. Is the catching of a fish of 50-lb the ultimate? Does not the method by which a fish is caught figure in the analysis? My fish of $46\frac{1}{2}$-lb was taken on a prawn. Would not the capture of a similar sized fish on a spinner, and then another of the same weight on a fly, make the catches progressively more significant? Is it the method or the fish that provides the deepest satisfaction?

For me the fish always predominates – but with definite reservations. It might be well to consider these reservations and their development. Frankly, I now dislike prawning and worming for salmon; but not from any stupid, sophisticated arguments that such methods are not 'the done thing'. I dislike the messy business of putting baits on the hook, damaging them on rocks, or the bottom, and having to bait up again frequently. This dislike originated no doubt, from practice of the cleanest, and possibly the easiest, way to fish for salmon; fly on the greased line. The fly is small and easily presented; the line floats; and the thrill of hooking and playing a salmon on such tackle is the greatest I know.

When we consider the intermediate methods between these extremes, there is the sunk fly; or the spinning lure; or the wobbling artificial bait. Dyed-in-the-wool greased-line salmon fly-fishers will cringe, I have no doubt, at any suggestion that such methods have merit; but in many ways the angler who uses the sunk fly or active lure has to think in a sort of third dimension – with method adjusted to thought. A novice can catch the odd salmon with modern spinning tackle, but to be consistently successful with this method there is a much broader canvas to be covered than is the case with fly on the greased-line. In the case of the fly on the greased-line, the salmon must rise deliberately and take the fly; and this reaction is entirely at the volition of the fish itself. In fishing the sunk fly and the spinner there is some element of skill and luck in whether the fly or lure hits the salmon on the nose, so to speak, and causes it to take – when in fact it is not really a 'taking' fish. Fly on the greased-line, for this reason alone, must retain a primary place among methods – and perhaps rightly so.

Until I began to fish the Lune, in the early sixties, I had been content to catch salmon by any sporting method I could devise: spinning, prawning, worming – anything, just to catch salmon. Those days were successful enough in terms of fish caught, as I have already indicated by recounting several occasions when I came home with bonanza catches. Slowly, this approach began to pall a little; and since I began to fish some lovely fly pools on the Lune, my approach has changed from predominant interest in sheer numbers of fish caught to interest in fewer fish caught by a more satisfying method.

There are times, of course, when the fly on a floating line is useless: early spring; late autumn; water at low temperatures, dirty or with prevalent acidity. These factors have a positive and detrimental influence on the inclination of salmon to take the high-swimming fly of the angler. In such circumstances, with me, it must still be the fish. If any other method pays the greatest dividends, regardless of its comparative lack of interest, the other method it must be. I see no rhyme or reason for plodding along with what is regarded as 'the done thing' when my experience tells me that such a method is useless on the day. If it has to be the Toby, or a big Black and Gold Devon – on they go. Let us set about getting fish!

Samuel Johnson commented that our brightest blazes of gladness are commonly kindled by unexpected sparks. The big salmon of the Vosso was something in the nature of such a spark. When I began to fish the river I desperately wanted to catch one of its monsters with fly. I had, at that time, yet to catch a salmon of over 20-lb with fly on the greased-line, but greased-lining was out of the question: hot sun; a river fed with the melting snows of the great mountains; low water temperature; and bank-top water level. Even the sunk fly was almost certainly a waste of time. I gave it a trial with a heavy line and a brass tube-fly; but I was well aware that the method was not getting the lure anywhere near the deep-lying fish. I turned to the big copper spoon, with additional lead weighting to get it down. The method resulted in the hooking of one fish; but it got off minutes afterwards. By the evening of our first day, the gillie was urging me to try the prawn. Who was I to argue? If it meant the hooking of one of their big fish, and the gillie went through the messy business of mounting the prawn on the tackle, why not? Better a big fish by any method than no fish at all.

The rest you know already. The fish took the prawn; fought as valiantly as a combination of any two fish I have ever taken; and gave me forty minutes of great excitement. It was exactly twice the weight of the biggest salmon I had taken from

British waters; and very much heavier than the two fish of
27-lb and 31-lb respectively I had previously taken from
Norwegian rivers. But where was the real achievement? As I
have said, eight fish of over 50-lb had been taken from the
beat during the short open period of the season before I fished
it. We are back to my earlier point. Should this fish of mine
have been accepted casually as the fish of a lifetime?

The truth is that the challenge still remained, and remained
in a much more complex form than mere ambition to take a
bigger salmon. The challenge was there, for instance, to catch
a 20-lb salmon on fly with the greased-line; then, perhaps, a
30-lb fish with the same method; then again, a fish of 40-lb
with a spinner; and if life and opportunity give the chance,
a fish of the same weight on the fly. Ultimately, the challenge
is to achieve what Richard Waddington described as his lifetime ambition when he hooked a 51-lb fish on a salmon fly
of his own design, and beached it without assistance on the
bank of the Norwegian Aarø river.

Goethe was undoubtedly right: the best thing we get from
history is the enthusiasm it arouses.

## 23
## A Few Haraldsen Tours

In the years that followed my great success in 1966 I was to strike up an increasing friendship with Odd Haraldsen. The following year Eric and I were once again on our travels over there. This time we were to fish some new rivers, and in the space of two weeks were to take in the Vefsna, Forra, Tengs, Aurland and Sand, not to mention a further brief visit to the Vosso – where I incurred my host's wrath by taking a mere tiddler of 10-lb on the fly, and thus helped to lower the 28-lb *average weight* of fish for his beat! All in all, I have now fished a total of ten Norwegian rivers when including, during the following year, a further visit which covered the Laerdal, Namsen and Bindal rivers.

The Vefsna river is reached by a six-hour train journey from Trondheim. The river empties its waters into the North Sea near Mosjöen. It is still a little south of the Arctic Circle, but enjoys a great reputation for big fish. Leering down at us from the wall of the lodge at Laksfors were woodcuts of Vefsna monsters of the past, the most notable one topping the 65-lb mark. Like many other Norwegian rivers, however, the Vefsna suffers from inadequate fish passes, although it should produce some really fabulous fishing if adequate fish passes are installed. In the short time I was there I took a lovely fish of 17-lb on the fly, and a small grilse of 4-lb.

The Forra river is small and, as a tributary of the bigger Stjordal river, is situated quite close to Trondheim airport. I barely had more than a few hours to fish this pleasant little river, but suceeded in landing two very fine sea-trout up to 4-lb while I was there.

The Namsen is truly a mighty river; undoubtedly the largest salmon river I have seen. Methods to fish it consist mainly of harling from a boat. It is, therefore, a dull river to fish; but does provide some very fine specimen salmon. In the short time I was there a fish hooked itself on my trolling rod, but only made the 5-lb mark. Another notable salmon river is the Sand; but I had barely one day on this river, and this day at a time when it was running a good ten feet above normal height. I should dearly love to go back there when the river is at more normal level. The Tengs river, like the Sand, is also down Stavanger way. It is a small river, but gets very good runs of grilse and small salmon. Some of the fishing on both these latter rivers may be leased from the Atlantic Hotel in Stavanger.

The Bindal river, also known as the Å-Elv, is one of the most inaccessible, and the facility of a float-plane is a decided asset. It is a most attractive river, and in addition to having good runs of salmon, it is a noted river for sea-trout. Much the same applies to the Aurland river in Songefjord. At the time of my visits to both these rivers they were either too low or too high. Perhaps the classic river for fly-fishermen is the Laerdal river. Again, I spent little more than a day plying a fly over its crystal-clear waters. All I got for my efforts was a lovely rise at my fly. I witnessed the entire incident, from the fish leaving its lie to the time when it returned *without* my fly in its mouth. It is truly a lovely river, and is yet another ear-marked for a return visit.

As a guest of Odd Haraldsen I have seen much of Norway's wonderland as we winged our way in small float-planes over that magnificent country. For me, however, the Vosso remains the real sportsman's river. On many of the rivers I failed to catch salmon. In fact the only ones where I have met with any success have been the Jolstra, Namsen, Vefsna and Vosso. But the fish taken on most other rivers have failed to match

the magnificence of those Vosso fish; and during the past two
years I have been fortunate in making two visits a year to
this lovely river. I have still to catch a bigger fish than the
one of 46½-lb which I took in 1966; but it is, I feel, only a
question of time before a fish of similar dimensions comes
my way. Who knows? It might just tip that magical mark of
50-lb! In terms of other success, however, I have been most
fortunate; the typing-ink was barely dry on my reflections on
Norway in Chapter 21 when my best fish on greased-line fly
exceeded the 20-lb mark. It was, of course, once again taken
from the Vosso, but this time during August 1968, a time
when all the best fish are reckoned to have moved upstream,
and the small summer fish are all that are likely to be
encountered. Late July and August are ideal for the fly on
this water, but the flies used to tend to be about two sizes
larger than would normally be used at home under the same
conditions. It had been a delightful day with brilliant sunshine. Daytime fishing had proved most difficult, and as my
gillie and I pondered on chances of sport for the evening we
waited patiently for the sun to sink behind the lofty mountains which surround the Bolstad valley. I had selected a
13½-ft Hardy 'Wye' rod, with a forward taper floating line
(AFTM 10), and had put up a No. 4 Silver Wilkinson tied
on a gilt hook. As the first shadows cast themselves upon the
water we commenced our operation; and I had barely extended my casts, so that they would cover the pool, before I
detected a lovely head-and-tail rise at the fly. My line slid
away very slowly; but as I raised the rod point I knew that I
was fast into a good fish.

The fish fought hard in the powerful water. At the end of
one spirited run it came crashing out of the water, and we
were able to get a rough idea of its dimensions. 'Nice fisshe!'
said the gillie. 'Maybe 15 kilos.' I was quick to realize that
there and then I was playing the biggest salmon I had ever
hooked on fly; and, moreover, that the battle was far from
complete, and that I should have all on to contain him within
the pool. I fought him as hard as I dared and within fifteen

minutes I had him laid on his side, ready for the gaff. I even had a notion to tail him, as I do with the bulk of my fish nowadays; but a glance at his jaw, and the fly hanging there by a thread of flesh, was sufficient to bring the gillie into instant action. The gaff went home. Out came my biggest fish on fly. 30-lb was his weight at the time of capture; but when the photograph was taken, two days later, he only made $28\frac{1}{2}$-lb. He was, indeed, a very unfortunate fish; for had the battle been protracted much longer it was plainly evident that the mere thread of flesh holding the fly would have broken to give him his freedom.

The salmon rivers of Norway enjoy a short season. The first breath of spring comes with the month of May. Quickly, it seems, the sun moves into the northern hemisphere and slowly wins over from the Arctic ice. As the snows melt, so the rivers rise until, by the end of the month, they are roaring down in full spring-time spate. The first fish to run the rivers seem to be the big ones, and it is not normally until the end of June that the bulk of the snows get melted. Even then, much snow remains; and the hotter the weather, the higher the rivers. As early as February Odd Haraldsen can often make a very good assessment of the season's sport, his prediction being based on the amount of snow. The more snow there is to melt, the better the chances. It is a pretty awesome sight which greets the angler who visits such a river as the Vosso after a heavy winter of snow. The river may well be six feet to ten feet above normal summer level, and any notions of traditional casting of fly or bait are soon put to one side. Heavy baits are required to get down to the fish and rods and tackle normally used at home have to be replaced with stouter equipment. Prawn fishing is very popular at this time of the season, and it may well require a good six-ounces of lead to ensure the bouncing of the prawn on, or near, the bed of the river. Alternatively, a big spoon bait up to six inches long – with additional lead weighting – will often lead to successful conclusions. It is not until the bulk of the snows have melted that the tackle we should normally use for early

spring fishing in Britain comes into its own. Usually, however, by the middle of July and into August, it is possible to
resort to traditional greased-line methods. There is not quite
the quantity of really big fish coming into the river at this
time; but as the *average* weight for the river is in the region
of 28-lb, it is not uncommon for the angler to encounter
several fish in the 30-lb bracket. In all my visits to the river
I have caught more fish over the average weight of 28-lb than
I have taken below that weight. It is truly a 'trophy' river in
every respect, perhaps only marred by the fact that the monsters of May and June may not be successfully fished for with
a fly on the floating line. Apart from excessive water height,
one of the greatest factors mitigating against this is the low
water temperature still prevailing at this time of the year.
Freshly melted snow takes quite a time to be so influenced
by the sun as to raise the water temperature. I have known
days when air temperatures hovered around the high 80s, yet
the water had to struggle to make the low 40s.

Techniques for prawn fishing, because of the torrential
current, are slightly different from those used at home. It is
still essential to find a suitable weight to get the bait down,
and the lead is mounted in ball form, with the amount of
balls dictated by the force of water (See Fig. 9.).

Great skill is required in keeping the lead weights banging
on the bottom, without getting hung up, as the angler makes
a slow sink-and-draw action. A rod with a strong tip is
required; and the heavy fibre-glass spinning rods now
marketed by Bruce and Walker, or one of Hardy's range, fill
the bill admirably.

During June 1969 I was once again on my travels to the
Vosso. This time, again, I had a television cameraman with
me and we were hopeful to make a feature-length film of
monster fish being caught – with the pleasure of being in the
company of Odd Haraldsen, of course!

The third member of our party was Mr T. B. 'Happy'
Fraser, of the Atlantic Salmon Association of Canada. Fraser
has done much over the past few years to highlight the grave

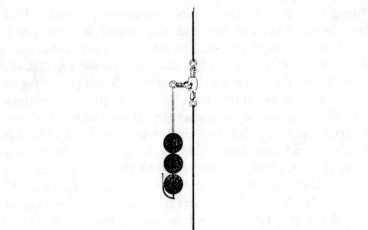

FIG. 9

dangers of salmon netting on the high seas (see Chapter 26).
He proved a very interesting companion; and there were
many evenings when, over a bottle of Scotch on the table, we
talked into the small hours. We were all, however, a bit
despondent. Odd Haraldsen had particularly reserved the
middle week of June for us as being the most likely to produce the bumper bags. But the fish had not come up in any
great quantity. We guessed that it would need some very hard
work to make a showing for the cameraman.

On the first morning it was agreed that the cameraman
should go with Odd who, with the pools he was going to fish,
seemed on the face of it to have the best chances. I was to take
my favourite pool, the one in which I had taken my big fish
in 1966; and as it was almost three years to the day I should
try the prawn again. I had not been fishing for more than
ten minutes when, in the identical spot where I had hooked
my monster, another fish took me. I fought it hard in that
strong water and did not let it get the better of me. Within
eight minutes I had it ready for the gaff; and out it came,
dripping sea-lice and topping the scale at 30-lb. Later that
evening one of the local gillies caught a fish of identical
weight – but, alas, the cameraman had not been on hand for
either!

The following day it was decided that the cameraman
should come with me. I might have known that it would now
be someone else's turn to catch a fish! So it was; at lunchtime
that day 'Happy' Fraser came in with one of exactly 30-lb. By
now, of course, the cameraman was tearing his hair; but it
took him to our final day there to admit defeat. He was
spending the last day with me, while higher upstream Odd
Haraldsen was about to do battle with the best fish of the
week – a magnificent salmon of 42-lb. At the time of writing
(autumn 1969) another Haraldsen tour is being planned for
June of next year. I know that I should be content with
takings of the past; but I am still hoping for that 50-pounder!

AUTHOR'S NOTE:—*'Happy' Fraser died in 1972 following a long illness.*

## 24
## More Tales of Norway

SINCE the previous chapter was written I have been most fortunate in making at least another four visits to Norway. All of these visits, however, were confined to the Vosso river and it has been a period when the fortunes of Norwegian fishing have ebbed and flowed. Three of these seasons on the Vosso were dramatically poor in terms of numbers of fish caught, but they could be explained by a lack of winter snowfall and excessive commercial netting in the fjords and at sea.

By far the majority of Norwegian rivers are dependent on a good winter snowfall to sustain them throughout the spring and summer. Additional rain, later in the season, also helps considerably, but if snowfalls have been modest there will never be the heavy weight of water to assist upstream migrations of the salmon. It is not usually until mid-May that the sun melts the snow on the high hills and it is then that the rivers rise and the really big fish start to run. Following a winter of heavy snow, the rivers may be sustained at a good height throughout the short season, and experience has shown that when this happens sport is likely to be good. During the years 1970, '71 and '72, however, the Norwegian winters were comparatively mild with only modest amounts of snow. Fishing during June of 1971 was hard work and I had to be content with one fish for my week. It was, however, a most unlucky fish and it might be interesting to recount how I came to catch it.

I had been fishing for four days without so much as an offer.

No fish had been seen and enthusiasm was waning rapidly. On the evening of the fifth – and another blank – day I was ready to throw in the towel and admit defeat. As I retrieved my bait for another cast I leaned over to the gillie and told him that I was about to make my last cast of the day. I cast out and the bait swung round nicely. Quite suddenly it stopped and I felt convinced that, once again, I had got hung up on a rock. I tugged and heaved impatiently, then all of a sudden the 'bottom' started to move and I realised that a miracle had happened and that I was into a fish. The salmon made a spirited run upstream and then it jumped. It did not take us long to realise that it was a good fish – probably in excess of 30-lb – as it continued with its headlong plunge against the strong current. Slowly the gillie moved the boat towards the shore where he landed me. The fish seemed to be well-hooked as it fought strongly against the current; but quite suddenly I felt something give as all went slack and I was just cursing my luck when I became conscious that tension had been renewed. With that the fish turned and fled downstream and we had no alternative but to jump back into the boat and try to keep pace with it. My reel was emptying at a high-pitched scream as I urged the gillie to make the boat go faster down the torrent of water. Out of the pool headlong we went, down through the next pool and thence into fierce rapids at the neck of the third pool. Under normal circumstances I would have feared for our safety, but I had a fish on and a good one at that. So we threw caution to the wind and headed for the maelstrom.

By yet another miracle, when I wound in the slack line my fish was still on and had taken up station in a quiet backwater beside the roaring torrent. We moved the boat quickly ashore and it was then that I caught a good glimpse of the fish. He was certainly not as big as my monster of 1966, but he was by no means a tiddler. As I worked the fish closer inshore my gillie began to get excited and suspicious of the hookhold. 'I think we lose him if not very lucky,' he said. I must confess that I too had detected two bare hooks hanging from the mouth. However, the fish was still firmly hooked, and I proceeded to haul him to within gaffing distance.

Both the gillie and I breathed a sigh of relief as the gaff went home and the fish landed on the bank. It was a fine, fresh-run fish with the sea lice still on it. By some strange quirk of fate the mouth hookhold had broken from the trace, but the remaining hooks were firmly embedded in the muscle of the pectoral fin. Little wonder that my fish had taken-off when the mouth-hold had broke. But for the gillie, the boat and the blessing of the Almighty, the fish would still be in the river.

My fish was short and deep, but I doubted whether he would quite make the 30-lb mark. Back at the lodge all estimates put him at 30-lb plus, and I was surprised and delighted when the scale swung down to $33\frac{1}{2}$-lb For the remainder of that week I fished with renewed interest, but to no avail. Another year would have to elapse before I would get a further chance of that elusive 50-pounder.

During June of 1972 I was once again on the Vosso, but apart from enjoying the company of my host, Odd Haraldsen, and the delightful scenery of the Bolstad valley, I need not have bothered. I fished all week for nothing – not even a good pull – and came home reflecting on my sanity. 'What was wrong with Norwegian fishing?' I wondered. The river had been maintained at a reasonably good height, but the fish were just not there in any quantity. Back at home the situation was little better. The Lune sweltered, low and clear, under a hot sun and I caught my last salmon of the season during the first week of August.

During the first few months of 1973, however, heavy snow was being reported in Norway. A letter from Odd Haraldsen virtually promised that this time we would hit the river right and that the fishing would be good. Like many other salmon anglers of long experience I am highly suspicious of such promises, but the visit to Norway is always a highlight of my angling year.

On arrival in mid-June it was raining heavily and the river was higher than I had ever seen it before. Catches prior to my arrival could only be described as modest. But I was to have my choice of pool for the first evening and I elected to try one of the top pools where I had hooked the $33\frac{1}{2}$-lb fish back in 1971. On my second cast in this pool, the bait – a big Norwegian klepper spoon – stopped abruptly and it was not long before I was contesting the odds with a strong fish. It fought well, but without any spectacular developments and it was not long before my gillie gaffed out a lovely fresh-run fish of 25-lb. Moving down to the next pool, my very first cast produced another solid pull and after ten minutes of tough fighting I was able to lead ashore another beauty of 22-lb. 'Not bad for my first evening out,' I thought, but the rain continued to pour down and I needed little encouragement to call it a night and take some light refreshment in the lodge.

The following morning the river was a good 2-ft higher and still rising and only an odd fish was caught by one of the gillies. By the third day, it was up to the 6-ft mark, but I did take a fish of 26-lb by deep-spinning in the slack corners near the bank. That evening, however, the river began to fall and we retired to our beds in the hope that there would be no more rain.

On the morning of June 17, 1973, the Vosso was fining down into good fishing ply. The day was soft with a suggestion of humidity, but it was not actually raining. Odd Haraldsen and I both commented on the fact that it seemed a good fishing day and I was to spend the morning in the Upper Bolstad pool – the pool where I had taken the fish of $46\frac{1}{2}$-lb back on June 18, 1966. The river was still fractionally too big for perfection, but I elected to begin my operations fishing from the bank with a heavy Bruce & Walker spinning rod and an Ambassador 7000 bait-casting reel. My terminal tackle was the same big Norwegian klepper spoon I had used for most of the week, but I added a spiral lead to assist in getting the bait down to a reasonable depth.

Beginning at the head of the pool I fished down to the tail without so much as an offer. My last cast had to be a long one so that it would get well across to the other side of the river and then swing into the exact lie where I had taken the $46\frac{1}{2}$-pounder. The cast was a good one, but the reel overran slightly and I paid out the extra few loops of line before closing the reel. The bait seemed to be swinging out of the main current very nicely and I was just about to begin the retrieve when the rod was nearly pulled out of my hand. I was into a fish. Thinking that it might just be another fish in the 25 to 30-lb bracket I tried to walk it upstream, but it seemed very reluctant to be led. Fortunately I had Einar, a very experienced Vosso gillie, with me and he urged me to get into a waiting boat in case we had problems. I did as I was bid and we tried to row the boat slightly upstream to give ourselves some room for manoeuvre. The fish was still very reluctant to leave its lie and many minutes passed as it lay there log-like without any apparent movement. The thought occurred to me that it might have got off and left me hooked into the bottom, but Einar knew better. 'I think this a verra big fish,' he quietly observed.

After a few more minutes the fish seemed to be getting annoyed and it cruised about in its lie with vicious shakes of the head and tail. Then, quite suddenly, it took off in a mad downstream dash with my reel emptying as though I were attached to an atomic submarine. We set off in hot pursuit as Einar swung the boat into the main current to assist his rapid rowing – it was like 1966 all over again. Within seconds my reel was empty and I was just bracing myself for the inevitable twang, when, as it reached the tail of the next pool below us, the fish turned and started swimming back upstream. My next problem was to make the line knot bite at the reel spindle to get some line back. For some nerve-racking seconds I wound the reel and nothing happened, but by handlining some line back through the rings I got sufficient slack line to make the knot bite on the drum. Moving down quickly, I soon got the bulk of my line back onto the reel; with the fish seemingly content to take a rest in the quieter water near the bank. Soon, however, it was off again as it pulled into the main draw of the current. It was now quite obvious that it would go down through the rapids and into the nearby fjord. We had no alternative but to follow as best we could. The ride down those rapids in a small boat can only be described as hair-raising. Half-way down everything went slack and I feared the worst. But our boat was merely gaining on the fish and by winding the reel handle as rapidly as I could we eventually regained contact.

It was not long before we smoothed out on the placid waters of the fjord. The fish was still far from being tired and we had to follow it around in the boat for several more minutes. During this time Einar was slowly making for the shore where he landed me. By now I had an audience who were just as aware as I that this was no ordinary fish. We got occasional glimpses of it as it desperately tried to shake the hook. I say hook (singular) because it had become painfully apparent that there was only one hook of the triangle in its mouth. Slowly and quietly I eventually led the fish to the shore. The first gaffing stroke missed and there were further moments of tense anxiety; but the next time the great fish came in, the gaff went home and out he came. All immediate assessments indicated that I had at last got my fifty-pounder, but when the fish was hung on the scales he was just a few ounces short of that magical mark. It was, however, the biggest fish from the Bolstad beat of the Vosso for the past three years and at the end of 1973 it was also the biggest for the season.

On my last day on the Vosso that year I was accompanied by a French photo-journalist who wanted some good action photos. I am always reluctant about catching fish to order, and after I had tried the spoon to no avail, I decided to have a try with the prawn. This means fishing from a boat and, as explained in earlier chapters, using heavy lead weights banging on the bottom. It is a very efficient way of taking dour fish and I had not been casting for very long when I got another heavy tug and a fish was on. Thinking that it might be another monster I was careful at first, but the fish played with more dash and sparkle and when it jumped we saw that it was of more modest proportions. As I brought it to the gaff the hooks fell out as the gaff went home. Then, suddenly, it fell off the gaff and there was an anxious gillie bundling it into his arms to get it ashore. He just made it and at our feet lay another gleaming fish of 25-lb.

Of the 24 fish we got for the week, all had carried sea lice and some even still had their teeth. Not only had I caught the biggest and my personal best, I had also caught the smallest (22-lb) and the most. My own catch averaged out at 29-lb per fish and I cannot think of another river in the world where this might be possible.

When all the Norwegian rivers closed for 1973 I got an overall report on some of the more notable rivers. Some, indeed, had suffered from too much winter snow, but in the main they all reported exceptional sport. In a letter from Laerdal, Mr R. J. Brooks wrote: 'There is no doubt that in 1973 all Norwegian rivers have seen one of the biggest runs of salmon for many years. The Laerdal, although the water was high, was never out of order and the lowest beats had phenomenal catches with the best fish weighing 54-lb and with over 300 salmon from one pool. I have personally landed 93 salmon averaging slightly over 18-lb – ninety per cent of which were taken on fly. I am sure that a good angler, fishing full time, could have multiplied this take by five times.'

From the information I received and my own limited experience, it would seem that in 1973 the Norwegian salmon made a dramatic return. Only history will prove if it is to be sustained, but there seems an increased awareness on the part of fishery owners, management and authority of the vast potential of the sporting resource. Already schemes are being undertaken to increase, yet again, the number of fish passes and more rivers are being stocked with fry and smolt. It is hoped that the Norwegians have now got it right. It is my opinion that they could curtail their commercial catches even more strictly, but then I have a bee-in-my-bonnet about our own level of netting here at home.

There is still no sign of disease in Norway and comparatively little pollution or abstraction of these virgin rivers; but rents are now high and going higher. In the meantime, if the Norwegians will nurture their resource and develop the potential, there is no doubt that Norway could still be the great Mecca for the salmon angler.

# 25
## The Salmon of Spain

TUCKED away in the north-west corner of Spain lies a vast region with magnificent scenery, lush valleys and foaming rivers. It is known as Asturias and to anglers who have fished there it is as much a byword for salmon as Perthshire, Inverness-shire, New Brunswick or Finmark. As Spanish provinces go, however, Asturias has escaped the attention of the average tourist, and if you incline to the belief that all Spain has to offer are golden beaches, bullfights, brilliant sunshine and sherry, you are very sadly mistaken.

It was my good fortune to see and fish in this part of Spain in 1971, and my companion for this salmon safari was Mr Hilton Pierpoint, of Blaydon. He had seen many of the rivers on an earlier visit and had thought them well worth further exploration. It was our intention to fish three of the best-known rivers and take in some lake fishing for rainbow trout, and mountain stream fishing for brownies.

To get to the heart of Asturias we had to fly from London to Bilbao by scheduled Iberia Airlines service. A good, four-hour drive brought us to Colombres and the San Angel Hotel. This was our overnight stopping place, but it was also handy for the Cares river where we fished later on. Our immediate destination was the River Narcea to take in the end of an international salmon fishing tournament with anglers from all parts of the world.

To describe fully the breathtaking scenery we passed through on our journey would involve more superlatives than I can muster. It is truly magnificent. The entire county is framed by the high Picos de Europa, rising to some 9,000-ft and the rivers Cares, Sella, and Narcea all have their sources in this high mountain country. Road surfaces vary from very good to pretty grim, and ample time has to be allowed for comfortable motoring.

On arrival at Cornellana, we were dismayed to find the Narcea in roaring flood. Excessive snows on the high Picos were melting and the river was barely fishable, except with a worm. We were shown some lovely fresh fish taken a few days before our arrival, but barely troubled to wet a line ourselves.

Much information on Spanish salmon fishing potential may be gleaned from *The Atlantic Salmon – A Vanishing Species,* by Anthony Netboy. In this book Mr. Netboy deals at length with the situation there, past and present. It is doubtless true that over the years Spanish salmon fishing has suffered in much the same way as our own. Rivers were polluted wantonly, and commercial interests were ever ready to take the lion's share of the salmon resource.

At the end of the Spanish Civil War, in 1940, only a dozen reasonably good salmon rivers remained. But General Franco, himself an ardent angler, inspired a law in 1942 which was designed to prevent further deterioration of the inland fisheries. Its prime aim was to ban all forms of commercial netting, leaving the entire salmon resource to the sport fishermen. In later years the fishing on the top rivers came under the control of the State Tourist Bureau, and is now readily available to residents and foreign visitors at modest fees. It is essential, however, that beats (known as *cotos*) should be booked well in advance. Costs vary, depending on the beat and time of year, but generally average around £3 per day. Hotels are not too plentiful, but if luxury is not a prerequisite there are an adequate number of smaller hotels at modest cost.

Most of the fishing on the rivers mentioned is carefully controlled and maintained. Casting platforms have been built and each section of a river is under the control of a local game warden. It is necessary to take out a national fishing licence and I do not recommend anyone to try to fish without the necessary licence and beat reservation. Gillies are readily available at around £3 per day, and, although few have any knowledge of English, they make excellent and conscientious guides.

Much the same tackle as would be used on the Spey or Dee would be more than adequate on the rivers I saw. Fly sizes and patterns differ little from ours, but there is great enthusiasm for a weighted Mepps spoon for those who would wish to spin. For the fly-only fisherman May and June should bring the best sport, and because of the sheer banks on some of the rivers, it is highly desirable that the angler be reasonably competent at Spey-casting.

During the early months the rivers are snow-fed, but this part of Spain also produces a high rainfall, so the rivers rarely get too low. It is quite possible to be basking in the sun on the coast when 10 miles inland there are those lovely soft rain showers which only a salmon fisherman can appreciate.

With the Narcea out of order, we made our way back east to visit the River Sella at Cangas de Onis. Here we were to fish the Sierra beat, and our gillies, Ramon and Angel Sierra, were enthusiastic about our chances. Once again the Sella looked fractionally too high for perfection, but we fished hard in the hope that we would connect with an Asturian monster. There was some excitement when we connected with a couple of big brownies, but the salmon did not want to know.

It is difficult from a brief expedition like ours to assess the ultimate fishing potential. All I can say is that the rivers looked fishy (in the best sense of that word) and well worth our efforts. We were most unfortunate that heavy rain and melting snow combined to produce big rivers, and I would dearly love to go back another year and find the rivers at more normal height. Recorded catches from the rivers we fished left us in no doubt that the bulk of fish top a 10-lb average and are caught in sufficient numbers to make a visit there worthwhile. When we were there in June 1971 catches since the season opened on March 1 had totalled 254 salmon from the Sella, 187 from the Narcea and 150 from the Cares and Deva.

On our way back to Colombres we took a scenic route from Covadonga down the Cares valley to Panes. Here we fished briefly at 4,000-ft, in the lakes of Enol and Ercina. Rainbows up to 12-lb have been reported from these lakes, but we caught only the smaller fish around the 1-lb mark. Driving along the steep slopes of the Cares river we saw many anglers, most of whom were worming in the swollen waters. Cat-walks and casting platforms abounded, and we were shown and fished from many of the places where General Franco has caught his share of salmon.

Perhaps one of the greatest advantages which Spanish salmon fishing offers is a chance to take a family holiday. Leave the family on the beach and within half-an-hour's drive you can be fishing on one of the named beats of a famous river. At the little fishing port of Ribadesella, for instance, there is a first-class hotel and virgin beach. Yet no more than 20 kilometres away are the middle beats of the Sella river at Arriondas and Cangas de Onis. Similarly with the Hotel San Angel at Colombres, where barely a kilometre away is an unspoiled beach, and fishing on the Cares and Deva is only a short distance by car.

Iberia Airlines and Swedish Lloyd Shipping Lines are developing travel to this part of Spain for the tourist angler, and if the demand grows there may be improved facilities for flights from London to eliminate the long drive from Bilbao. The town of Oviedo is more centrally placed for the fishing, but at the time of writing it deals only with domestic flights from Madrid and Barcelona. All in all, a salmon-fishing holiday in northern Spain should bring a new horizon to the British salmon angler. It offers magnificent scenery, lovely rivers and a chance of the same silvery salmon which would cost the earth in Norway or Iceland.

With a toast of *Salud, Pesetas y Amor* we sipped our glasses of sherry on our last evening there. It was true we had not caught an Iberian salmon, but we could not recall such lovely scenery as yet unspoiled by the march of progress and mankind in general. It is to be hoped, perhaps, that some of my readers will go to

Asturias and have greater success than we, but I have a private hope that it will not become too popular and that in the years ahead it will be spared the ravages of mass tourism.

# 26
## Disease and Netting

DURING the years leading up to 1966 it was becoming apparent
that numbers of salmon entering British and Norwegian
rivers were on the increase. Classic rivers like Spey, Tweed,
Tay and Dee were all producing better bags to both salmon
anglers and the estuarine nets. Returns from the River Eden
district of the Cumberland River Authority and the Lune
area of the Lancashire River Authority showed an all time
high in 1966, of salmon taken from these areas since 1945.
There was a general feeling of optimism about the future.
True, there was vague talk about netting in the high seas off
Greenland; and of an outbreak, during 1964, of an uniden-
tifiable fish disease in the rivers of Ireland. But these were
just wispy clouds on a distant horizon when all was serene in
Britain. The angler could have his fun on well-stocked
rivers, and the coastal netsmen could reap a modest harvest
without any thought or worries for future stocks. During the
early sixties it was not uncommon for the lower beats of
Tweed to be so full of fresh-run fish, in the month of February, that anglers could regularly catch into double figures
of salmon during the brief period of daylight of a winter's
day. As winter warmed into spring, the migrating salmon
would surge upstream to the middle beats and thus provide
wonderful sport for the fly-fishermen. Indeed, towards the end
of 1966 it was very apparent that the Lune, at least, held such

great stocks of fish that, should disease break out, the mortalities would be very heavy indeed.

I have already recounted how 1966 was a good year for me personally. The seasons, it was felt, were getting better every year. Why worry about the high seas netting off Greenland, or the bumper catches being made by the coastal netsmen? There were sufficient salmon, and more, for everyone.

During October of that year, however, what had been a distant, wispy cloud on the horizon, suddenly manifested itself as an anvil-shaped cumulo-nimbus in the form of an outbreak of the disease. Small white patches, the size of a sixpence, appeared on many of the fish being caught; and it was then realized that the Irish salmon disease, as it was then called, was now showing in the rivers on this side of the Irish sea. The west-coast rivers of England and southern Scotland were the first to suffer mortalities; and it was left to local river authorities to net out the dead fish and bury them in quicklime.

On the Lune, as one instance of the disease-attacked rivers, somewhere in the region of ten thousand salmon were thought to have been infected. As the waters cooled with the onset of winter, quiet pools and shelving banks became littered with dead and dying fish; and by the early spring of 1967 it appeared, to the casual observer, that the river was devoid of life. Very soon the fresh-run springers were arriving; but within a few days of their move into fresh water the disease took hold. The entire run, it seemed, was quick to die. Other rivers, too, were now being affected; Tweed, Spey and Dee all reported outbreaks; and it gradually became apparent that we had a plague on our hands that would, slowly but surely, thread its venom into the entire river systems of the British Isles.

A sight of the river Tweed in the November of 1967 was sufficient to make the most hardy angler vomit. Hundreds of diseased and dying salmon cruised about aimlessly in the backwaters, not strong enough to complete their spawning task, but apparently awaiting their untimely and inevitable end.

Scientists seemed slow to get to work on the disease. Several labels were applied; but eventually someone came up with *Ulcerative Dermal Necrosis* (UDN) as the best description of the malady. The initial infection was thought (and still is) to be a viral infection; which was followed by secondary bacterial infection; and the subsequent killer was the fungal growth on the diseased tissue. It was observed, however, that diseased fish could sometimes stay alive for a long time. Some fish, with only minor infected areas, would die quickly, while others would become completely covered with fungus before eventual death. Of those fish seen and removed from the river systems, there must have been thousands unseen that were swept down to the estuaries at times of flood.

The advent of disease in our rivers seemed to make many of the apparently healthy fish more difficult to catch. Previously effective fly and bait patterns did not produce the same response; and throughout the summers of 1967 and 1968 I could not catch fish under conditions in which, previously, I should have banked on providing sport. Fish were caught almost entirely by accident. They gave me the impression that, although unmarked with any outward signs of disease, they may well have been sick, and fearful that the cold water conditions would bring the disease to a head.

During the long dry summer of 1969, there were few fish in our rivers and very few signs of disease. Some of us, in our flights of fancy, even pondered on the possibility of the long, hot weather killing the disease bugs; but it was not to be.

Apart from the serious winter-time mortalities, the effects of the disease have not yet had time (1969) to affect the runs of salmon still coming up from the sea. With a minimum two-year life span in fresh water before the young salmon makes its way seawards on its first migration, there has not yet been time to note the effect on the reduced spawning stock. In 1968 that excellent book by Anthony Netboy, *The*

*Atlantic Salmon – A Vanishing Species* appeared on the book-stalls. It left the analytical reader in no doubt just where we in Britain were bound with our destructive policies. During the same year it was also very obvious that something, apart from the disease, was affecting our runs of fish. Reports from rivers were very dismal, with rod and net catches down on earlier years. This brought into highlight the 1965 contentions which Mr T. B. Fraser of the Atlantic Salmon Association of Canada put forward to publicize the dangers of the high-seas fishing for salmon off the coasts of Greenland. Greenland has few salmon-producing rivers of its own; and it soon became obvious that, at long last, man had found one of the hitherto elusive feeding grounds of salmon while they are at sea. These self-same salmon had their origins in the rivers of Canada, Great Britain and Ireland. If the toll of commercially taken salmon continued to mount, it appeared that it would not be long before the effect of this high-sea fishing would become reflected in the reduced numbers returning to our rivers.

Many of us, in Britain, were so concerned with the disease problem that we were slow to realize the full impact of this high-sea fishing; but by spring 1969 it was obvious that disease alone could not account for the grave shortage of fish now entering our rivers. At a meeting in Warsaw during the month of June that year a majority of the fourteen member nations of the International Commission of Northwest Atlantic Fisheries (ICNAF) voted in favour of a ban on all high-sea fishing for salmon. Those voting against the ban contained the names of Denmark and West Germany; and as the Danes and Faroese had been the principal offenders in the past, the high-sea fishing will continue until the process of international law has gone full circle, and an enforceable ban has been imposed.

Meanwhile, for the few fish entering our rivers, the disease still rears its ugly head, and has, I am given to understand, now spread to the rivers of Normandy and Brittany. Just how long the disease will flourish seems difficult to estimate. From

records of the late 1800s it seems obvious that the self-same
disease affected our rivers at that time. All in all, it took
around twelve years to abate; and during some of those years
it was more virulent than during others. Scientists working
on the disease seem no nearer a solution than were their for-
bears of eighty years ago; and even if the disease were
identified, and an antidote discovered, it would seem well
nigh impossible to administer the antidote to wild fish. The
disease, therefore, appears to be something with which we
shall have to live. But we can, and must, do something about
high-sea netting, estuarine netting, and excessive catches by
anglers and poachers. The major blame for the bulk of the
decline in British salmon fishing may well be laid at the
Danes' door. That country's fishing fleets proved very effective
at virtually eliminating the tunny from the North Sea. Latest
reports indicate that they still operate a vast fleet of long-
range fishing vessels, and are landing increasing tonnages of
salmon in their home ports. Despite pleas by the Danish
Ambassador, they appear to have little thought for conservation; and it must be presumed that as soon as the high-sea
salmon fishery is no longer worth their efforts, they will
doubtless turn their hands once again to deep-sea fishing for
marketable sea fish.

Not all salmon, however, spend sufficient time at sea to
make the distant journey to Greenland. It has been note-
worthy, during the latter half of 1969, that many rivers have
received modest runs of small salmon or grilse which can
only have spent a year at sea. A theory put forward by many
old anglers and gillies is that it is possible that our rivers are
slowly reverting to an autumnal cycle, when the bulk of the
fish will come in to complete their spawning activities
quickly. A century ago the Tweed, as an example, was a fine
autumn river. Then, since the Second World War, the spring
runs predominated until a few years ago. The autumn runs
then began to attract more and more anglers. All forms of
coastal netting ceases, by law, around the end of August or
the middle of September; and those fish which prolong their

sea-feasting have, at least, the advantage of not having to run the gauntlet of these nets.

At the time of writing (December 1969) the rivers of Britain have suffered a long and dry summer and the salmon found it difficult to obtain the required access. Commercial netsmen in several estuaries (notably that of Tweed) made fantastic catches as the fish came in and out during the ebb and flow of the tides. In the September 1969 issue of *Trout and Salmon* one boat alone was reported to have caught two thousand fish in the period of a week. Meanwhile anglers were having a tough time to find any worth-while fishing. Quantities of fish entering the rivers were well down on earlier years, and the catches were only modest. Little wonder that anglers became indignant; and that the letter pages of many angling publications called not only for a ban on all high-sea fishing, but also that national administration authority should take a long look at our own destructive policies, so that we might do something to put our own house in order.

With the arrival of the colder weather in late 1969 the disease once again made its appearance, although it would be true to say that on Tweed, for instance, it did not seem anything like so bad as in the years of 1967 and 1968. At a meeting in London during October 1969, it was obvious that little was being done to attempt the controlling of the disease. It seems more than likely that the disease will have run its course before man even gets to the threshold of worth-while knowledge. We can and must, therefore, do something about all forms of netting. We can no longer afford to let the Danes 'milk a cow' that they neither own, nor feed! We can no longer tolerate the vast plunder which takes place on our own coasts and estuaries. The time for conservation is right *now* – even if, in order to achieve it, the angler has to accept limit bags or restricted seasons.

The salmon is indeed a fine and noble fish; a fish that has won the admiration of all mankind for its great strength and tenacity in performing feats of great endurance. At the moment, however, this fish is being faced with the last straw. We must hope that man will see sense before it is too late; and take firm action to prevent devastation of one of our greatest sports. Otherwise, this book will be nothing more than history.

AUTHOR'S NOTE:—*Since this chapter was written there have been several notable developments on the question of high seas fishing for salmon; but there is a distinct lack of useful development on the question of excessive netting around our own coastline. An up-to-date review is to be found in the next chapter.*

# 27

# Further Thoughts on Commercial Netting and the Salmon Angler

A STUDY of all the classical literature on salmon angling will reveal that from the advent of salmon fishing with a rod-and-line there has been a growing division between those who fish for sport and those who fish for profit. Such a situation was almost inevitable. Without doubt, the netsmen have had the right to take salmon from our coasts and estuaries long before salmon angling was even a vague possibility. This age-old right has remained and it is only in comparatively recent years – in terms of salmon fishing history – that commercial and sporting interests have conflicted. It may be interesting to examine the background to this present state of strife.

In the days before salmon angling tackle was successfully evolved it seemed perfectly natural for mankind to crop the vast harvest of salmon which ran our unpolluted rivers. In our greed, however, we eventually took too much for granted and the resource dwindled as the suitable environment for salmon was polluted or overfished. By 1861 the sense of man prevailed and the fishery laws imposed during that year were expressly designed with conservation in mind. By the turn of the century, however, the demands for a sporting resource were on the increase. Salmon angling had become a fashionable sport, even though our best sporting rivers were only available to the riparian owners and their personal guests. Angling pressure was never very high at this time and there was little real conflict between those who fished for sport and those who fished for profit.

As far back as 1922, however, there were many far-seeing anglers who were predicting that increased commercial catches could not be sustained if the sporting resource were to have a fair crack-at-the-whip; but the status-quo continued and it was only in the bad years that the angler raised his pen, dipped it in vitriol, and complained about the other lot. Quite by accident, it seemed, mankind had struck a balance between sporting and commercial interests of the correct crop to be taken. Overall stocks in the rivers at the termination of a season were generally regarded as adequate for the benefit and survival of the species.

At the end of the last war, the situation changed drastically. Riparian owners began to see the full value of the sporting resource and certain fisheries, for the first time in their history, were let to ordinary mortals who could pay the rentals involved. All around us mankind was seeking more leisure and by the mid-'sixties the sport of angling in general and salmon fishing in particular was attracting more devotees and the rents were increasing. A beat that had previously accommodated two rods was slowly being made available for four rods and then six. The wealthy angler, it seemed, was prepared to pay almost any price for a chance of sport. Many rivers did produce higher catches than ever before in their history, but there was still no let-up on commercial fishing and with nothing more than hit-and-miss husbandry, our advisers assumed that everything would be all right and that salmon could take the increased plunder without placing the species at jeopardy.

By the mid-'sixties, and as previously explained in earlier chapters, there was some heavy clouds on the horizon. By the autumn of 1966, many of our rivers were suffering the scourge of U.D.N. and reports from Greenland indicated that mankind had, at long last, found one of the sea-going destinations of salmon and was indiscriminately scooping up increased tonnages by commercial fishing. As far as the disease was concerned there was very little which could be done – despite honest attempts by biologists to isolate and contain it. We may all have moaned about the apparent lack of activity on this score, but we had little

more than a *fait accompli*. On the question of high seas netting for
salmon, however, there were many anglers who again dipped their
pens in the acid. But little was done by those in authority and it
was amazingly accepted by many of them that the poor salmon
could continue to suffer the vast inroads on their species without
stocks suffering too much. No attempt was made to put our own
house in order, and commercial netting at home continued as
before. It took a U.S. President to successfully bring about an
ultimate ban on high seas fishing for salmon by the Danes and
others in the north-west Atlantic, but this will not be fully effective
until 1976. Additionally, the Danes have refused to accept a
similar ban on high seas fishing in the north-east Atlantic so we
may well expect some more of their skulduggery and mayhem in
that area.

At the time of writing, Britain is the one remaining salmon-
producing country not to have lifted a finger to curtail commercial fishing or impose limitations on angling methods. Where
authority is challenged, back comes the stock reply, 'The Depart-
ment, which is in close touch with river authorities, is satisfied
that the level of salmon stocks in England and Wales gives no
cause for concern from the point of view of conservation.' One is
forced to wonder how this conclusion is drawn, for if reports from
anglers have any semblance of truth it would appear that there
are some strong differences of opinion. Many rivers which produced good rod catches a few years ago are now showing
fractional returns, but the returns from commercial fishing activities seem to be maintained. When, however, it is suggested that
commercial fishing be curtailed to benefit the sporting angler,
not to mention the breeding stock of salmon in a river, we are
told that excessive stocks in the river are not desirable. The
pundits tell us that this would only result in over-cutting of the
redds; that it would bring an increased risk of disease, and that
the progeny of an increased spawning stock would be hard-put
to find adequate rations during the two years of their infant river
life. There may well be some truth in any or all of these statements, but in those countries where commercial fishing has been

severely curtailed the sport resource has increased beyond wildest expectations. Iceland and Eastern Canada are the classic examples.

At this moment in time there is but one organisation with the sole aim to protect the interests of the salmon angler and the riparian owner. It is the Scottish Salmon Angling Federation, but sadly this caters only for Scotland and those of us in the rest of Britain, who may regard the level of commercial fishing to be too high, have no platform for our grievances. As an example of what I mean I will quote from the Association of River Authorities Year Book for 1973. From pages 256 and 257, of this report on catches in 1971, we can extract the following figures. Rod licences for migratory fish issued that year totalled 79,687 to bring a revenue of £124,089, and the number of salmon caught on rod-and-line, in all these areas, totalled 19,639. By my simple arithmetic this means that an average licence fee of £6.30 has been paid by the angler for every salmon caught. On the commercial side we see that 1,167 netting licences were issued for a total revenue of £14,063. The gross commercial catch, however, is declared at 89,905 salmon. The average cost of these fish, therefore, in licence dues is only 15p each. Bear in mind that the figures involved only refer to licence dues. Anglers would also be called upon to pay substantial rents or subscriptions – not to mention rates – some of which would be returned to the Government or local authority as taxes.

It is easily seen from the above figures that the anglers are getting a raw deal. Most of us would readily admit that angling is not the most effective way of catching fish and that if a crop has to be taken then netting is the obvious method. But which of these two methods brings the most benefit to the total economy of the country? I submit that it is not commercial fishing, and that every effort should now be made to enlarge the sporting resource. It is one thing to angle unsuccesfully in a river known to be full of fish, but quite another to cast in desperation over pools where there is barely a fin to be seen. When this happens, as it did to me on the Lune in 1973, and we are told that the netsmen in the estuary had bonanza catches, I feel entitled to get a little indignant. If there were too few fish for me to try and catch there were too few fish left to fulfil their prime task on the spawning grounds.

As a prime example of over-commercial exploitation we need look no further than the figures for the Northumberland River Authority area. These show that in 1971, 4,264 salmon rod licences were issued for a total revenue of £7,488. The number of salmon caught by these rods came to 440. Yet in the same area 325 netting licences were granted for a revenue of £3,573 and the declared total net catch came to 54,201 salmon! In this area, therefore, the anglers paid an average licence fee of £17 per salmon – not to mention all the other costs outlined before.

I have before me, as I write, a copy of a cutting from the Devon *Sunday Independent* dated August 5, 1973. Reporting on the salmon situation there, Brigadier Bertram Cripps says, 'Last year the fifty members of the local association caught only 40 salmon compared with 1,267 taken by ten netsmen at Shaldon.' The report goes on to say that anglers on the lower stretches of the Teign are horrified at the number of salmon netted compared with those caught by rods. They claim that the ratio is sometimes as high as 40-to-1 and that, despite pleas to the river authority over the past twenty years, nothing has been done to ensure a more equitable distribution of the resource.

In these days, therefore, when the great cry is for more leisure facilities, how can such a level of commercial netting be justified? For how long must the angler and the conservationist suffer these netsmen – mostly part-timers – and for how long will the angler subsidise the bulk of the operation. I have no wish to see anyone genuinely out-of-work, but commercial licences could be slowly withdrawn as present holders die or retire. Is there not anyone in authority with sense enough to see where our priorities lie?

# 28
## Casting Hints and Tips

---

SUGGEST to an angler that he might be fishing with the wrong fly or bait and he will gladly accept your advice. Tell him, however, that his casting and presentation are bad and you will have made a mortal enemy for life. In so many instances it is bad casting, and therefore bad presentation, that causes failure; so that some discussion on these topics may not come amiss.

I do not propose to go into casting techniques at any great length. Several books have been written on this topic; and practically every book on salmon fishing gives 'chapter and verse', with detailed diagrams, on how to execute various casts. I have never yet been able to learn the first thing about casting techniques from a book; but for those who wish to try, I can only recommend two books worthy of note: *The Anglers Cast,* by Captain T. L. Edwards and Eric Horsfall Turner; and *Casting,* by Captain Terry Thomas. In both instances the authors have tried to reduce the detailed techniques into print. Whether they have failed or succeeded is not for me to say. The attempts were sincere and carefully executed; and all three of these men were first-rate anglers, and top performers with any type of game-fishing tackle.

My own shortcomings in casting were dramatically highlighted, in 1959, by the methods of which only the late Tommy Edwards was capable. I had gone up to Grantown on Spey to act as photographer for Tommy and Eric, before the publication of their book. Tommy was in charge of the angling courses, run in conjunction between the Scottish Council of Physical Recreation and the Palace Hotel; and at the end of my photographic session, I thought it an opportune moment to seek Tommy's opinion on my casting techniques. At the end of an hour I was left in no doubt that, in the nicest way Tommy could put it, I was well below full potential. I learnt a lot that first year; and was surprised and delighted when, the following year, I was invited to attend the Grantown courses as one of Tommy's assistants. From that time on it was to be an annual event; and over the years, until his death in 1968, I was not only to learn how to improve my own casting techniques, but to learn the intricacies of passing on that knowledge to other people. Following his death it was a great honour for me to be asked to take his place as chief instructor at Grantown. Even now I continue to learn, since all my assistants are very competent casters and anglers; and in quieter moments we pick each others' brains, and discuss techniques.

For those novices or experienced anglers keen to polish up their techniques, the courses at Grantown (details from the Palace Hotel at Grantown on Spey) represent remarkable value for money. There is a seven-mile stretch of the Spey to fish and those wishing to have instruction have a wide talent from which to choose. Among the instructors there are such well-known names as Jack Martin, the ex-British amateur casting champion over several years, and finally the all-round amateur/professional champion. He has recently become a professional instructor. There is local tackle dealer and Spey expert, George Mortimer, who is a very competent instructor and talented Spey-caster. Dr Alastair Perry from Wales also lends a hand. His British record cast of 63-metres with the salmon-fly rod, achieved in the 1969 British Casting Championships, gives some indication of his prowess.

Apart from the fancy casts like the Spey, Roll and Double-Spey the basic fly-casting action is fairly straightforward. Most novices quickly learn the primary techniques; and at

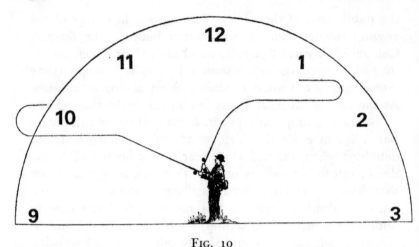

FIG. 10

The main arc of power with the fly rod

the end of a week are certainly sufficiently competent to be
let loose on a river. Troubles arise when contrary winds make
conditions difficult; or, after they have perfected their techniques when standing on a river bank or platform, they
attempt the same performance when immersed up to their
armpits in breast waders. Like everything else in sport, it is
all a question of timing; and it so frequently happens that the
timing of the power has to be varied slightly, depending upon
the angler's height above the water level. Every good forward-
cast must commence with a good back cast. A common fault
with salmon-fly fishermen, using a double-handed rod, is for
the backward cast to be commenced too late. The rod point
should be well down below the horizontal, if water levels permit; and the backward cast should be so made as to drive the
line and fly, in a tight loop, over the angler's head, and up
into the air at a position on our dial of 2 o'clock.

Attempts to raise the rod point before commencing the
backward cast must be checked, since there is a grave danger
of bringing the rod too far back, and thus driving the fly into
the ground behind. Even if such a backward cast is successful,
there will be every likelihood that the forward power stroke

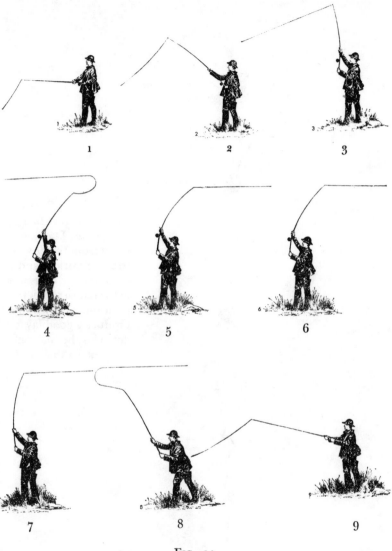

FIG. 11

The sequence of the good overhead cast. The lift is commenced at
1 and carried on to 3. A slight drift and pause is permitted
between 4 and 5. Then the return power should be applied
between 6, 7 and 8, bringing the rod down to 9 as the cast
straightens out

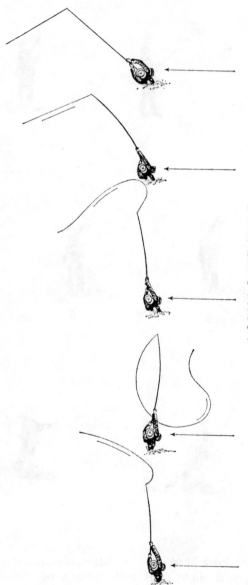

FIG. 12

Circling is very bad
technique. The line is
lifted from the down-
stream position, and
becomes circled as it is
delivered to the new
position. This will not
produce a good lay
down on the line, and
will restrict distance

will come too early. The line will then extend well above the water level and be subjected to any contrary winds before it comes into contact with the water surface. Such a cast may well be used when shooting a lot of line; but for normal casting it must be considered bad practice. Another common fault which will take the power out of the cast, and restrict potential distance, is circling.

This means in effect that the angler has lifted his fly from a downstream position and then the line makes a circling motion as it is delivered to its new position across the current. Invariably the line does not extend straight out; and if there is any element of downstream wind, the line lands with a very pronounced downstream belly. We have already discussed the great undesirability of this in our chapters on tactics; and if this downstream belly can be half-eliminated before the cast is completed, it only leaves a slight 'mend' to be thrown into the line in order to make the fly itself move correctly in the water in the early stages after delivery. On streamy water, of course, it is quite feasible to make an initial circling cast; then to lift the line once again to ensure a tight loop over the rod tip, and a straight backward lift. This leads to a good and straight delivery of the final forward cast. On some gliding water, of course, such a double manipulation may well frighten the fish. Elimination of this circling can be avoided if, before the angler lifts the line into his initial back cast, he points his rod in the direction the new cast is to go. It is sometimes troublesome in excessive wind conditions; but is normally the correct style. Many anglers try to aerialize too much line. It is far better to have full control of a comparatively short lifted length of line, then to release some hand-held backing as the forward cast extends fully.

Basic casting faults with a salmon-fly rod, to sum up, generally involve: (1) Commencing the backward cast with the rod above the horizontal or at too high an angle to get the best lift. The backward cast does not discharge the line firmly, to stay high in the air; and as the backward power stroke reaches its ultimate extreme, instead of being extended straight

FIG. 13

In the normal cast the rod should have a pendulum action near the body

Any form of pushing and leaning in the final fore-cast only kills the spring of the rod and reduces distance

behind, the line tends to be coiled to some extent. The effect is a clumsy bundle forward of the line, so to speak. The initial requirements of the good cast are that the line must go straight back with a tight loop and without appreciable coil; and must then be driven forward in complete straightness until it turns over the rod tip. (2) Imparting a circling motion to the line, instead of keeping the backward and forward casts in exactly the same plane, with a tight loop over the tip of the rod. (3) Pushing the rod forward violently, with lack of complete smooth movement throughout. This does nothing whatever to extend the distance of the cast; and only serves to kill the power of the rod flex. It is the smooth, springing, pendulum action of the rod which gives the power; and any excessive drive only serves to cause a jerky and ineffective spring in the rod.

I find it virtually impossible to put down in print just what a good cast should look like; and for those novices keen to learn, I suggest that they seek out one of the top professional casting instructors. At the expense of a pound or two, they will see at first-hand what they themselves can achieve with thorough practice. I am still amazed how an angler will spend a small fortune in hiring a beat on a classic river, and yet make no effort to ensure that his casting techniques are as near perfect as he can make them. Without a shadow of doubt, the main cause of angling failure, under ideal fishing conditions, is due to indifferent technique. The general casting standard in Britain is abysmally low; and this alone can well account for indifferent fish-catching results. There is no magic requirement for good casting. It is, basically, a mathematical operation; and, once mastered, is capable of adaptation to cover all contingencies. It was the lack of good professional instruction which first prompted the formation of the Association of Professional Game Angling Instructors in 1969. The conception was good, but the birth of the Association was a little painful! We were not without our critics! The founding of the Association was, however, a sincere attempt to raise the standards of game fishing generally; and the passage of time will show its ultimate value. Few golfers have reached any great standard of perfection without having had, at some time in their career, a few lessons from the club professional. We live in the age of professionalism in sport of all types; but there is still an element of taboo in the angling world against the professionals. It is the wide contention that angling is a solitary, contemplative sport, and, as such, should not be tarnished with anything that savours of professionalism. With the greater modern demands for fishing, and the fact that there are more participants in this sport than in any other, I should have thought it high time that standards were improved – even if only for the benefit of those who fish behind the clumsy angler!

Casting techniques with spinning tackle, while not so painful to watch as bad fly-casting styles, are still pretty bad when general performance is examined. The modern casting reel, be it fixed-spool or multiplier, is comparatively easy to use. With power applied at the right moment, the bait will invariably land at a reasonable point on the water. Here again,

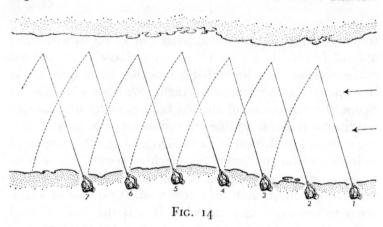

FIG. 14

precise timing is all important; and it is the power of the
rod, and not that awkward push, which transmits itself into
the weight of the bait to send it hurtling out over the water.
As with fly-fishing, many anglers want to push at the final
cast. They should practise into realization that this very act
kills correct rod action, and drastically reduces potential
distance. With a little practice, the spinner should be made
to land in a precise area of water; and subsequent casts should
be so controlled that the bait travels the same distance, and
in the same direction, as achieved by earlier casts. (See Fig. 14.)

Good casting is not an art. It is purely a craft that can be
quickly learned by any able-bodied person. There is no magic
in it; but the reasonable standards must be learned and can
only be reached by developing a thorough understanding of
what is happening – and why. An hour with a competent
professional instructor will do more for the indifferent performer than reading a hundred thousand words in print!

# 29

## Thoughts on Wading, Playing, Gaffing and Tailing

---

THERE can be no doubt that in order to fish at full potential there are many rivers where breast waders are essential, particularly if fly-fishing is the angler's main choice. There are, of course, many big rivers where the use of a boat becomes necessary; and there are also quite a lot of rivers where wading or the use of a boat are not desirable tactics.

Some anglers have a thing about deep wading. It is perfectly true that such wading in heavy water is not without its moments of tension – or even danger. The use of a wading stick may well be a great help; but care must be taken to ensure that its use does not lead the angler into parts of the river where he should not be. Most of my moments of tension have come when I relied upon a wading stick to get me out to an awkward place. I then stumbled and faltered, and had the added curse of my shooting-line fouling around the stick. Nowadays, I rarely use a wading stick and definitely prefer to go quietly on my way down a pool, making sure that each step takes a firm foothold before transferring the weight. I rarely get into serious difficulty, but like all anglers, I have had the occasional ducking. The most notable occurred when I was deep wading in the River Tengs in Norway. Suddenly I ran out of river bed and a cameraman was on hand to take a picture. I must confess to a feeling of near panic; but I quickly got control of myself and let the current swing me on to a shelf of gravel. Some writers argue that waders should not be too tight around the waist. I don't think that it matters very much. If the angler is deep wading, all the air is expelled from the waders by water pressure; and it seems to me merely a question of keeping one's head above water, and letting the current carry one down. All the time, of course, one should make slight arm movements to edge closer towards the bank.

Like everything else in fishing, confidence in wading is only achieved by doing it constantly. When my wife first took up salmon fishing she was like a nervous kitten. Nowadays, however, she will think little of wading across our Lune water on her own; and although she uses a wading stick on rivers like the Spey, she is not frightened of getting in deep. Greatest care in wading must be taken when the angler is working his way down a shelving run of gravel, with deep water on either side. It may well be easy enough to wade down; but when the time comes to get out, it will be sheer hard work to walk back and upstream against the current. There will also be the hazard of shifting gravel, and a few unpleasant moments may occur. I well recall one instance when I was fishing in the company of a friend on the river Spey. We went our separate ways. Some two hours later he appeared on the opposite bank. 'How did you get across?' I shouted. 'I waded across,' said he, with, unknown to me, a broad grin on his face. Walking downstream, I found the place where I *presumed* he had waded across. I started to cross and eventually made it; but not before I had seen all my sins flash before me a thousand times. I should not have gone back across there, at that height of water, for all the money in the world. Upon reaching my friend, it was only to learn that he had been pulling my leg. He had, in fact, walked down to a bridge and crossed that way.

While deep-wading can be well nigh essential in order to fish some pools correctly, there may well be a danger of wading so deep that the angler disturbs the salmon in their lies. For this reason alone it is very important to know your river, and eventually you will find a route down the water which brings best water-coverage – and wading without tears! Care must also be taken when wading in rivers subject to rapid rises of water. I have known occasions when there has been barely time to get out before the flood hits. It can be pretty frightening.

Over on my section of the Lune, it is customary to wade across the river before commencing fishing. The river fishes best from the opposite bank from that on which the car is easily parked; and it is only a very high water which makes it impossible to wade across. I well recall one instance when I had waded across to do some night sea-trout fishing. In the space of an hour the river rose quite rapidly, but in the darkness I failed to observe it until it was too late. I had a long walk that night! Moreover, I trod upon many a sleeping cow until I finally stumbled into a small village. Once there, a kindly soul was just leaving the village pub at 1 a.m. He gave me a lift round by the nearest bridge and back to my car.

Wading, therefore, is not without its hazards; but it must be resorted to on occasions in order to be in with a chance of a fish. There are, of course, many rivers which do not lend themselves to wading, since any form of wading would only frighten the fish, and do little or nothing to extend the useful casting range. Wade only when compelled to do so by the conditions; and use a little forethought before committing yourself to the water!

The playing of a fish sometimes poses problems for novices. The fact is that there can be no hard and fast rule in salmon fishing. A freshly-hooked fish has a few definite ideas of his own; and it may take some time before the angler is the complete master of the situation.

No matter by which method you have hooked a fish, the fish is a long way from being safely on the bank; and many a hard-earned fish has been lost through careless handling. In the first few seconds, following firm hooking, you may quite casually put your rod over your shoulder and wade or walk to the nearest vantage point to play your fish. Make sure

G

that the reel runs freely if the fish wants to take line; and take care not to let any slack line offer a chance of his gaining his freedom. You should aim to get slightly downstream of the fish, so that he is not only fighting against your tackle but against the current as well. Attempts to hang on while the fish flounders downstream should be discouraged. In this movement he can lean on your tackle, so to speak, and thus get assistance to swim against the current. Don't be in too great a hurry to hustle him out of the deep and fast water. It is in this part of the river that most of the steam is taken out of him. Many fish are lost through over-anxiousness; and the time spent in keeping a steady strain on the fish, whilst he fights the current, is well spent. A minute of play to each pound weight is a rough guide to the time it should take you to play out your salmon; but bear in mind that in the early stages the fish has not seen you, nor has it felt in any real danger. It is only during the final moments of play, when seeing the moving angler makes him realize his danger, that he will make some desperate bid for freedom. If you intend to gaff your fish, wait until he is lying quietly on his side before striking the gaff home. If, on the other hand, there is a shelving gravel beach handy, you may draw him to the side, get hold of him firmly by the tail and slide him up the beach. This method of handling, however, is not safe unless you are absolutely certain that he is played out. Any form of over-anxiety at this stage may well send you home with the tale of a big one – that got away! This brings me to the general question of landing salmon; and during March 1969 I wrote the following article for *The Shooting Times*.

Remarkably few salmon fishermen venture very far these days without the comforting feel of a gaff beside them. Indeed, there are many who would feel an air of nakedness without such a weapon on hand. There are, of course, a few occasions when the use of a gaff can save an otherwise embarrassing situation. But, in my opinion, it is used much too widely; and for many occasions when it would be perfectly simple to beach or tail the fish out by hand.

In my early days of salmon fishing, of course, the gaff was always by my side; and in the great excitement and anxiety to have the fish ashore it was inevitably stabbed into the fish's vitals at the very first opportunity. 'Let's get the fish out at all costs,' was the simple creed of those early days. My reasoning was not hard to comprehend. I had spent a long time fishing. Every salmon hooked was like a piece of elusive jade, to be snatched from its environment by the quickest means known and available. I think, for this reason, that the novice is to be excused for his reliance on the gaff; but it might pay to ponder on the inevitable feeling of anxiety which the possession of a gaff automatically bestows upon the angler who continually relies on one.

I should think that, in nine cases out of ten, the angler who is unaccompanied by a gillie invariably attempts to gaff his fish before it is fully played out. He looks round and there is no one on hand to help. With great trepidation, he makes ready with his gaff; and, as sure as fate, will have an early stab as the fish swims past on one of its final passes before being fully played out. With a bit of luck he may well get the gaff home and come lunging ashore with his prize. The fish will doubtless be dripping blood and stabbed through the vitals, wherever fate planned the gaff should strike. With normal luck he may well miss the first time – and even the second and third. By now he is getting anxious, and in danger of completely losing any of the sound reasoning that led to the successful playing of the fish in the first place. He desperately wants it out; and it is at this stage that he is quite likely to do something so irrational that, in a fraction of a second, fish and line part company. The doleful angler is then left with memories of a big one that got away! Rarely would the angler dream of blaming himself; and the size of the fish and its immense strength, gradually grow in proportion to the number of times the story of its loss is related to friends! It has happened to me; and I have witnessed it happen to others, who were completely rational human beings. They appeared to be driven from the rational to panic when they saw the fish, just beyond or just within their grasp – so near or yet so far! If only they had forgotten the gaff and had tried to steer the fish during play to some convenient place where they could have beached it conveniently when it was completely played out! If, at the eleventh hour, no such place emerged, and the fish was lying on its side, it would be a simple matter to lower the gaff and place it into the gills of the fish so that it would do the least damage, and would not cause unsightly effect. There are, however, occasions when the use of a gaff is both sensible and desirable but there are also many more occasions when its use is not at all necessary.

For the bulk of my normal salmon fishing I rarely carry a gaff when I fish regularly on a piece of water with shelving pebble banks, where it is a simple matter to wait until the fish is played out; and either push him, head-first, up the gravel or (if a small fish) lift him out by the tail. It is quite remarkable how the fish, even a big one, will respond to being pushed up the bank head-first, when there might be a chance of losing him if he were picked up by the tail. Fish are frequently inclined to kick when picked up by the tail; and it sometimes requires a firm grip to prevent them slipping out of the hand and falling back into the water. I have used the beaching technique many times with fish up to 25-lb, and have tailed several up to 20-lb without great difficulty.

Before the beaching or tailing techniques become acceptable to the angler, however, there has to be a basic change of philosophy. No longer must the successful killing of the fish be the sole objective. There must be a personal reappraisal of what really matters in a day's sport with the salmon. Is the killing of the greatest number of fish still the prime objective? Or is the maximum pleasure of the sport derived from hooking and playing the fish? When the angler comes into the second category, he may well have to pay for his experience by the loss of a few fish; and it would indeed be sad if a lost fish happened to be one of the really big ones.

In the spring of 1967 I firmly resolved to fish throughout the season without a gaff. In terms of fish actually caught, it cost me something. It was a season during which, for me, fish were hard to come by. I lost the first three by stupid tactical errors on my part. On the first occasion, I tried to beach the fish on a part of the river covered with chain-link gabions. One of the hooks on the triangle was showing outside the mouth of the fish, and quickly caught in the chain-link. The fish un-hooked itself quickly and was back into the water like a flash. Similarly stupid tactics caused the loss of the other two; and I almost went back on my resolve! A few days later, however, I had my tenacity of purpose rewarded when I beached a lovely fish of 22-lb I had taken on a small fly. I did not use the gaff again that year; and have not, personally, carried a gaff since.

This does not mean that I shall never carry a gaff again. There are certain waters I fish where the possibility of beaching or tailing fish is either difficult, or well-nigh impossible. These rivers have high banks which drop steeply into deep water; and where trees or other obstructions prevent the angler from moving upstream or downstream, to more suitable places. Under such conditions, I would have no hesitation in taking a gaff; and on certain wild rivers of Norway have been very glad to have one handy. The alternative on such occasions for lack of a gaff would be to break the tackle and let the fish go free! There would be no way of getting it out of the river.

An amusing incident comes to mind. I was fishing with a friend who decried the use of a gaff on *every* occasion. The river was carrying extra water, and was coming down like thick coffee. For some obscure reason, I was attempting to fish while my friend stood close by. We were both up to our knees in water when, in a startled voice, my friend whispered, 'Look at this.' Glancing down towards his feet I saw the broad expanse of a salmon's tail. The fish had literally come and laid over his feet as it paused in its upstream migration. 'Now's the chance to show me your tailing technique!' I jokingly said to my friend; whereupon he quietly lowered his hand and made a sudden grab around the tail of the fish. There was a violent cascade of spray. The fish came half out of the water – and then 12-lb of untamed fury was let loose. The end was inevitable. Within split seconds it was back in the river, as though the Devil himself were after it; and quickly tore across the surface and into deep water. My chum was soaked; but complained, with a huge grin, that he did not consider that a fair test! Fair enough!

Shortly after publication of this article on landing salmon, I received a letter in the following vein.

Dear Sir,
Further to your article on gaffing. Tailing with one's hand is most effective and very easy. However, I was surprised to see a photo showing you holding the salmon the wrong way. When tailing salmon with your hand, always have your thumb and

forefinger towards the tail. With your little finger towards the
tail, as in the picture, your fish is much more likely to slip through
your hands. With large fish, or when my hands are cold, I always
put a wet handkerchief in my hand before tailing the fish, as this
greatly increases 'grip' and reduces 'slip'. Never try this method
with sea-trout, as they have no 'bone' in their tails and slip
through one's hand.

Yours faithfully,

T.T.

My subsequent commentary was as follows: I was not aware
that anyone established a right and wrong way of tailing
salmon; just as there is, as yet, no stipulated method for pick-
ing up a pint of beer. One does it in certain ways out of
habit, or for most comfort and effectiveness. I have read very
contradicting reports on this question of tailing; and I came
to the conclusion, many years ago, that it did not matter. I
have tailed fish by both methods. I have seen very many
experienced salmon anglers also tail their fish out by both
methods; some have a preference for T.T.'s way, others for
mine. It is not a method about which I would like to pontifi-
cate. T.T. is certainly clear on the question of sea-trout,
although I have known occasions when my method worked
successfully *for me*. There are times, with really big salmon,
when it pays to beach them. This can easily be done by pushing the fish, head first, up the bank. The rod is pointed in
the direction you want the fish to go, and then the fish is
pushed up by the tail. Under these circumstances I think
that my grip would be the more effective and comfortable.

On the question of sea-trout: I was always under the impression that these fish were anatomically the same as salmon,
except that they are much thicker around the 'wrist' of the
tail and therefore slip out of one's hand much more readily.
One of the old rules of fish recognition (between salmon and
sea-trout) for those who could not readily tell the difference,
was to pick the fish up by the tail to see if it slipped. If it
stayed, then it was a salmon; and if it slipped out of one's
grip, it was presumed to be a sea-trout. Like many rules, it
was not infallible; but it was a good guide.

I have since been at great pains to pick the brains of as many experienced salmon anglers as I could. At the Knock-ando salmon hatchery on the River Spey I was shown a selection of colour slides of salmon being trapped for arti-ficial spawning; and noted carefully that all the fish handled by the bailiffs were tailed after my own fashion. An angling film show recently revealed the fact that well-known angler Hugh Falkus also tails his fish the same way as myself; but that American expert, Lee Wulff, tails them out after the fashion of T.T. My vast library of angling photographs has depicted many anglers tailing out salmon. I can only find one which shows fish being tailed in any other style than my own.

In order to test the matter further I put the question to a doctor, who readily agreed on the adaptability of the human hand; but after some thought felt that my way should pro-duce the better grip. I must confess that I am still left wonder-ing, and would certainly never be so bold as to say, whether there is a right and wrong way of doing the job. I think that every angler must find the best way to suit himself, dependent upon the size of his hand and the strength of his grip.

## 30
## Gillies and Boatmen

ACCORDING to my dictionary a 'gillie' is an attendant on a highland chief; a servant who carries the chief across streams, or one who attends sportsmen in the Scottish Highlands. In general usage the term 'gillie' has come to mean a guide or servant in the specialized sense of salmon fishing; and the one writer who commented, 'they are a dour lot!' was not far from the truth!

Gillies come in several shapes and sizes, and have varying degrees of affluence (I well recall one who had a chauffeur-driven Daimler). Some are part-timers, with limited knowledge of their beat of the river. Others know literally every stone, and every conceivable lie, under every condition or height of water. The good ones are like rare jade; but the bad ones can well spoil an otherwise enjoyable outing.

In general, however, I must confess that I think that gillies are a dour lot. It does not need great powers of reflection to find the causes for such dourness. The man who turns to gillieing as a means of livelihood is usually a native of the area; he knows the river intimately and knows the perfect conditions and seasons when the best sport is likely to be had. Small wonder that the edge is taken off some of his enthusiasm when he has an indifferent angler fishing a period of the season which is not likely to produce very good sport. Whilst I have often felt it a strain to have a bad gillie, it must be infuriating for a good gillie to be burdened with a bad angler.

A gillie is only important to me during the period I am fishing a new water. If he is up to his job, he will tell me the best lies, and can give facts about the water which, fishing alone, I should take years to find out for myself. I well recall being eternally grateful to David Cook on the little Yorkshire Esk. He taught me more about the river in a year than I could have learned in ten years by myself. Nowadays, however, I rarely need the services of a gillie to land a fish, and I am still sufficiently agile to carry my own tackle. Moreover, there are times when I positively dislike the presence of a gillie, particularly if I sense some form of resentment at the way I am doing things.

Gillies' habits differ greatly from one river to another. Many of the gillies on the Scottish Dee refuse to wear waders. The head gillie of one famous beat was very indignant when I refused to let him gaff a 20-lb fish I was bringing in, because it was obvious that unless he could wade away from the shallows it would take me ages to play the fish out so that he could gaff it dry-shod. 'Give me the gaff.' I said, 'and I'll gaff it.' 'What am I here for then?' was his quick retort. 'I don't know,' I replied; 'unless you clothe yourself adequately to gaff my fish, I would rather do it myself.' He handed the gaff over and I duly brought the fish ashore; he was a bit sullen for the rest of the day, but I respected his knowledge of the water, and a more friendly relationship was established during the rest of the week.

There must be a subtle difference between gillies and boatmen. When fishing a river like the Tweed, a good boatman is fairly essential for success on the lower reaches of that river. As with gillies, there are good boatmen and bad ones; but most have a long experience on the water, and their enthusiasm waxes and wanes with the experience of their angler and the chances of sport. Watt Lauder, my own regular Tweed boatman, is a good barometer to the sport to be expected. If I arrive all full of enthusiasm and he appears lazy and indolent, I know that chances of sport are not very good. If, however, he is raring to go and hustling me to get ready, it is a pretty safe bet that we shall have a few fish that day.

I know of few gillies who do not have a taste for whisky. One of my acquaintance, on a West Highland river, could down a bottle without batting an eye! The only noticeable difference at the end of the day was that his Spey-casting became a bit tatty. On one occasion everything looked to be going smoothly until the fly circled over his head and removed his hat! Suddenly he was base-over-apex in some swirling water. He was quickly ashore, however – where another dram soon put him right!

The great feature about Norwegian gillies is their youth. Many hamlets have their younger generation away at schools; but the short fishing season of the country almost coincides with school or college vacation times, and the young men are back at home with time on their hands. Small wonder that they use the period to earn some extra money and, with their agility and nimbleness, they make excellent assistants on those violent waters. It seems a point of honour for all Norwegian gillies to gaff the fish in the head. The market value of fish gaffed through the body is lower than that of the fish gaffed in the head, and it is only when a really big fish has to be taken from dangerous water that these gillies will forsake their commercial principles.

If not all gillies are perfect, neither are the anglers who fish with them. A good angler will listen to the advice of a gillie, and will weigh that advice against his own experience. Although I have a wide experience in salmon fishing, I always make a point of consulting the gillie or boatman. 'You know this water better than I do,' I say: 'what tactics would you adopt?' Usually the advice is worth hearing; and after a few years on a portion of a river, the angler and the gillie will have built up a mutual respect for each other. It is important, I think, to let your gillie know, at the outset, just what you expect from him. On a river like the Dee, for instance, all

I could ask of my gillie is that he position himself, unseen, so that he can peer into the clear water and give me information about any response to my fly. I do not yet require a burden-bearer, and have sufficient experience of gaffing and tailing my own fish to look after this job myself. A good gillie on a strange water, however, is still a gem; and to get the best from him he should be treated with respect, courtesy, and as a fellow sportsman.

# 31
## Tackle Tips

---

THROUGHOUT the preceding chapters we have touched upon the various types of tackle which the all-round salmon angler may well require to see him through a season. There are few ways to short-circuit the vast amount of tackle required if the angler wishes to be at full potential. We have seen the desirability of at least three rods for differing types of fly-fishing, and a similar number for every aspect of spinning. Such a comprehensive outfit is not entirely necessary, however; and if I had to limit myself to two only, I think that I should go for a medium-weight 14-ft fly-rod, and a 9-ft double-handed spinning rod. A lot would depend upon where I was to do the bulk of my fishing; but to cope with Tweed in early spring or late autumn I should require something a little more substantial than the normal 12½-ft Hardy 'Hollolight' I use for greased-line fishing. The heavy rod I now use on Tweed in spring, again, would be far too cumbersome to cope with the latter method. A good compromise may well be found in the 14-ft Hardy 'Jet' or the 14-ft 'Expert', now being marketed by Bruce and Walker. I have, of course, a few treasured Hardy cane rods; I should be loath to part with my 14-ft 'LRH', or my 13½-ft 'Wye'; not to mention the 12½-ft 'Hollolight' on which I have taken the bulk of my fly-caught salmon. There is no doubt that the latest types of fibre-glass rods now coming into the market have a decided advantage in the question of weight. I am not yet fully convinced that the lighter ones will lift a heavy sunk-line as efficiently as a good split-cane rod; but the latter are very expensive, and in the longer versions do become a bit of a weight at the end of a tedious day's fishing. I tend to retain my opinion, however, that, despite the weight, a good cane rod is the best for fly-fishing. But I have no doubts that the day is not too far distant when the cane rod will be a thing of the past, much as greenheart rod disappearance showed itself to the 'Spey-cast' enthusiasts as cane rods gradually became the only available type they could obtain. I think that I am now too old to be wooed completely over to glass. I have become accustomed to the action of cane, but have retained a sufficiently open mind to see the merits of glass. I do, in fact, have many glass fly-rods and have no qualms about using this material for spinning rods. The trouble with a lot of glass rods is their tendency to excessive tip action; and I have no use whatever for fly-rods with this action. The rod should have action through to the butt; and I have only found this quality in the glass rods I have named.

There are, as well, very few glass rods which will do an effective form of Spey or roll cast. It used to be argued that even cane was not the ideal material for Spey casting; and there are still quite a few die-hards who cling to their long greenheart poles. Until quite recently it was true that continued Spey casting would damage a good ferruled-cane rod. The continual twisting action could soon dislodge the wood from the male ferrule – mine usually went in the middle section – and many of my rods had to have attention from Hardy's at the end of a week's hard Spey casting. Recently, however, they seem to have overcome this problem. I suspect that the heavy gauge wire now used to bind the ferrules has something to do with the improvement.

Quite apart from choosing the right fly-rod for your purpose, it is very important to match the rod with a suitable line. Most modern fly-rods have the Association of Fishing Tackle Makers (AFTM) number engraved near the rod handle; and this is the number of the line best suited to the rod. In order to work at its ultimate, a rod is designed to

carry a certain *weight* of line. This weight is computed from
the ideal length which may be aerialized to get best rod
action. I find that many of the course students who come to
Grantown-on-Spey have lines which are either too light, or
too heavy, for their rods; and in order to get the best from a
rod it should have a perfect marriage with the line. The list
below will give some indication of the lines available for
selecting the best suited to rod action.

| AFTM Number | AIR-CEL | | | | | | KINGFISHER | | |
|---|---|---|---|---|---|---|---|---|---|
| | Double Taper | Forward Taper | Level | D/T | F/T | Level | D/T | Balanced Taper | Level |
| 3 | HEH | | F | | | | 1 | | 1 |
| 4 | HEH | | E | | | | | | |
| 5 | HDH | HDG | D | | | | 2 | | 2 |
| 6 | HCH | HCF | C | HEH | | E | 3 | 2 | 3 |
| 7 | GBG | GBF | B | HDH | HDG | D | 4 | 3 | 4 |
| 8 | GAG | GAF | A | HCH | HCF | C | 5 | 4/30 | 5 |
| 9 | G2AG | G2AF | | GBG | GBF | B | | 4/40 | 6 |
| 10 | G3AG | G3AF | | GAG | GAF | | 6 | 5 | 7 |
| 11 | | | | G2AG | | | | | |
| 12 | | | | G3AG | | | 7 | | |

   Current descriptions of fly lines have been much simplified.
For instance, a Double-Taper floating AirCel line, in size
GAG would now be labelled DT-8-F; and a Forward-Taper
line in the same size would thus be termed WF-8-F. The
initial lettering indicates whether the line is of Double taper
or Weight Forward. The number corresponds with the
AFTM number and the F or S indicates whether the line
floats or sinks. The code number of a WetCel line, therefore,
always terminates with the letter S.
   The choice of line size, therefore, is largely dictated by the
rod you wish to use. Whether you go for sinkers or floaters,
double-taper or forward-taper is again largely a matter of
where, and how, you are going to fish. The 'Kingfisher' silk
lines still have great merit. They can be greased to float, or
rubbed down with Fuller's Earth paste to make them sink.

These lines tend to be less bulky, weight for weight, than the
floating lines; but it is sometimes a little tedious to be continually greasing them throughout the day's greased-line fishing; and invariably some grease gets on the leader, and may
well cause the fly to skate. They are, however, extremely nice
lines to fish with.

Of the fully floating and sinking lines, the 'Air-Cel' and the
'Wet-Cel' are the most popular makes imported into Britain.
There are, of course, several other makes; but, like the 'Air-
Cel' and 'Wet-Cel', they are generally imported from
America. One of my favourites is a line made by the Cortland
company, which was presented to me when I lectured in Pitts-
burgh in 1967.

If we rule out the silk lines there is, as we have seen in all
our chapters on fly-fishing, a great need to have both floaters
and sinkers on hand to cope with the changing conditions
throughout a fly-fishing season. It is not really possible to
make a floating line sink effectively, nor to make a sinking
line float. Having said this, however, it must be emphasized
that all floating lines are not as buoyant as the makers would
have us believe. If there is any suggestion of an eddy in the
water, it will often make the line sink; but for general purposes they float effectively enough provided that they are
cleaned periodically, and any scum removed. Furthermore,
dirty water with surface scum has a tendency to make these
lines sink; but in good streamy water they work very effectively, and must be considered a boon to the greased-line
salmon fisherman.

Many of these lines come in various colours; and we have
already discussed, in Chapter 6, occasions when it might pay
to use a darker coloured line than the more normal white
one. Generally speaking, however, the floating lines are
white (but are available in light green), and the sinking ones
dark green. This, at least, enables easy recognition.

The choice between forward-taper or double-taper for
greased-line fishing is a little more difficult to determine.
Much depends upon the type of water to be fished, and

because I fish a wide variety of rivers I like to have both types of line on hand to cope with differing techniques. For a medium-sized river there is a lot to be said for the forward-taper variety. The line is so constructed that the bulk of the weight is in the forward section. This section, therefore, is the maximum amount which can be aerialized. The rest of the line, with much smaller diameter than the forward section, is designed to be 'shot' when the final cast is made. This leads to an ultimate distance beyond which it is very difficult to cast. Techniques for using a line of this type involve hand-lining the back section of line through the rings and then, as the forward cast is made, the hand-held line is released so that it may be taken out more easily by the heavy forward section. As I have said, it is virtually impossible to aerialize more than the forward section; and there comes a limit to the amount which may be shot. Because of the small diameter of this back taper, however, it does shoot much more readily than would be the case with a double-taper line. It is, however, virtually impossible to do any form of worth-while Spey or roll casting with such a line.

It is quite possible, with a double-taper line, to aerialize a great deal more line than would be possible with the forward-taper line. It does not shoot quite so readily, but has a decided advantage when any form of Spey or roll cast is required. The final choice, therefore, must remain with the angler. For my own personal preference I tend to use the forward-taper line on a river like the Lune or the upper reaches of the Scottish Dee; and the double-taper line for Spey, Tay or Tweed. There are, of course, as we have discussed, great merits in the shooting-head system for sunk-line fishing. Indeed the same technique may be used with a floating head; but it is then much more difficult to make any worth while 'mends' in the line. The method, however, finds great favour with some anglers.

On the subject of sinking lines there is little to be said. My own definite preference is for the double-taper variety on the simple basis that I get two lines for the price of one. There is little point in having the forward-taper variety when the normal double-taper line may be cut in two and spliced to monofilament backing. It is not possible to lift a great deal of drowned line anyway, so that the forward-taper principle is still involved. Even then, it may well be found that 15 yards of shooting head is a little too much; and for this reason, I invariably cut my 30 yard line in half; keep one section in reserve, and then remove a further three yards of the centre section before splicing it to the monofilament backing. This last-named type of line should be of fairly substantial diameter, since it will bear the brunt of casting work; and, moreover, fishing with very heavy flies and tackle will subject it to harsh treatment. For this reason I tend to go for backing of about 25-lb test, and splice it with a needle knot to the heavy back-taper of the line. Great care must be taken with this knot, or the occasion will come when you suddenly see your fly-line sail off into the blue. This happened to me on one occasion. Fortunately my gillie was able to recover it; and I then increased the security of the knot by applying a bit of plastic cement.

With this type of fishing it is a good plan to pre-stretch the backing before starting to cast, and some advantage may be gained by using oval section monofilament marketed by Don's of Edmonton (246 Fore Street, Edmonton, N.18). When wound on the reel, normal monofilament backing quickly develops a coil. If it is not pre-stretched, there will be a grave danger of bunching, and an inevitable snarl-up into the butt-ring once a hefty cast is made. With a bit of practice, some remarkably long casts may be made with this technique; but it is true to say that they are more easily accomplished from a boat or bank where the backing will be laid on a still and clear surface than from a deep-wading position, in which the water inevitably imposes drag on the pulled off backing. If the current is strong, this drag is substantially increased, and reduces the distance of the cast considerably.

Perhaps the most surprising feature about many talented salmon fishermen is their very limited range of knotting

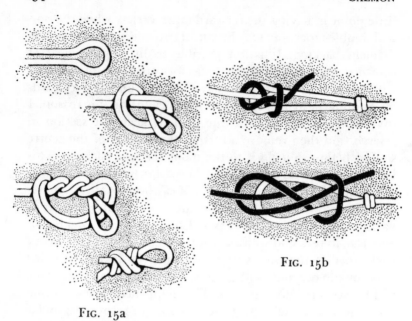

Fig. 15b

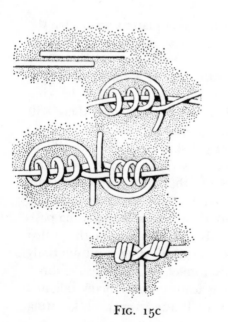

Fig. 15a

Fig. 15c

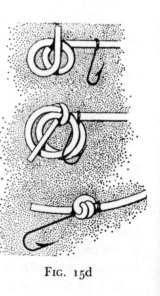

Fig. 15d

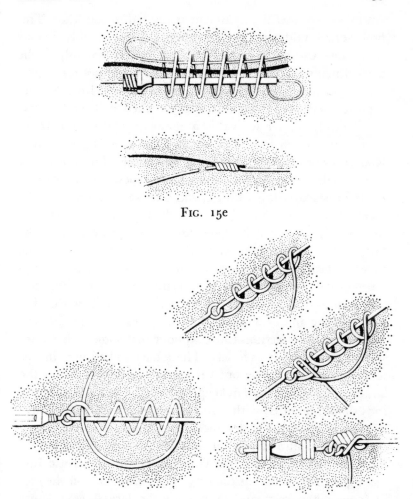

FIG. 15e

FIG. 15f                    FIG. 15g

techniques. There are several very good knots which have
been evolved since the advent of nylon monofilament. Descriptions of most knots can be found in many tackle cata-
logues; but the illustrations in Fig. 15 are a simple diagram-
matic guide to the junctions I require most frequently, and
the method of meeting requirements to ensure absolutely
secure junctions.

Another very useful attachment is the half-blood knot. This however, should not be used when fly-fishing, since it may well cause the fly to hinge, and the fly will not fish in the correct manner. It is, however, the most used knot for attaching a spinning bait, or swivel, to monofilament line. A more sophisticated version of this is the tucked half-blood knot; but I rarely bother with this refinement, and cannot recall ever losing a fish by the standard version letting me down. Rod rings pose other interesting reflections. There is still a great tendency to go for flashy agate types. These are perfectly satisfactory until they crack. The short margins of the crack then cause serious shaving damage to monofilament line. I like big, open bridge-rings, with a large ring at the butt and plenty of room in all the other rings to enable the shooting-head and backing to move smoothly with a minimum of friction. When recently trying a rod by one maker I was surprised to find that the rings were so narrow that the knot joining my backing to the line would not go through those on the tip section. Little wonder that some rods do not shoot line as readily as others! There have to be limits in this sort of thing, of course; but I think that it pays to go for the largest rings which look in keeping with the rod. All spinning rods should be fitted with a good-sized butt ring, particularly if the rod is expressly designed for use with the fixed-spool reel, and it is also important to have the ring well stood off from the rod if line friction is not to be caused by the line hitting the rod as well as the ring. The line comes off the reel in loops when cast; and even with the largest ring, some bunching is inevitable, thus causing friction, and restricting distance.

Reel-fittings and reel-seatings are also bones of contention. It is high time that the AFTM adopted standards which would eliminate reels flopping about on the rod; or reel-fittings being so tight that it is difficult, or even impossible, to get the sliding reel fittings over the reel-holders. A good supply of strong adhesive tape accompanies me on all my fishing trips, since I find, on occasion, that the required reel will not fit the rod in hand. The reel then has to be bound on with the tape.

I have already highlighted the importance of having the weight figure stamped on a spinning bait. This is something which could well be done to advantage for the angler. It would also be desirable if spinner manufacturers were to take up the challenge of producing a certain length of bait in three alternative weights, with a wide variety of size and weight permutations on which the angler could base his choice. The angler would be better equipped, with this type of guide, to face a season's salmon fishing.

Apart from these minor grumbles, I think that it is fair to say that the British tackle industry is now providing the angler with better products than ever before. Much of the tackle now being produced is the result of long periods of experimental trial and error by experienced anglers and casters. Tournament casting has done much to bring these findings to the notice of both manufacturers and anglers; and although a lot of tournament tackle is as far removed from practical angling needs, as a racing car is from the transport facilities of the family saloon, the tournament world has been the breeding ground for a lot of useful ideas. 'Race bred' is a much used term in car advertisements; and I think that we could well apply the term 'tournament bred' to some of our tackle and techniques. For this reason, we owe a lot to the tournament world for present day rod action and casting techniques.

AUTHOR'S NOTE :—*I will concede one contradiction in this chapter for I have now, almost completely, been wooed over to glass-fibre rods. The range currently marketed by Bruce & Walker are excellent for their specific tasks.*

# 32
## Fly Tying

As I have already stated elsewhere in this book there is a great deal of satisfaction to be obtained from catching salmon on flies which the angler has tied himself. I make no great claim to expertise in fly-tying; but I have tied flies for the last twenty years; and while few of my flies would catch fishermen, they have proved quite successful as catchers of fish. I am more than convinced, however, that flies tied by a good professional dresser will be just as successful as my patterns. The trouble is that nowadays, a well-tied salmon fly may well cost a small fortune to buy in the shops; and if the angler is to have a worth-while range of patterns and sizes he might well have to invest a very large sum of money on these items alone.

In order to make flies that conform to the old recipes, a great deal of material preparation and dexterity are required. I would not presume to be able to tie such a fly as well as any professional dresser. I therefore avoid those traditional patterns, and seek only to make a fly of the simplest materials; and to construct it so that it will stand a deal of hammering, and not fall apart at the first cast. In order to do this I may break some rules of the craft. I have had no tuition in fly-dressing, but have just picked it up from watching other people – which is not, in fact, the best way to learn! My flies, however, must have some merit if they continue to catch fish; and this is the only yardstick I set them against. For this reason I have now discarded practically all flies with feather-wing dressings. Instead I go for hair-wing flies, relying on the movement of the flowing fibres to represent a small fish or large insect. My flies have to look as though they come alive in a current of flowing water. Unless they do this, even if they contain the most beautiful feathers and have cost the earth to buy, I discard them out of hand. I have a large collection of such flies. They are all mounted in a beautifully bound leather hold-all and are most attractive to look at. They have been exquisitely tied, but will never find a place on my leader – unless, perhaps, on one of the wild rivers of Norway where the extra strong current may invoke some life from their dressing. Traditionally-tied flies are still quite popular in Norway; and this may well be the reason.

The trouble with most of the big traditional flies is not their basic inability to raise and hook a fish, but their inability to retain the fish on the hook during the tense and frantic moments of play. There is too much leverage with the big, old-fashioned flies; and I rarely fish with anything larger than a No. 4 double or single-hook fly. When conditions demand larger flies than this, I tend to rely almost exclusively on the tube-type of fly with an articulated treble-hook at the tail.

For small flies, therefore, I rely on the simplest dressing. The selected hook is placed in a suitable vice and the shank covered with clear bostick. A few turns of binding silk are then spun on to the shank and wound down to the point where the tail will finish. A length of fine tinsel wire is then bound in, followed by a split length of marabou silk. The tying silk is then taken to the head of the fly, and the body silk is bound round the shank until it is locked into position at the head. Following this, the tinsel is wound round in open spirals until it too is tied in position at the head of the fly. It is fairly important to bind in the tinsel in a different direction to that taken by the body silk. The tinsel then helps to keep the body silk bound in if a fish should cut the silk at any time. A few hackle fibres are then taken from a suitable feather and then bound in underneath the eye of the hook. All that is then left to do is to select some squirrel or bucktail winging of a suitable colour, and tie this in on top of the shank. The whole is then bound in with the tying silk and further additions of clear bostik. A final whip-knot completes the dressing and the knot is layered with black enamel to give a professional finish to the head.

Big flies on tubes are even more simple to dress. I now rarely bother with any body materials, but tie in the various colours of bucktail winging and finish off as before. The point at which the triangle of hooks are to extend should be carefully assessed and the fibres allowed to extend beyond the length of the tube so that they will adequately give a little masking of the hook. I am not a great believer in having fibres extending any further than the hook since there is a possibility that the fish might nip the end of the fly without coming into contact with the hook. There are those who argue that this does not matter; and that if a fish takes the fly, it will take it with a bang. If, however, anyone has seen the way a salmon sometimes plays with a shrimp, they will feel as apprehensive as I do about fishing with flies with long hackles beyond the hooks. In my glass tank of flowing water it was quite surprising to see how the triangle-hook has a vague resemblance to the caudal fin of a fish. I feel, therefore, that it does not matter greatly if the triangle-hook is a little bare. If the fish attempts to take the fly properly, there should be little doubt about a good hook hold. It is well to make sure that the strength of the treble is in keeping with the width of its gape. I have lost many a good fish through having the hook straighten out, or break at the shank.

On most of my big flies I like plenty of dressing; but on the very small flies it is sometimes difficult to keep the dressing sparse enough. As I have already indicated I am not greatly concerned with pattern, but do like to have a wide variety of sizes, with further variables on the amount of dressing those sizes contain. Experiment a bit, even if you are ashamed to show your flies to more talented fly-dressing friends. The only yardstick by which they should be judged is whether they catch fish!

# 33
## American and Canadian Methods

I HAVE not fished in North America. It may seem strange, for this reason, that I intend to comment upon salmon fishing in that continent. In the autumn of 1967, however, I had the great pleasure in visiting the United States to lecture and demonstrate on British game-fishing methods in both Pittsburgh and New York. While I was there, I met many well-known American anglers. They gave me a first-hand opportunity to compare our methods with those practised in that country.

It must be said at the outset that most of the worth-while salmon fishing in the North American continent lies within the boundaries of Canada. This must not be confused with fishing for salmon on the Pacific coast where the salmon are of a different species from the Atlantic salmon, the latter being mainly concentrated along the north and south shores of the Gulf of St. Lawrence, Labrador and Newfoundland. The provinces of Quebec, New Brunswick and Nova Scotia offer some of the finest fishing for Atlantic salmon anywhere in the world; but it is closely controlled, and much of the best is in the hands of small, wealthy American syndicates. Short of a personal invitation, it would be impossible for the casual visitor to wet a line.

Perhaps the river with the greatest reputation is the Resti-gouche. This, along with several other legendary rivers, has its home in the Gaspé peninsula and is world-renowned for its fine fishing, as are the Grand Cascapedia, the Matapedia, the Kedgwick, Upsalquitch and the Matane. Further south there is the well-known Miramichi river; and on the northern shores of the St Lawrence, in the province of Quebec, lies a vast territory with many fine, though lesser known, rivers. The Natashquan, Moisie, Romaine and Etamamiou are very fine rivers; and the Moisie is said to hold larger salmon than any water in that area.

While many of the salmon rivers are virtually closed to visitors, there are quite a few rivers (or sections of rivers) where fishing is free on payment of licence dues. Many of the rivers of Newfoundland and Nova Scotia come into this category. Controls vary from province to province. Most New Brunswick rivers are leased to outfitters; and there are Crown waters available for a fee to non-residents, and free to residents of the province. Quebec has many rivers leased to private clubs and outfitters; and for fishing of certain rivers, such as the Matane, only a licence is required since they are set aside for public use.

Outfitters are individuals or small companies who lease the fishing from the government agency, and sub-let a rod or rods. Normally they provide a full package deal with lodge accommodation near the fishing site; float-plane transportation; guides; and canoes. Costs vary, but £40 per day would seem about normal; and this may well be exclusive of transportation charges. The season, generally, is over the three months of June to August. Fly-fishing *only* is allowed by law; and there are many rivers where it is quite common to fish the dry-fly. Limit bags are in force on all rivers. Taking a general view, the greased-line methods as founded in this country are in general practice; and for many years the flies and tackle popular at home have found great favour. For the past few years, however, North American anglers have tended to regard our traditional flies as over-dressed, and have favoured the hair-wing flies which are now becoming more popular over here. Sizes are usually No. 6 to No. 8 singles or doubles, with similar dressing patterns to those used in UK. As a compromise between traditional greased-line and dry-fly methods, some anglers tie a fly on to their leader with a final half-hitch. This causes the fly to hang at right angles from the leader, and may be put on at either side of the fly, depending from which bank the angler is to fish. When the fly is cast out, it drags around in the water with a wake-form. I am told that it is a very effective way of taking fish on occasions; and I know of one gillie who has tried the method with some success on the Scottish Dee.

There is a general tendency to use single-handed rods, usually around 8 to 10 ft in length. A few old-timers on the Grand Cascapedia, however, still cling to their double-handed cane rods. It must be remembered that quite a deal of fishing is done from canoes, where casting a long line, or Spey-casting, is not required. Other waters are easily waded, with little bank vegetation to hamper overhead casting. Perhaps the ultimate in light tackle has been propagated by Lee Wulff. The light rods he has designed are occasionally used by some anglers, but certainly cannot be used on every type of river. The trend, however, is to greater lightness and small flies. Serious inquiries for fishing in Canada may be addressed to the Atlantic Salmon Association, Marine Building, 1405, Peel Street, Montreal, Canada.

# 34
## Future Trends

WHAT lies in store for the salmon angler of the future? This is a tough question. I should need a computerized crystal ball and some of the Almighty's perception to be able to look very far ahead. The rods of our forefathers were long and cumbersome; and the 17-footers of bygone days have all rotted away or are treasured possessions as family heirlooms. Rarely are they used for fishing these days. Instead, we have seen a slow trend to shorter and lighter rods. Inevitably (with American influence as shown in the last chapter), this trend will continue; and the double-haul cast, so popular nowadays on our reservoirs, will ultimately find its way to the cascading shrines of the die-hard salmon angler. Many of my generation will be loath to part with trusted tackle now in use. There is still a lot to be said for a long rod. It gives better line control, once the cast has been made; and the longer the rod, the greater the distance that may be achieved when Spey-casting. It will be a long time before rods much shorter than 10 feet make their full impact on the classic Scottish streams. That the time will come, however, I have no doubt – with ultimates in lightness, perhaps, along the lines of those practised by Lee Wulff in Newfoundland at the present time.

We have already noted many changes in the materials used for rod construction. When I was a boy, greenheart was still a popular material. Then came the slow change to split-cane. Now the move seems to be to fibre-glass; and it must be admitted that improvements with this material have been

244

quite marked. We now hear talk of carbon-fibre, with its ultimates in lightness and strength. This may lead to further exciting changes.

Nylon monofilament will doubtless be with us for a long time yet; and we may expect diameters to decrease as test strength increases. Doubtless also, we shall see minor changes (I avoid the word improvement) in fly-design; and if I were to make a prediction in this respect, I should think that as the floating-line with a sinking tip finds greater favour, fly sizes will tend to increase slightly. In the past, I think that we reached ultimates in smallness of dressing; and I am strongly of the opinion that there are few occasions when flies of less than size No. 10 are required. Fly and spinning reels will stay much as they are for some time yet; but we may well expect refinements in the form of slipping clutches, or geared re-winds on some fly reels. I don't expect to see any great advance in bait design; but it would be nice if manufacturers made a range of baits of variable sizes and weights, *with the weight stamped on the bait.*

If there is to be little change in tackle within the next decade, there may well be some drastic changes in the law affecting salmon fishing generally. Catching salmon with rod and line is still the most ineffective way of taking them. Figures from the Lancashire River Authority indicate that for every rod-caught salmon in the Lune river system, eighteen are taken by the estuarine and coastal nets. This, in my opinion, is an unfair proportion; and it behoves all anglers to press for greater restrictions on netting, to increase conservation of our salmon stocks. It is sheer nonsense for authority to try and compare the two methods. In order to achieve this, however, the angler may well have to suffer further restrictions on his methods of fishing; the length of the season; or the limit of bags. It is still the legal right of any member of the public to demand a netting licence from the local river authority. That they might have difficulty in finding a place to operate in a worth-while manner is beside the point. Our netting laws are outdated, and with the hue-and-cry about high-seas netting off Greenland, and the ravages of the salmon disease, it is high time that we took some steps to put our own house in order. The whole of salmon husbandry is too much of a hit-and-miss affair. The disease problem is only receiving lip-service; and despite all the warning signs of increasing shortages of salmon returning from the sea, we have done nothing (except the prohibition of drift-netting around our Scottish coasts) to restrict estuarine and coastal netting. We may have to accept a trend towards the fishing of more rivers becoming restricted to fly-only. There may be an abolition of many forms of natural bait fishing; but if all these come as a result of a concern for conservation, and are backed up by sensible and properly enforced netting laws, then it will not be a bad thing.

Perhaps the largest cloud on the horizon is the greater demand which will be made on river authorities and water boards for industrial water supply. The next ten to twenty years will see a further population expansion; and with many of our rivers already suffering from abstraction, we may well expect the decline in content and flow to continue. There is vague talk of de-salination of our sea water; but this is still a costly process, and I doubt if I shall live to see the day when it comes into operation. Trouble has arisen from the fact that we have been so wasteful with our water resources in the past. The present annual rainfall in Lancashire alone is more than ten times the national requirement. Land drainage and deforestation get the water into the rivers as quickly as possible; and our rivers are subjected to much faster flooding, shorter natural dropping of the flood, and longer periods of drought, than ever before.

The whole future of our migratory fish stocks seems to hang in the balance. The salmon are faced with too many odds; and if mankind does not offer a positive helping hand, in the very near future, they may well pass into history as the greatest, but extinct, fish of the sporting angler.

AUTHOR'S NOTE:—*My comments on commercial netting are amplified in Chapter 27.*
*See also Chapter 9 for new thoughts on flies.*

# Index